CRACKS IN THE
IVORY TOWER

CRACKS IN THE IVORY TOWER

*THE MORAL MESS OF
HIGHER EDUCATION*

J ASON B RENNAN
P HILLIP M AGNESS

OXFORD
UNIVERSITY PRESS

OXFORD
UNIVERSITY PRESS

Oxford University Press is a department of the University of Oxford. It furthers
the University's objective of excellence in research, scholarship, and education
by publishing worldwide. Oxford is a registered trade mark of Oxford University
Press in the UK and certain other countries.

Published in the United States of America by Oxford University Press
198 Madison Avenue, New York, NY 10016, United States of America.

© Oxford University Press 2019

First issued as an Oxford University Press paperback 2021

Library of Congress Cataloging-in-Publication Data
Names: Brennan, Jason, 1979- author. | Magness, Phillip W., author.
Title: Cracks in the ivory tower : the moral mess of higher education /
Jason Brennan and Phillip Magness.
Description: New York, NY : Oxford University Press, [2019] |
Includes bibliographical references.
Identifiers: LCCN 2018058356 | ISBN 9780190846282 (hardcover : alk. paper) |
ISBN 9780197608272 (paperback) | ISBN 9780190846299 (universal PDF) | ISBN 9780190846305
(electronic publication) | ISBN 9780190932824 (Oxford scholarship online)
Subjects: LCSH: Education, Higher—Moral and ethical aspects—United States. |
Education, Higher—Economic aspects. | Universities and colleges—United
States—Sociological aspects.
Classification: LCC LB2324 .B75 2019 | DDC 378.001—dc23
LC record available at https://lccn.loc.gov/2018058356

1 3 5 7 9 8 6 4 2

Paperback printed by Marquis, Canada

CONTENTS

CRACKS IN THE
IVORY TOWER

I

Neither Gremlins nor Poltergeists

GREMLINS, AS YOU KNOW, are horrid little beasts. At night, they creep around and sabotage your stuff. Is your dishwasher broken? Probably gremlins.

Poltergeists are even more insidious. Poltergeists are incorporeal spirits that *possess* your home. They smash the dishes, trash the furniture, and play white noise on your TV while you sleep. You can't trap or kill a poltergeist, unlike a gremlin, because poltergeists lack physical bodies. Burn your house down and they'll just move elsewhere.

Both gremlins and poltergeists are mythical saboteurs. But it's not surprising that people invent such legends. As anyone who's ever taught economics, sociology, or biology knows, most people have trouble understanding how an event could happen without *someone* or *something* making it happen.

Witness how ancient peoples tended to believe a god or spirit haunted every tree, bush, and river. Witness how contemporary people stand over their ruined homes and wonder why God decided to send a flood their way. Witness how when an election goes badly, partisans blame hackers. When the stock market plummets, people blame Wall Street. If their football team loses, they think someone tampered with the balls or the field.

People have a hard enough time understanding how natural events could result from natural laws, rather than supernatural will. They have an even harder time comprehending how many things that happen in society could be the product of *human action* but not *human design*.

When people observe social trends—inequality rises or falls, people get richer or poorer, mores about sex become stricter or looser—they jump to the conclusion that some powerful person or group *chose* to create the change.

You see this trend most especially in politics. What caused the Big Bad Thing? Blame George Soros, or Charles Koch, or the Russian hackers, or the Rothschilds, or the. . . . Really, these are just newfangled, slightly more respectable versions of gremlins and poltergeists. You can make a lot of money selling such conspiracy theories.

What economists and political scientists have discovered, but most people don't know, is that social trends and systematic behaviors rarely result from puppet masters pulling strings. We explain systematic behavior not by suggesting bad character or malicious intent, but instead by examining the incentives and constraints that individuals face. When people are rewarded for doing something, they will do more of it. When they are punished, they will do less. If lots of people do something bad, it's probably because the incentives induce them to do it.

In turn, we can explain the incentives people face by examining the *institutions* under which they live. As the Nobel laureate and economist Douglass North puts it, institutions are "the rules of the game in a society or, more formally, are the humanly devised constraints that shape human interaction."[1] Furthermore, the rules we live under often appear by accident, or emerge spontaneously from previous trends, or result because of external constraints. There is rarely some mastermind behind the curtain. Good and bad things happen, but not because anyone—or any gremlin or poltergeist—planned for them to happen.

In short: Big trends emerge from individual behavior without anyone running the show. Institutions create incentives, and incentives determine behavior. Econ 101.

Now, that's a simple story, maybe too simple. Sometimes we need a fancier story. Sometimes we'll even discover bona fide gremlins and poltergeists are to blame. But even the Ghostbusters would tell you not to start with the supernatural explanations. The bump in the night is probably just your furnace. You start with the simple, natural story first and then invoke evil monsters and spirits only *after* you rule out natural causes.

AGAINST GREMLINS AND POLTERGEISTS IN HIGHER EDUCATION

What does this have to do with higher education? Many people, on both the Left and Right, from parents to students to faculty to staff, from outsiders to insiders, believe that higher education in the US and elsewhere faces various crises and suffers from various flaws.

We agree! That's what this whole book is about. Indeed, we're here to say the situation is *worse* than you think.

But many people blame these flaws on gremlins or poltergeists. "Gremlins" are corporeal individuals who sabotage higher educa-tion for their own sinister ends.[2] Such gremlins might include, say, state or federal legislatures, donors, various corporations, or the Reds. "Poltergeists" in this case refers to intellectual movements, ideas, ideologies, and attitudes that possess and corrupt academia. Some such supposed poltergeists include "neoliberalism" or "the profit ori-entation" or "the practical orientation" or "leftist ideology" or "social justice."[3]

This book is titled *Cracks in the Ivory Tower: The Moral Mess of Higher Education*. We think higher education suffers from serious moral flaws. From a business ethics standpoint, the average university makes Enron look pretty good. Universities' problems are deep and funda-mental: Most academic marketing is semi-fraudulent, grading is largely nonsense, students don't study or learn much, students cheat fre-quently, liberal arts education fails because it presumes a false theory of learning, professors and administrators waste students' money and time in order to line their own pockets, everyone engages in self-righteous moral grandstanding to disguise their selfish cronyism, professors pump out unemployable graduate students into oversaturated academic job markets for self-serving reasons, and so on.

What sets this book apart from many other critiques of higher ed is that we believe academia's problems are ingrained. Bad behaviors result from regular people reacting to bad incentives baked into academia. No specters haunt academia. Normal people just take the bait.

BAD INCENTIVES EXPLAIN BAD BEHAVIOR

To illustrate, let's list some examples of bad behavior we've witnessed firsthand. These cases are not so serious. In the rest of the book, we'll go on to discuss far worse scenarios. We chose the stories that follow because they're simple, and the causes of the problems they illustrate are easy to see. We want to warm you up before we get to the more complicated stuff.

Breaking the Law, Breaking the Law

Years ago, Jason was involved in a tenure-track job search. The search committee picked three candidates (out of hundreds) for fly-out interviews. After the interviews, the department voted to hire a particular candidate, who happened to be a white male. Their second choice candidate was a white woman.

On paper, the man's résumé was superior to the woman's. Both candidates came from equally and highly ranked graduate programs, but the man had published more articles in better peer-reviewed outlets, and his experience showed a more original, higher-stakes research trajectory. The man had previously taught successful classes like those the hiring department offered; the woman had not. The man had received competing offers, but indicated he was likely to accept an offer from the university in question; the woman had indicated she was likely to turn down any offer from the university in question because she was unsure about the fit.

The department asked to hire the male candidate. The provost—let's call him Jeff—said no. He claimed that the female candidate was superior and they should hire her. That seemed odd and flew against the evidence, because the male candidate had a far superior publications record and possessed related teaching experience.

Jeff, for his part, was strongly committed to hiring a more ethnic and gender-diverse faculty. He would carefully craft statements about hiring that would induce professors to inadvertently violate Title VII of the Civil Rights Act. (Title VII of the 1964 Civil Rights Act forbids preferential hiring *unless* done in accordance with an affirmative action plan.[4]) For instance, Jeff sent out one memo to faculty reminding them that "every search is a diversity search, and everyone involved in every search has an obligation to think and act on that assumption." Jeff didn't exactly *order* faculty to break the law, but most faculty— utterly ignorant of the laws in question—interpreted his directive as saying they should discriminate in favor of non-white, non-Asian, and female candidates. Furthermore, Jeff never once informed faculty that the Civil Rights Act *forbids* them from considering or giving weight to race, color, religion, sex, or national origin after the pool of candidates has been established.

Why did Jeff do this? Maybe Jeff thought the 1964 Civil Rights Act was unjust, because it *prohibited* discrimination in favor of minorities, and thus wanted to circumvent it. Or, maybe the problem was that Jeff faced bad incentives. Jeff was stuck between the clichéd rock and hard place—or Scylla and Charybdis for you more literary types.

The rock: The department in question was mostly male. According to federal and local regulations, the department could thus be presumed guilty of discrimination by *disparate impact*. If someone sued the university, it would automatically be considered guilty unless the school could somehow prove the disparate impact was justified.

The hard place: Jeff wanted to avoid a disparate impact suit, so he had an incentive to actively discriminate in favor of women. But this is *also* illegal, as it is a form of *disparate treatment*. You aren't allowed to avoid disparate impact by disparate treatment—except in accordance with a valid affirmative action plan, which the university lacked.

Regardless of what Jeff did, he'd put his university at legal risk. In the end, after faculty protested, Jeff tried to solve the problem by granting the department two lines; they extended offers to both candidates. The male took the job; the female did not. Today, the male candidate is a full professor and endowed chair at a research university; the female candidate is an untenured assistant professor at a liberal arts college.

Note carefully: We take no stance here on whether affirmative action or preferential treatment for underrepresented groups is good or bad. We also don't know what really went through Jeff's head. We just want to illustrate how Jeff had strong *legal* incentives to skirt part of the law and to discriminate, regardless of his underlying beliefs.

Nancy at the Aspen Institute

In each of his classes, Jason asks students to complete the "Ethics Project." The Ethics Project's instructions are simple: Do something good, something that adds value to the world. Jason provides each student group with $1,000 (from corporate and alumni donors) to help them complete their projects. Students are free to do almost anything: Start a business, run a fundraiser, teach others valuable skills, hold a seminar, fly high school students to a leadership summit, create a new club. At the end of the semester, students must analyze and defend their decisions using economic and philosophical tools.

Students do amazing things. One group created an iPhone screen repair business that grossed tens of thousands of dollars per semester. Another group created an "Unsung Heroes" club, which celebrates and aids blue collar staff at universities. Unsung Heroes received national news coverage and is starting new chapters in multiple US universities right now. Another group raised $12,000 and sent two full truckloads of supplies to a town destroyed by a natural disaster.

Nancy, a former high-level administrator at Georgetown's business school, invited Jason to present on Ethics Projects to the Aspen Undergraduate Business Education Consortium's annual meeting. During the talk, Jason mentioned that one group of first-year undergraduates had created and sold "Hoya Drinking Club" t-shirts for a hefty $700 profit.

A dean from another university asked Jason, "So, you allow students to do things that carry genuine moral risk. Why? Why not forbid them from selling such t-shirts?"

Jason explained that an Ethics Project grants students freedom but also holds them responsible for their choices. It requires students to reflect on their choices and on how they might improve in the future. While most business schools ask students to reason through hypothetical business ethics case studies, Jason has his students *create* and *live through* their own case studies. Wharton undergrads play *Dungeons and Dragons* while Georgetown undergrads slay actual dragons. The students in Jason's example were conflicted and spent a good deal of time reflecting on whether they'd made a poor choice. The dean agreed that this strategy was better.

Nancy did not. Immediately after the talk, she asked Jason, "Can we chat for a moment?" For ten minutes, she cajoled Jason to reconsider his permissive treatment of his students. "What if something bad happened? What if another bad thing happened? You should require students to tell you ahead of time what they will do and how they'll do it. You should forbid projects that have *any* risk!"

Jason stood his ground and politely refused. "Sorry, Nancy, but what you see as dangers and flaws I see as *the very point* of the project."

As Nancy reproached him, a different dean interrupted, "Hey, great project! Make sure to eat lunch with me so we can discuss doing this at my university." Another dean also interrupted to praise the project. None of this deterred Nancy, who spent the next month trying (and failing) to impose new regulations on the Ethics Project.

Why was Nancy so upset when everyone else *loved* the idea? Nancy explained, "If students do something that bothers parents, such as selling beer pong shirts, the parents won't call you, Jay. They'll call *me*. *I'm* the one who has to placate angry parents. And I don't want to deal with that."

There you go. Nancy agreed that Jason's project worked. She admitted that its moral risk was good for the students to confront. She even admitted that parents could be made to understand the pedagogical value of the project. She saw that her peers admired the project. Still, she said, she didn't want to worry about possible angry calls. (For what it's worth, no parent has ever complained.)

Nancy tried—and failed—to destroy one of the most success pedagogical innovations at her university. But to explain Nancy's bad behavior, we need not posit that she's a bad person. Rather, her job was not to educate students or produce scholarship. Her job was to raise money, manage lower-level administrators, placate parents, and curate outsiders' opinion of the school. She wanted to avoid any chance of a headache.

No Cookies for You Unless I Get Some, Too

In 2009, Brown University's president and engineering faculty wanted to convert the "division" of engineering into a distinct *school* of engineering. From a regulatory and academic standpoint, these labels ("division" vs. "school") matter. Becoming a school enables Brown engineering to raise more money from different sources, to increase the number of faculty, to attract better graduate students, and to create more diverse programs.

To make the change, engineering needed a majority approval vote from Brown's assembled faculty. Before the vote, the division carefully presented its case. They showed how they would seek new sources of funding unavailable to other departments at Brown; in other words, creating such a school would help *them* but not come at anyone else's expense. They also explained how they planned to hire eight new engineering professors with outside funding.

During the meeting, a professor (Jason thinks she was from the sociology department) rose and issued a public threat. She acknowledged that the change would not hurt her department. Nevertheless, she said she opposed allowing the change unless the new school agreed to devote at least one faculty line to hiring a sociologist who would study engineers and engineering from a social scientific perspective. She also said she had already assembled a bloc of professors who would vote to block the change unless the engineering division met her demands.

Obviously, we the authors have nothing against studying academic engineering from a social scientific perspective. This very book is a social scientific and philosophical study of academia. But Brown engineering was understaffed in genuine engineering professors. It needed *engineers*, not a sociologist of engineering.

Still, we can understand why the professor responded in the way she did. She believed that she had the power to veto someone else's gain. The power was tempting. In effect, she said, "I won't let you bake cookies for yourself unless you give me some."

Great Teaching! Now Shape Up or You're Fired

Years ago, a national magazine extolled a colleague's exceptional teaching. Nevertheless, when the colleague came up for a pre-tenure review—an evaluation intended to advise a professor about whether he or she is likely to earn tenure—the tenured faculty gave the rock star teacher a rather negative evaluation.

Why would they do that? Well, at Carnegie Classification "R1" universities, tenure and promotion are almost entirely a matter of research productivity. Research brings the school prestige. Teaching does not. Star researchers—people who can publish year after year in high-prestige outlets—are rare and hard to find.

Furthermore, we faculty—the ones who vote on tenure—don't personally benefit from our colleagues being good teachers. We benefit from them being star researchers. They help us write better papers and publish more ourselves. They also bring the school research prestige, which rubs off on the rest of us. If our colleagues are smart, people assume we're smart. Teaching helps students (sort of . . . see Chapter 3), but students don't vote on tenure.

Why Jason Bought a Standing Desk

Let's be clear: We the authors also respond to incentives. We're not saints either.

To illustrate: Jason automatically receives at least $7,500 a year to spend on books, travel, data, copy-editing fees, or anything else related to his work, plus $2,000 every two years to spend on a work computer. Since *other* universities pay for most of his travel, he usually has a few thousand dollars left at year's end.

But the university doesn't allow him to roll over any unused funds to the next year. If he's frugal or conservative, *other* people benefit, not him.

So, one May, when Jason still had $2,000 left in his account, he decided to experiment with a standing desk. Guess how much he spent? Similarly, when Jason attends conferences, do you think he books nice rooms at nice hotels, or budget rooms at budget hotels? Do you think Jason has a budget-friendly PC or a top-of-the-line, 27-inch iMac?

The problem here is clear: People respond to incentives. That includes us, the authors. If we could keep 25 percent of our unused budgets, we might well conserve. But if we're not rewarded for being frugal, we might as well spend $2,000 on a standing desk or buy the nicest computers and hotel rooms our budgets permit.

ACADEMIA WITHOUT ROMANCE

Academics often express a romantic view of academia. They believe higher education serves a number of noble purposes. It discovers new truths and transmits those truths to the masses. Scientific research fights hunger and disease. Social scientific research fights oppression and poverty. It cures students of ignorance and provinciality. It shapes students into passionate, purposeful human beings in service to society and democracy. Furthermore, it advances social justice by eradicating inequality and promoting social mobility.

Maybe these are good *ideals*. But beware. Although many people believe academia *should* promote such ideals, it doesn't necessarily follow that academia, in fact, promotes them or that it even could. Perhaps higher education is not the right tool for the jobs we've assigned to it.

There's no guarantee that the kinds of people who want academic jobs are motivated solely or even predominantly by such ideals. They may just be regular people, with their own private and selfish concerns. Many will just pay lip service to these ideals, perhaps, in part, to inflate their own self-esteem. As the psychologists Nicolas Epley and David Dunning have discovered, most people have an inflated view of their own moral character.[5] People believe themselves to be more virtuous than they are. And as Kevin Simler and Robin Hanson show, we are hardwired to *deceive ourselves* about the goodness of our own motivations—we often act selfishly while simultaneously tricking ourselves into thinking we're acting morally.[6]

Sure, the people who want academic jobs may be somewhat different from the kinds of people who want to become used car salespeople, politicians, or business executives.[7] But people are people. Academics aren't saints.

Suppose you believe that because academia is supposed to serve noble goals, academics will mostly have noble motivations. Of course, you'll then be flabbergasted when bad things happen in academia. Of course, you'll want to blame outsiders—gremlins and poltergeists—for disrupting the system.

Economist James Buchanan won the Nobel Prize in Economics in 1986, in part, for pointing out how silly and misguided this common way of thinking is.[8] Before Buchanan's time, economists would often just assume that government agents or people working in non-profits would always be competent and motivated to do the right thing. They'd pretend, for modeling purposes, that governments and nongovernmental organizations (NGOs) are made up of saints and angels rather than real people. For instance, economists would identify some market failure and then note that, *in principle*, a well-motivated, smart government bureaucracy could fix it, at least if every citizen automatically went along with whatever rule or regulation the government imposed. But, Buchanan said, we cannot assume that *real* government agents have either the desire or knowledge to identify or solve such problems. We shouldn't presume that people will always comply with the law, either.

Buchanan's apparently earth-shaking idea was that government agents and NGO workers are people, just like everyone else. Crowning someone or giving him the corner office at the Red Cross doesn't make him an angel. The power to save the world is also the power to sell favors, smite one's enemies, and promote one's own agenda . . . or to do nothing at all. Once the government can distribute favors, he said, we should expect people to compete to win those favors for their own private ends. People will still often break or game the rules if they can. Buchanan was right—nowadays, if you're pretending governments are omnibenevolent and omnicompetent, you aren't doing serious social science.

So it goes with higher ed. As we'll demonstrate throughout this book, many of the tools Buchanan and other economists use to explain political behavior also explain higher ed.

To be clear, we're not recommending you take the other extreme view that academics are selfish sociopaths who care nothing about justice. That's a different kind of romantic theory. In the same way, Buchanan didn't claim that all politicians—or market actors—are entirely selfish. Rather, the point is that people are people. People are, on average, fairly selfish, but some are more altruistic than others, and some are neither selfish nor altruistic. People sometimes sacrifice their self-interest to promote moral ideals, they sometimes *pretend* to do so in order to gain favor among others, and they sometimes violate their proclaimed ideals to promote their own interests.

Higher education has a purpose only in the way hammers have a purpose. Just as hammers can be used for any number of purposes—for example, to build a hospital or to murder a romantic rival—so can higher education be used for any number of purposes. Individual "users" of the tool have their own purposes, which may conflict with the noble purposes higher ed supposedly serves.

A slightly different romantic view regards academic politics (and politics in general) as a battle between the good guys and the bad guys, the Light Side versus the Dark Side of the Force. According to this view, there are good people and bad people. Bad things happen when bad people rule; good things happen when good people rule. You get success by empowering good people and constraining bad people. In this romantic view, when something bad happens, you shouldn't try to change the rules; you try to change *who* rules. In this view, you fix a country by electing a new leader and fix a university by hiring a new dean.

Academia without romance looks different. When you see bad behavior, you ask:

- What incentives do the rules create?
- Who bears the costs of people's actions and choices?
- Who benefits?
- Why are the rules the way they are?

When you ask those sorts of questions, you'll rarely have to identify good guys and bad guys, or look for external gremlins and poltergeists.

Imperfect rules create bad incentives that, in turn, create bad behavior.[9] The downside of this simple insight is that changing the rules is *hard*—it's much harder to amend a constitution than to replace a president. Once we identify the cause of our problems, we often can't do anything about it.

Sometimes we don't even know *how* to change the rules. For instance, development economists both Left and Right largely agree that certain institutions—stable governments, open markets, robust protection of private property—are *necessary* for sustained economic growth and to end extreme poverty.[10] But economists don't know how to induce the countries that lack these institutions to adopt them. We know Zimbabwe would be much better off with Australia's institutions, but we have no idea how to make that happen.

So it goes with higher ed. As you'll see later in this book, sometimes we'll be able to diagnose why academia suffers from bad behavior or produces bad results. But sometimes, when we diagnose the problem, we'll see there are no obvious solutions. It may be too costly to change the rules, or we might not know how to, or we might know that the people in power have no incentive to change the rules.

It's too bad the romantic theories are wrong, because the romantic theories make saving the world look easy. That's probably why people *want* to believe romantic theories. Romantic theories of politics are the intellectual equivalent of penis-enlargement pills.

SEVEN BIG ECONOMIC INSIGHTS

Since economics will be central to our argument, we'll start by listing seven basic economic ideas and principles. These are platitudes, perhaps, but platitudes people—including people who write about higher ed—routinely ignore.

1. *There are no free lunches. Trade-offs are everywhere.* The most basic, important, and frequently evaded economic idea is that everything you do comes at the expense of everything you didn't do.

Time spent at a rock concert is not time spent calling your mom, learning Mandarin, or watching a movie. Money spent building a rock climbing wall is not money spent on scholarships. Earning a bachelor's degree in eighteenth-century Romanian poetry comes at the expense of a bachelor's degree in chemical engineering.

Yawn. Everyone agrees, right?

Well, no. For instance, around the US, adjuncts' rights activists demand that universities pay adjuncts better salaries, provide them with more benefits, and give them more status. In previously published work (which we'll discuss later in this book), we calculated how much it would cost universities in the US to give adjuncts what they demand. A *low* estimate is $30 billion extra per year, which turns out to be a 30 percent increase in faculty costs. In the past, we pointed out the banal and obvious truth that spending $30 billion more per year on adjuncts means $30 billion is not being spent on, say, scholarships for poor, first-generation, or underrepresented minority students.[11] People didn't respond by saying, "Yes, that's obviously true, but we should prioritize adjuncts over poor students because. . . ." Rather, they got angry and denied any such trade-offs existed. But such trade-offs *always* exist, and someone who refuses to acknowledge them lacks minimal moral seriousness.

In response to campus protests, Brown University recently created a $165 million "Diversity and Inclusion Action Plan." This plan does not itself include provisions for funding undergraduate financial aid. But instead of allocating $100 million for twenty-five endowed professorships, Brown could have spent that money on scholarships.[12] A $100 million endowment could provide full rides for least one hundred minority students each year into perpetuity. As philosopher Tom Mulligan points out, that money came from donations that could have instead gone to save lives—so, quite literally, Brown's Diversity and Inclusion Action Plan equals fifty thousand dead African children.[13] That's not to argue Brown should have spent money on financial aid rather than faculty, or that it should not have raised the money at all. We take no stance. It's just to say that—ironically—funding a Chair of Justice and Poverty Studies comes at the expense of putting poor students through college or, more fundamentally, saving poor children from starvation. Of course, no one wants to admit that.

To take another example, faculty and political pundits often complain that students are too concerned with getting jobs and don't care to learn for learning's sake. But college is expensive: four years of unpaid labor and tens of thousands of dollars in fees. Students could "learn for learning's sake" by downloading free course materials from MIT.[14] In the four years they spend in school, they could easily have earned over $60,000 with a minimum wage job. So, *of course*, they want a financial return. Going to college for the sake of learning is like booking an international flight for the sake of the meals. (Remember that when we get to Chapter 3, where we discuss how little students learn, or Chapter 9, where we discuss how much they cheat.)

2. *There are always budget constraints.* Consider this a corollary of the last point. American universities spend about half a trillion dollars each year.[15] Overall, US higher education is a $500 billion industry.

The US is a rich country, and many American universities are rich. Princeton has over 2 million endowment dollars per student.

Nevertheless, limits on spending exist. There is not some unlimited pile of gold out there waiting to be used.

Indeed, it turns out that most universities spend their entire discretionary budgets and tend to have little freedom to spend or raise more.[16] Furthermore, universities rarely have one single fund or account, similar to the sole checking account you might have. Rather, they typically have multiple funds and accounts, each controlled or owned by different entities (the state, the board of regents, the physics department, the Johnson Center for Happiness Studies, the student union, etc.), and subject to different spending controls and regulations. It's sometimes difficult or even illegal to move money between units. (*Note:* To some degree, this mitigates the opportunity cost problem we just discussed.)

Thus, whenever somebody demands universities do something, we should ask, "How much will that cost?" and "Where is the money going to come from?" And, of course, as we just discussed, we have to ask, "Why raise money for *that* rather than this other cause?"

When talking about matters of justice, activists often refuse to ask these questions. If something is a matter of justice, then it feels callous to ask whether we can afford it. How can you put a price on justice?

The economist and philosopher David Schmidtz responds, "Some things are priceless. So what?"[17] We might decide that dolphins are the world's priceless heritage. But if it costs $2 billion to save one priceless dolphin, that's still $2 billion we're not spending on saving all the other priceless things out there. Schmidtz's ultimate point: The world doesn't care what we regard as priceless. We still have to choose, and every time we choose, we are forced to put a price on everything.[18] We have only a limited supply of money, power, resources, time, effort, and goodwill. The world doesn't give us the luxury of treating things as priceless, not even justice.

3. *Incentives matter.* When we want to predict or explain behavior, we should ask, "Who benefits? Who pays?" If people are rewarded for doing something, they'll tend to do more of it. If they're punished or made to bear a cost, they'll tend to do less of it. If people can reap the benefits of something but push the costs onto others, they'll tend to do so.

For instance, faculty at Georgetown's McDonough School of Business receive annual raises. Officially, assistant professors' raises are based 60 percent on research, 30 percent on teaching, and 10 percent on service. But tenure and promotion seem to be almost entirely a matter of research—a star teacher who doesn't publish will be fired, while a star researcher who can't teach will be promoted. Faculty who publish "A-level" articles each year receive a course reduction plus a summer research bonus worth 2/9ths of their base salaries. Furthermore, the more a professor publishes, the more invitations she receives to give paid talks at other fancy universities or to do consulting. A well-published professor can earn an additional $50,000 per year from talks, royalties, and consulting fees. Some famous professors get $25,000 per talk. Nobel laureate economists can charge $50,000 or more.

Thus, it should not surprise you that many professors try to minimize the hours spent teaching, attempt to teach only one "prep" per year, only hold the required minimum number of office hours, and reuse the same learning materials year after year. Receiving the university teaching award might be gratifying. But publishing a big deal book could be worth $75,000 in the short term and $300,000 or more over the course of a career. For the rare few, books are worth millions.

Did we mention we're not selfless either? Also, thanks for buying this book. Tell your friends!

4. *The Law of Unintended Consequences.* When we pass a rule making a change or advocate a policy, we can say what we *hope* to accomplish. But we don't get to stipulate what we will actually accomplish. In general, almost every change brings unintended and unforeseen consequences.

For instance, suppose universities offer more counseling or extracurricular services to students. Suppose they create centers to promote scientific, social justice, civics, or environmental causes. Suppose they improve the school's network and infrastructure. These benefits all increase the operating expenses of the university, and thus increase tuition and fees, and thus tend to make college less affordable.

Or, to take an example that students should find troubling, consider the two main ways in which the US federal government has tried to help more students go to college: federal grants and subsidized loans. The logic seems simple—the price of college is too high for many bright but needy students, so we can fix that by giving the poorest of them additional cash to spend on tuition, or offering them loans at discounted rates.

Imagine what would happen if the government did something like that to help people buy cars. Suppose decent new sedans sell for $20,000. But the government thinks too few people can afford them. So, it decides to give a large number of people $10,000 grants to help them buy cars.

Of course, car dealers would respond by raising their prices—the subsidy means there is higher demand for their cars. If the government subsidizes car purchases, it thereby unintentionally but unavoidably *increases* the price of cars. That's textbook econ 101.

But, you might hope, colleges surely wouldn't do the same. Car dealers are just trying to maximize profits, while universities are supposedly guided by noble, public-spirited ideals. But, in fact, when economists do the research, they find that universities act like auto dealers. In response to tuition subsidies, American universities jacked up their tuition rates. This induces politicians to increase subsidies even more, and the cycle continues on.[19] Why is college so expensive? Answer: because politicians want to help the poor. If you want to make college more affordable, you'll need to find a different solution, or perhaps regulate and restrict college tuition prices.

5. *People often break the rules when they can.* Or, in fancier language: People engage in strategic noncompliance.

Consider this a corollary of the last point. Rules are not magically self-enforcing. We can pass a rule requiring people to do something good. We can pass a rule forbidding them from doing something bad. That doesn't mean they'll obey. They may even game the rules to their own advantage.

So, for instance, forbidding students to drink beer in a dorm may just lead them to drink more, and in more dangerous ways, at frat houses or bars.[20] It may also cause them to continue drinking in the dorms, but switch from beer to booze. It's easier to conceal a bottle of vodka in your dorm room than a case of beer. It's easy to hide vodka or rum in mixers. So, when universities forbid students from drinking beer in their dorms, they inadvertently induce some students to switch to more dangerous hard liquors. That's strategic noncompliance.

Strategic noncompliance explains why many well-intentioned rules lead to bad unintended consequences. For example, consider laws forbidding texting while driving. Texting while driving is roughly as dangerous as driving drunk. Yet there's some evidence that *banning* texting while driving actually leads to *more* crashes. Why? The evidence suggests that people continue to text and drive even when it's illegal. But instead of holding their phone over the steering wheel as they text and drive, they now keep their phones low and out of view from policemen. This means they're even more distracted.[21] The law is supposed to save lives, but strategic noncompliance means it kills people.

6. *Rules shape the incentives*, which in turn affect how people perform their jobs, interact with one another, and use the scarce resources of their positions. Recall the example of Jason buying a standing desk. The university's rule meant that budgeted funds expired if they were not spent by the end of the fiscal year. Buying Jason a standing desk was not the best use of that $2,000. Perhaps that money could have been applied to tuition relief, applied toward upgrading the computer system in a classroom, or carried over into a future semester as a rainy-day fund. The university's rules, though, constrained the way it could be spent, incentivizing Jason to purchase superfluous office furniture.

Now consider not just one rule on office supply spending, but hundreds or even thousands of similar rules governing everything from faculty hiring to scholarships to university facilities to the way that student recreational and activities fees must be spent. Consider their effects on how a department sets its curriculum, or what classes a tenured professor chooses to teach.

7. Our final lesson is that *good rules economize on virtue*. Most people are neither devils nor saints. They sometimes do the noble thing, often do the selfish thing, and sometimes do the wrong thing even when it doesn't serve their interests. Sometimes they act badly because they think they can get away with it, and other times because they're on autopilot and don't notice what they're doing. At any rate, when designing rules to govern any group or organization—society as a whole, the government, a business, or a university—we should as much as possible try to create rules that align the public interest with individuals' private interests.

THE BAD BUSINESS ETHICS OF HIGHER ED

Whether we like it or not, universities are a kind of business. They sell education, prestige, research, status, credentials, fun—and a few other products—to customers. Universities maintain a wide portfolio of investments, maintain contracts with a wide range of vendors, and employ a diverse range of contract employees, many of whom only have an arms-length relationship with their employer. Non-profit universities generally try to maximize their endowments, their operating revenue, and their prestige. Some universities and colleges are run for profit. Despite this, little serious work has been done on the "business ethics" of universities.[22]

Some people find it offensive to describe universities as a kind of business. But nothing in our argument hinges on the word "business."

The reason we call this an inquiry into the "business ethics" of academia is that business ethics asks the right questions. The field of business ethics asks *normative* questions, such as:

1. To whom is an organization responsible? Whose interests must it serve?
2. What moral limits do organizations face in the pursuit of their goals?
3. Whom should organizations hire and how should they treat employees? Customers? Suppliers? Others who have a stake in the organization?
4. What do individual employees owe the organization and society as a whole?

The field also asks descriptive questions, such as:

5. Why do people in an organization sometimes act unethically? What explains how they make decisions about right and wrong?
6. What physical, mental, organizational, or budget constraints do individuals and organizations face?
7. How can we use the answers to these last six questions to produce better behavior?

Business ethics at its best combines philosophy, management theory, sociology, economics, and moral psychology. To do it well, you've got to know something about each of these subjects.

This book examines higher education through an economic, sociological, and psychological lens. We'll examine how rules create weird incentives, and how such incentives motivate real people to behave in suboptimal ways. At the same time, we also recognize that, as our friend Pete Boettke puts it, "Economics puts limits on our utopias." There are limits on how much positive change we can expect. It won't be enough to say, "Don't do that! That's bad!"

For instance, consider the problem of cheating. Most undergraduates cheat, plagiarize, or engage in some form of academic dishonesty at some point.[23] Sometimes this happens because students are genuinely confused about what counts as plagiarism and what doesn't. But a great deal of it happens because students lack time management skills, get behind on their work, or are stressed or tired. And quite a bit happens for strategic reasons.

We want this book to expose some of the problems associated with higher ed, but we don't want it to be a left- or right-wing book. Thus, we plan to avoid criticisms that rely on or presuppose left- or right-wing political beliefs.

For instance, people on the Left often believe the university has a duty to promote social justice. They worry universities instead reinforce social privilege, racism, and sexism. In contrast, people on the Right often believe universities are chock-full of leftist ideology, that half the classes are little more than leftist indoctrination, and that half the research is ideological claptrap. The Left complains that private donors pay libertarian and conservative professors to shill for capitalism; the

Right complains that government grants and other private donors pay leftist professors to shill for big government. The Left complains that universities fail to admit enough minority students; the Right complains that universities actively discriminate against smart Asians and whites in favor of less qualified black and Latino students. People in the center and Right worry that universities now deny due process rights to men accused of rape; some people on the Left think universities are too easy on those same men.

We want to expose and discuss problems people from all sides—or no side—can appreciate. Thus, we will mostly *avoid* these complaints and problems, even if these represent universities' largest moral failings. We want to show that, regardless of your underlying politics, you should agree that universities suffer from flaws in their fundamentals.

2

What Academics Really Want

A DECADE AGO, THE professors at Georgetown's McDonough School of Business agreed they needed to improve the MBA program. But many faculty, including the star teachers, preferred to teach undergrads, not MBAs. The faculty believed the MBA curriculum was important, but they wanted *someone else* to teach it.

It's no great mystery why. Consider the incentives: Georgetown's undergraduates are generally smarter than its MBAs. Furthermore, thanks in part to incentives, undergraduates are curious and interested in big ideas, while MBA students demand practical knowledge with an immediate financial benefit, rather than the subjects faculty like to teach.[1] So, all other things equal, teaching undergrads is more fun.

But other things aren't equal. In fact, there's a structural disincentive to teach MBAs. Tenure-track business faculty owe the university either nine or twelve credit hours of teaching per year. A 45-student undergrad class is worth three credit hours, but a 120-student MBA section is worth only four credit hours. The course lengths are different, but it turns out that teaching MBAs has a higher work per credit hour ratio.

We could wring our hands and complain that faculty are too selfish. That complaint would be both true and utterly useless. There's no army of altruistic angels out there waiting to replace current faculty. We must make do with what we've got.

The more important lesson is that academics, including faculty, staff, and students, respond to incentives. Many of the behaviors everyone complains about—that professors don't care about teaching, that administrative staff waste time and money, and that students don't care about learning for learning's sake—are explained by these incentives. Sometimes the university itself created or could change the incentives its members face. In those cases, a solution exists. Sometimes the incentives are beyond any individual university's control. We may just have to shrug and learn to live with the problems.

In this chapter, we explain the basic incentives that faculty, students, and administrators face, especially at what are called "R1" (doctoral-granting with the highest research activity) universities. Of course, different people have somewhat different motivations. Some people are more driven by fame and prestige, some by money, some by intellectual curiosity, some by love, and others by a desire to push their ideology. And, of course, different institutions structure their incentives somewhat differently. This chapter is impressionistic. We paint with broad strokes, but the fine details will vary from place to place and from person to person.

WHAT THE FACULTY WANT

A Job, Period

What potential faculty want first and foremost is a job. But there are many different kinds of faculty jobs, and they are not all the same.

Long-term, full-time faculty jobs—even bad ones—are hard to get. In most fields, a PhD trains you for exactly one thing: to be a professor. (And it barely trains you for that.) But most fields also graduate more PhDs per year than there are jobs for PhDs. (We'll discuss why they do so in Chapter 8.) Princeton's politics department alone pops out around five political theorists per year, but the entire United States typically offers only twenty long-term jobs for such theorists each year. Not surprisingly, the last time Jason's department hired a tenure-track professor, they received five hundred applications.

At the bottom of the pay and status barrel are *adjunct* teaching positions. Adjunct faculty earn a small fee (about $2,700 per course, according to a 2010 survey[2]) in exchange for preparing their classes, teaching, grading papers, and meeting with students. They have no job security. Their classes could be canceled at a moment's notice, and there is no guarantee they'll be hired again next semester. They often receive no benefits, no office, no research account, no computer, and no other perks. Typically, no one invites them to campus events and they are not permitted to march at graduation. The university often doesn't even list them on its website.

A "full-time adjunct," or a professor who strings together multiple single-class appointments at different universities in the area and teaches a total of eight to twelve classes a year, might make only $30,000 at the typical current per-class rate. The full-time adjunct faculty falling in this category are rare and only a small minority of the adjunct population.[3]

Some adjuncts are retirees who want only part-time work. Others are working professionals with full-time careers who moonlight in the classroom. (These professionals often make much more money than other adjuncts—think of an accomplished litigator who teaches one class at a local law school.) Other adjuncts are only adjuncts and have no other job. Many adjuncts are recent PhDs who hope to land a permanent full-time academic job one day. Many more adjuncts never advanced beyond a master's degree, but still prefer teaching to other career paths in the private sector even if switching careers would pay them more. Unfortunately for this group, the lack of a terminal credential practically ensures that they will never obtain a more permanent academic appointment.

One step up the status-perks-security ladder are postdoctoral research fellows and visiting assistant professors. These are temporary jobs, usually lasting one or two years, that come with full benefits and acceptable pay (say, $50,000 in the humanities or $75,000 or more in business, engineering, or economics). Postdocs have minimal teaching duties and are expected to pump out publications. Senior faculty actively mentor them. Visiting assistant professors are usually paid to teach; they might teach six or so classes over the course of a single year. Senior faculty largely ignore them. Both receive offices on campus and associated perks, benefits such as health insurance during the time of their appointments, and are usually expected and encouraged to take part in departmental activities and other aspects of faculty life. Most faculty in these roles are aiming to improve their résumés so they can secure a more permanent appointment in a future hiring cycle.

Another step up (in terms of pay and prestige) are long-term, full-time, non-tenure-track *teaching* positions. Teaching faculty carry a higher course load than their tenure-track counterparts, but fewer or no research expectations apply to them.

In US and Canadian colleges, these teaching faculty are often called "lecturers." (In the UK, "lecturer" is analogous to a tenure-track assistant professor.) In business or medical schools, such faculty are sometimes called "professors of the practice" or "clinical professors." Sometimes teaching faculty have a clear hierarchy with paths for promotion. One starts as an instructor (especially if one only has a master's degree), but can then be promoted to lecturer (upon earning a PhD), and finally to senior lecturer. Or, one starts as an assistant *teaching* professor, can then be promoted to associate teaching professor, and finally to (full) teaching professor.

Teaching faculty receive long-term contracts (for instance, three- to five-year rolling contracts renewed yearly), full benefits, offices, computers, expense accounts, and some power in faculty governance. Although they are ineligible for tenure, many of them are assured automatic renewal of their contracts, contingent on decent teaching, after they pass a grace period. They have far more job security than, say, private businesspeople.

Finally, the gold standard faculty jobs are *tenure-track* professorships. Professors on the tenure track start as assistant professors. At the end of a six- to seven-year probationary period, they are either tenured and promoted to associate professors, or *fired*. Up or out. Associate professors can then become full professors, and some full professors will win endowed chairs or "university professor" status, which come with increased perks, pay, and prestige.

What professors must do to earn tenure or promotion varies. At some lower-tier liberal arts colleges or state universities, even the tenure-track professors have minimal research obligations and are promoted mostly for their teaching and service. However, at research-intensive universities, such as the Ivy League schools and their peers, or the big research-oriented state schools like Michigan, Berkeley, and Ohio State, promotion and tenure depend almost entirely on research output.

Which publication outlets count for tenure varies from university to university, too. At a third-tier research university, publishing an article in *The Southern Idaho Journal of Theoretical Political Science* (yes, we made that up) could count toward tenure; at Harvard, publication in that venue would count against it. Just as rock stars only date supermodels and drive Ferraris, rock star researchers only publish in the best outlets. You'll notice this book was published by Oxford University Press, not Nowhere State University Press. That's no accident—our employers expect us to hit the best presses.

Tenured professors enjoy fabulous job security. They generally can only be fired "for cause," such as misconduct on the job, or during gross financial emergencies (and then only after all the nontenured faculty and a bunch of administrators have been fired). They also enjoy full rights to faculty governance, the highest status, and the best package of pay and perks. A full professor might make more per week than an adjunct makes per class per semester.

Knowledge

College professors care about their fields. They are nerds. They enter academia because they find certain problems, ideas, people, places, or periods fascinating.

An academic job thus isn't all work—it's partly a consumption good for the professors. It's not merely an instrument for getting other things, but something professors want for its own sake.

To say that professors want knowledge isn't to say that they want *useful* knowledge. Some professors want to cure cancer. Others want to explore the religious semiotics of fourteenth-century Estonian tavern songs.

To say academics want knowledge is not to say they are dispassionate truth-seekers. Some college professors are open-minded and switch sides as soon as the evidence demands it. Others enter graduate school believing they already know all the answers. Their five years of graduate training merely help them produce better rationalizations for whatever they already believed. Some professors are activists rather than scholars.

Money, Fame, and Status

No one becomes an academic just for the money. Most professors could have made more money as surgeons, lawyers, or engineers. They choose quality of life over higher salaries.[4]

But that's not to say the money's bad. In 2017, across *all* four-year colleges and universities in the US, on average, full professors made $104,280, associate professors $81,274, and assistant professors made $70,791.[5] At private and doctoral-granting universities, professors earn much more. In contrast, the median *household* (rather than individual) income in the US in 2015 was about $59,039, while *mean* household income was approximately $72,000.[6] Even badly paid professors make more money than most other people in developed countries.

These numbers are US national averages. But there is tremendous variation in pay, which depends on (1) how rich the college or university is, (2) which field the professor works in, and (3) how famous or important a particular professor is. To illustrate:

- Harvard University, with its $38 billion endowment,[7] pays full professors, on average, about $220,000 and assistant professors about $122,000.[8] In contrast, Tusculum College in Tennessee, with its $16 million endowment, pays full professors less than $43,000 a year.[9]
- Brand new tenure-track assistant professors in business, computer science, engineering, and the law tend to make about $30,000 more to start, on average, than professors in history, psychology, or English.[10] The business school parking lot at Georgetown University is loaded with BMWs, Jaguars, and Mercedes.
- Universities compete to hire and retain star professors. Top professors make far more than others. Some star medical and business school faculty receive multimillion-dollar salaries.[11] In general, the more and better you publish, the more you make. Even star humanities professors at elite schools can earn well over $200,000 a year as their base salary, while also securing significant honoraria, speaking fees, and book royalties. Harvard pays John Bates Clark Medal–winning economist Roland Fryer over $600,000 a year.[12]

Professors earn more money than most people; a few earn much more than average.

Professors also want fame and prestige, among their fellow professors, if not among the lay public. After all, professors work hard to research and produce new ideas and insights. They want other professors to read and approve of their work. (Imagine how bad it would feel to spend a decade writing a book that sells ten copies.) It's a nice bonus if reporters call you for your opinion, if you appear on TV, or if the lay public decides to read your book.

Fame pays. If you're famous, other professors keep track of and automatically read and respond to your new work. Famous professors receive frequent invitations to deliver paid talks (for thousands of dollars per talk) on their research at other universities or for a public audience. Lecturing on one's research is a fun way to tour the country or even the world.

Just as TV celebrities hang out together, academic fame means other famous professors will want to talk to you. Fame also means that the professors will be invited to contribute papers to edited anthologies and journal issues, thus further increasing their fame and influence. In academia, the rich get richer while the poor wither in obscurity.

The fame of your university helps, too. You might be a nobody, but if your name tag says Stanford, other attendees of the Big Academic Association Annual Meeting will assume you're somebody and chat you up. A yale.edu email address means people will respond to your emails.

Freedom

One attraction of academia—especially a research-oriented job—is *freedom*. Although professors already enjoy far more freedom at work than almost anyone else, they want even more.

Some professors get to choose which courses they teach, while others are assigned courses by their department heads or by a departmental committee. But almost everyone, including adjuncts, may design their own syllabi, choose their own readings, and organize their courses as they see fit. Some classes have less freedom in terms of content than others: Even a chaired professor must cover supply and demand and elasticity in ECON 101, while even an adjunct may turn Introduction to Composition into a bully pulpit for her pet interests.[13] Still, within broad and flexible guidelines, the instructor is queen of her course.

Research is even freer. The job description: Research *anything you find interesting* so long as you can publish it in a *good enough peer-reviewed outlet*. For instance, our deans didn't ask us to write this book.

We work on this topic because we find it interesting. We can switch to another topic as soon as we get bored. How's that for a job?

Professors don't have bosses the way most workers do. Department heads are less like managers and more like suckers working for everyone else's benefit. Officially, above each professor is a dean, a provost, and/or a president/chancellor. However, faculty contracts contain academic freedom clauses that limit administrative power over faculty research. An exchange between a president and a tenured professor could go like this:

PRESIDENT: "Your research makes people mad. Would you please write about something nicer?"

PROFESSOR: "No."

PRESIDENT: "Oh, okay."

Ideally this conversation would never even take place, because the president would know better. When we hear about an aberrant administrator attempting to quash disliked research or other forms of faculty speech, it is usually in a news story about the violation of the expected norms of academic freedom. But this sort of bad behavior by administrators attracts notice precisely because it deviates from a long-cherished norm of academic life. The freedom to pursue your own research without such scrutiny is one of the nonmonetary benefits that faculty consume.

Professors also have tremendous freedom in their monthly schedules. They must show up for class and a few meetings here and there, but in general, they can work when and where they want. When and where they do their writing is their prerogative. Again, though, the amount of freedom varies from job to job. A professor at a small liberal arts college with a 4-4 load and heavy service obligations may work 8 a.m. to 5 p.m., five days a week.

More Colleagues

Faculty want more tenure lines in their department.

Professors are nerds who like to discuss nerdy things with fellow nerds. The more people in their department, the more fun and productive work becomes. Adding new faculty also makes it easier for individuals to publish—their colleagues can teach them what's at the cutting edge of each subfield, help them write papers, and so on.

Furthermore, the greater the prestige a professor's department has, the more prestige she personally has. People assume that if you work for the #1 program, you must be pretty good. Adding a new faculty adds to the department's prestige, which, in turn, adds to your prestige.

You'll rarely hear a department tell their provost, "Thanks for offering us another line, but we'll pass. We can staff the classes we need to staff, we're already impressive enough, and frankly the money is better spent on a different program. In fact, let's just keep tuition down." If adding another professor costs the school $300,000 a year, *others* will pay for that, while the department reaps the rewards. So, every department has an incentive to add more faculty, regardless of need. As we will see in Chapter 7, some departments seek out opportunities to expand their faculty footprint on campus regardless of need or demand.

Less Teaching

Students and academic outsiders often gasp when they discover that many professors, including world-famous scholars, can't teach and show no interest in learning how. There are many dedicated and excellent teachers in higher ed, but many professors regurgitate the textbook and reuse the same multiple-choice tests year after year. While high school teachers attend workshops to become better teachers, college professors instead attend conferences where they share research. Many hold only a minimal number of office hours. One of Jason's former colleagues advised him to hold office hours on Friday afternoons to ensure that no students would show up.

It's not because college professors are jerks. It's because they respond rationally to incentives.

Money, fame, and status depend on *research*, not teaching. A star researcher gets national or international prestige among her peers and the public. An exceptional colleague and star teacher will just win affection at her school.

Suppose Martha is a star researcher with a high citation count, who publishes major books or articles year after year, with legions of other researchers reading and responding to her work. But suppose Martha is a lousy teacher. Suppose Nate is an exceptional teacher, whose students love and cherish him. Nate can transform barely literate college freshmen into independent and creative thinkers. But suppose Nate rarely publishes, and no one reads what he writes.

How do their careers go? Martha will probably earn a base salary three to five times Nathan's. She'll receive another $20,000 to $50,000 or so in speaking fees each year; Nathan won't be invited anywhere. She'll end up working at a fancier and more prestigious university than Nathan. She'll enjoy extensive freedom to set her schedule, while Nate will have his week filled with classes and service meetings. Martha may choose where in the world she lives and work, while Nathan will be stuck living wherever he happened to land his first job.

So, of course, most professors who want the perks of a research career will invest in research more than teaching. It's no surprise when professors minimize their teaching time, or that they pump out articles (most of which no one reads) in the hope that something will hit. That's where the money is.

But this leads to a deeper question: *Should* that be where the money is? We suspect many people would argue that teaching is more valuable overall than research, and conclude that for this reason, good teachers should be paid more than good researchers. Furthermore, others might claim that teaching, rather than research, is the ostensible purpose of the university's operations and the ever-rising tuition it collects.

But note the following: First, universities become famous for their Nobel laureates, their groundbreaking discoveries, and so on. Their research brand attracts better students, who are rationally more concerned with the prestige of their university than the quality of its teaching. (We'll explain why later, when we discuss students' incentives.)

Second, the discrepancy in pay—that star researchers earn more than star teachers—could simply be an instance of the *diamond–water paradox*. Early in the development of economics, economists were puzzled why water costs more than diamonds. After all, you need water to live, but diamonds are mere trinkets. In the 1870s, they realized they'd been framing the question incorrectly. The question isn't whether *all* the world's water is worth more than all the diamonds—of course, it is. But what individuals have to decide is whether to buy the next *individual unit* of water or diamonds. All the water is more valuable than all the diamonds, but the next bottle of water is less valuable than the next one-carat gem.

Perhaps good teachers are like water, but good researchers are like diamonds. Part of the reason individual teaching specialists earn less than research specialists is that rock star researchers are more scarce than exceptional teachers. Overall, there are more teachers than research specialists in academia, and as a result, the teachers as a whole make more money than the researchers as a whole do. But because there are so many good teachers, they drive down the price of individual teachers, while the market for good researchers is far less competitive. So, individual teachers make less than individual researchers.

In a similar vein, people often complain that because K–12 teachers make less money than professional athletes, this means that the US must value sports more than education. Not so. The NFL, NBA, MLB, and NHL combined have a total revenue of about $30 billion, of which only a fraction goes to athlete salaries.[14] (Note that the NBA, MLB, and NHL also have Canadian teams, so some of that $30 billion comes from Canada.) In contrast, the US spends about $620 billion on K–12 education as a whole.[15] K–12 teachers as a whole earned about $174 billion in 2014.[16] (That figure does not include salaries for principals, school aides, secretaries, or other K–12 workers.) We spend more on teaching and education than professional sports, but individual star athletes earn more than individual star teachers.

The amount of time that average faculty spend in the classroom per week has declined over the past few decades. According to a nation-wide survey of faculty conducted in 1989, a clear majority of professors (66 percent) spent at least nine hours per week lecturing in the class-room, the equivalent of three courses per semester. When the same survey was taken in 2013, the number of professors reporting at least nine hours of classroom time had dropped to 45 percent.[17] One ca-veat should be mentioned here as well though: The decline in teaching hours is most pronounced at high-profile institutions where prestige is closely linked with research.

To Outsource Administration

In *The Fall of the Faculty*, political scientist Benjamin Ginsberg notes that before the 1970s, college professors engaged in far more of the actual *administration* of the university. "Faculty governance" used to mean something. (Although, in all fairness, before the 1900s, faculty had far less governance power than they did in Ginsberg's golden age.[18]) Faculty would take turns filling various administrative roles—they might serve as a dean, provost, director, president, and so on, for a few years, then "return" to the faculty. Faculty advised students, set the curriculum, and the like. But over time, faculty stopped volunteering to do such jobs. A new class of "professional administrators" emerged. The people running universities now generally "have no faculty experience . . . hope to make administration their life's work"; to them "teaching and research is less important than expanding their own administrative domains."[19]

Ginsberg thinks this was a mistake. Faculty ceded much power to a group of people who have far different priorities from the faculty. (We'll discuss administrators' goals and incentives soon.) As a group, they had more power and influence when they controlled administration.

But, Ginsberg would admit, it's also clear why faculty agreed to or even pushed to outsource administration. Faculty power was held collectively, but individual faculty had to bear the cost of maintaining it, by agreeing to do boring and tedious administrative work. Individuals had every incentive to let someone *else* do it. Individual faculty make far more money and obtain greater fame by focusing on research, rather than service. We the authors would benefit most from an arrangement in which the *other* faculty in our departments run the university, but we personally specialize in publishing and public speaking. But the same goes for almost everyone else.

Thus, over time, faculty choose to outsource their administrative work to professional administrators in order to specialize in research or, more generally, spend a greater portion of their time doing things they actually want to do. Collectively, this may be detrimental to both faculty and students, but on an individual-by-individual basis, it's perfectly rational. In the same way, an individual may want to pollute to his heart's content, even though collectively such behavior leads to global climate change or smog-filled cities.

WHAT STUDENTS WANT

Credentials

For five years, Jason led a seminar on entrepreneurship. In the second week of class, students read and discussed questions such as:

- Will getting a business school degree help you become an entrepreneur?
- How much and just what do students learn in college anyway?
- Why do college graduates tend to make more money than others?

We'll touch on some of these questions later in the book. (To preview: The answer to the second question seems to be "not much.")

During the class, Jason asks his students, Would you rather:

A. graduate from Georgetown with the Georgetown diploma, but literally learn *nothing* the entire time you were here?
B. graduate from East Podunk State College, but double your knowledge?
C. not graduate from any college, but triple your knowledge?

For what it's worth, five classes of elite students in their second week of college almost unanimously ranked A > B > C.

You might think these students are infected with a money-grubbing neoliberal corporatist ideology. Nope. In fact, most students are intellectually curious. But completing college requires four years of unpaid work. The sticker price of four full years at Georgetown is about $288,000,[20] although the US Department of Education estimates, on average, students really pay $110,000 (after financial aid/discounts and scholarships).[21]

The funny thing about college is that most classroom content can be obtained free of charge. Intellectually curious students can download free course materials from MIT,[22] watch free lectures from top professors at Berkeley,[23] or enroll in a free massive open online course

(MOOC) from Harvard.[24] They could do all this on the side while working at paying jobs. Sure, students in MOOCs or students watching Berkeley lecturers at LBRY.io will miss out on face-to-face interaction with professors and other students. Yet if *learning* itself were the goal, it's not clear this face-to-face instruction is worth $110,000 in tuition and fees, plus whatever income they could have earned over four years. It follows from the very fact that students are paying for college that they want the credentials, not just the learning.

The credential, not the learning, is what opens doors for them.[25] The fact that they've completed four years of college at an elite university signals to potential employers that they possess a desirable package of traits—namely, that they are smart and perseverant, willing to play by the prevailing rules and meet society's expectations.[26] It also helps ensure they'll be able to make the right kinds of friends and attract high-quality, high-status marriage partners in the future.

In contrast, imagine they chose option C, but had no clear way to *prove* they had tripled their learning. It's hard to see how they'd turn that path into a career. Potential employers aren't going to look for uncredentialed diamonds in the rough when they have piles of well-credentialed diamonds before them. Students who chose C might be able to attract venture capital, but only after they've already developed a proven start-up. Good luck with that.

In short: Given the incentives and trade-offs they face, what's most important to students is that college opens doors for them. Learning can't be the point. (And, as we'll see in Chapter 3, there is good evidence that most learn little.)

Less Work, More Play

Studying comes at the expense of fun.

Colleges concentrate generally young, healthy, but immature people at the height of their interest in socializing together in communal living arrangements for four years. Every hour spent studying is not an hour spent playing video games, working out, partying, or hooking up.

Students spend far more time on leisure now than in the past; indeed, they now spend more time on leisure and social activities than they do on academic work.[27] In the 1960s, average college students in the US spent 40 hours a week studying or in class. Now, they spend only about 27 total hours a week pursuing academic activities. In 1961, average students spent 25 hours per week studying; by 2003, that average had fallen to 13 hours per week.[28]

One reason they work less is that faculty *assign* less work. Since the 1960s, faculty have been assigning fewer pages of reading and shorter essays.[29] As many researchers on higher education have put it, there is an implicit bargain between faculty and students. The faculty won't ask much of students and students won't ask much of the faculty. Remember, as we discussed previously, that faculty want to teach less to focus more on their research. This arrangement benefits both sides— the faculty publish while the students play.[30]

Low Costs

Academia is a weird product. Back in 1970, economists James Buchanan and Nicos Devletoglou noted that, at least in the embattled University of California system, (1) students consume the product but don't pay for it, (2) faculty provide the product but don't sell it, while (3) the public pays for it, but doesn't consume it.[31] This bizarre market structure explained the weird incentives everyone faced, and why the academy was rather dysfunctional.

But, of course, the situation has changed since 1970. Now many public universities in the US are largely privatized, in the sense that the state provides only a small amount of direct funding. But at the same time, private universities are semi-public, as the federal government provides subsidized loans and grants that students use to pay tuition. Faculty still don't really sell the product, and the public (which doesn't consume the product in any direct sense) still pays part of the tab. However, students and their parents now pay a larger percent of the bill, and larger absolute cost, than they did in the past.

All things equal, students (and their parents or guardians) want lower costs. Students and their parents are consumers at the end of the day. They want to consume a certain kind of collegiate product— good credentials, prestige, a fun student atmosphere, and so on—but all things equal, they'd like to pay less for it.

Many of the "business ethics" problems we see in academia take the following form: A small subset of motivated faculty, students, or administrators push to implement some pet project. This project is expensive, but they can transfer the costs, through increased tuition or student activity fees, onto other students (or others in general) who don't benefit from it. Universities charge students differential tuition based on their ability to pay. But they do not usually charge them differential tuition based on the quantity or types of services, clubs, or projects they consume. You pay the same tuition and fees regardless of whether you join six clubs or none. At many universities, you pay the same tuition regardless of whether you enroll in classes that are expensive or cheap to supply.[32]

In general, students face a collective action problem whereby they have little incentive to lobby against projects that increase costs. They also have every incentive to lobby for projects that they personally want, knowing that they personally will bear only a tiny fraction of the costs. But when everybody has the same incentives, this leads to ever-increasing costs.

To illustrate, suppose Students for Organized Rock Climbing (SORC) want Big Public University to install an artificial rock climbing wall. Suppose the fifty or so SORC members value rock climbing at $3,000 per year.[33] They get a total value of $150,000 from the wall. Suppose all other students value rock climbing at $0. Suppose installing and then maintaining the wall will cost $300,000 a year. Suppose that the wall's cost will be spread equally among all 50,000 students through activities fees, so each student pays $6 for the wall.

Notice the bad incentives this plan will create. Installing the wall is a $150,000 net loss to the university's "society": The wall costs $300,000, but the students collectively extract only $150,000 of value from it. However, the benefits of the wall are concentrated among a few SORC members, while the costs are diffused among everyone. Accordingly, we'd expect SORC to lobby actively and intensely for the wall, while we'd expect the remaining students to pay little attention to it. It's not worth their time to lobby against it, or even take note of the proposal, because an hour spent lobbying against it will cost them more than just paying the additional $6 in fees for the year so that SORC members can climb a wall. Administrators also agree to build the wall so that the admissions office can show off its fancy new "amenity" to prospective students, even though most will never use it.

Now, rinse and repeat. It's not just SORC lobbying to get a new toy at others' expense, but every professor, administrator, and student group with a pet interest. So long as the benefits are concentrated but the costs diffused, we'd expect "special interest groups" to lobby continuously for new projects, even when these projects cost more than they're worth. College becomes ever more expensive. (Note, however, that we're not saying this is the main reason college is becoming more expensive. Other factors are more important.)

WHAT ADMINISTRATORS WANT

A Promotion

Administrators have less well-defined career paths than professors, but like others, they still tend to seek out better-paying, higher-status jobs. The highest-profile administrative jobs—those of president, provost, and academic dean—are often filled by former faculty who made the switch.

Prior faculty experience is usually a job prerequisite for top academic positions. It is common to see a college president who established herself as a well-published professor of chemistry, a provost who previously taught in a history department, or a dean of academics who previously chaired a faculty senate. These positions are held by academics who "made the jump" to administration at some earlier point in their careers but usually after establishing themselves on a traditional faculty track.

There are any number of reasons why some faculty cross over to administration as well. Some discover they have a knack for administrative work in a lesser position such as department chair and decide to pursue promotional opportunities outside of the classroom. Others are drawn to the prestige of a position, or its accompanying boost in salary. Many academics even know an administrator or two who was "offered" a role in the central office after years of being a troublemaking colleague in a department. After all, when tenure makes it difficult to fire a faculty member who creates problems in the classroom or department, one remaining option is to "promote" that person into a different role.

The reasons for filling senior administrative posts with academics derive from tradition and historical practice, rather than any particular training for the job. Some do advance through the ranks of administration, as might be the case with the dean of a major business school taking on the position of provost at another college or university as her next career step. Usually, though, people employed in this role have some level of academic accomplishment that may be traced back to their time as regular faculty members. The role of college president was once a way of conveying prestige upon an accomplished and long-serving faculty member. Until the mid-twentieth century, senior academic administrators from the faculty track would often teach an occasional class or two. At a few small liberal arts colleges, this is still the case today.

Senior administrators who follow the faculty path represent an ever-smaller portion of the lesser administrative ranks, however. Executive-level administrators have mostly tracked the pace of growth among faculty and student enrollments. By contrast, lower-level administrative professionals have more than quadrupled over the past forty years. In 1976, they sat just shy of 200,000, or less than half the number of full-time faculty. Today, there are over 800,000 lower-level educational bureaucrats—we'll call them "educrats" for short—in the American university system, placing them on par with or even a little ahead of full-time faculty numbers.

Educrats perform diverse tasks. They range from student affairs and activities to admissions and recruitment to college athletics to fundraising to regulatory compliance to political causes such as the "Office of Sustainability." Some of these roles have hybrid functions that require an advanced degree, for example, the student services counselor with an MEd who also teaches a one-credit "university skills" course in the general education curriculum. Others may only require a bachelor's degree, such as a student life manager who simply entered into an academic administration career after graduating from college and is now tasked with running a block of dormitories.

The motives for taking a lower-level administrative position vary. A non-profit fundraiser who excels at soliciting and securing donations may find that his skill is exceptionally suited to a university's development office, as might a marketing specialist who sees her skills are good for raising the public profile of a university's research. An admissions officer might simply enjoy the university atmosphere. A student activities administrator might have ideological reasons for taking a position, and view it as his job to "educate" his campus in the ways of carbon footprint reduction by insisting on "green sustainability" components for all projects under his budgetary control. An athletics program administrator may see a position as a pathway to a comfortable salary and relaxed work environment.

Money, Prestige, and Power

In many respects, administrators want the same things as faculty: money, prestige, and power.

To some degree, there's a trade-off between faculty and administration. The $250,000 spent employing two to three administrators is not money spent employing a physics professor. That's not say it's a complete trade-off. Administrators can also complement faculty. As we discussed earlier, professors have an incentive to outsource some of their former duties to administrators. Administrators can make professors more efficient, say, by taking over advising, admitting students, or running the computers, thus leaving professors free to do research. Of course, without faculty, administrators would have no jobs, period.

There's also a trade-off between administration and students. The $250,000 spent employing two to three administrators is money not spent giving some gifted or poor student a full ride. But, again, it's not a complete trade-off. Students have various needs and wants, and sometimes administrators serve those needs.

Just as economists find it helpful to model firms in a market as *profit-maximizers*, economist William Niskanen argued that we should model bureaucracies as *budget-maximizers*. To simplify his model: When trying to predict what a particular department will do, presume that the directors want to increase the department's budget, especially its *discretionary budget*, as much as possible. In fact, rigorous empirical work has found that this model explains several aspects of how higher education functions.[34]

In *The Fall of the Faculty*, Ginsberg expands on this model to explain how administrators face dysfunctional incentives. Suppose you want to increase your department's budget. Or, suppose you are more selfish than that—you want to increase your own personal salary, prestige, and status. Either way, you have an incentive to do two things:

1. *Hire more people.* The larger your staff, the greater your budget. The more people who report to you, the more important you are, and the easier it is to justify a raise.
2. *Expand the scope of your department.* Your department might be created to perform specific tasks. But if you can create *new* tasks, you can justify increased money, more office space, and new hires. Economists call this behavior "mission creep."

Administrators thus have strong incentives to *oversupply* their services. They have selfish incentives to create unnecessary jobs and hire unnecessary staff, which others will pay for.

Ginsberg claims that, in part as a result of these perverse incentives,[35] universities now suffer from severe administrative bloat. In the past forty years, US higher education increased its number of administrators and nonteaching staff by 300 percent or more.[36] In contrast, the absolute number of students grew by about 50 percent, with the number of full-time faculty keeping pace at around 50 percent. In 1975, colleges had nine full-time professors for every four administrators; by 2005, that statistic had changed to nine professors for every ten administrators. American universities now employ 100,000 more professional staff than full-time faculty.[37] Yale University spends $60,000 on administration *per student* each year, while Wake Forest spends $75,000 on administration per student per year.[38]

Ginsberg argues at great length that the proliferation of deans, deanlets, associate deans, assistant deans, assistants to the assistant deans, directors, and the like is pernicious. These expanding positions drive up the costs of college, but most of the new administrators, he claims, have a negligible value. (Consider this: Forty years ago, universities got by just fine without these administrators. So, why think we really need them?)

Note, however, that universities have a perverse incentive to raise their costs. *U.S. News and World Report*'s annual "Best Colleges" edition is the gold standard for undergraduate college rankings. Nearly everyone knows about them. Every president and dean wants her university to move up in these rankings. This means that they have an incentive to do whatever the rankings reward.

But—and here's the perverse incentive—in calculating each college's raw "score," *U.S. News and World Report* assigns 10 percent of the weight to the *amount spent per student*.[39] The more a college spends per student, the better it ranks. Imagine that the University of Chicago, ranked #3 in 2017 among all American universities, somehow managed to provide exactly the same quality of research and instruction, but—miraculously—without spending *any* money on faculty. It would *drop* approximately 8 percentage points in the rankings, down to #14.[40] If Yale University, tied at #3 with Chicago, somehow provided the same-quality output but magically spent $0 per student (except for faculty salaries), it would drop to about #11 in the rankings.[41] If both of them managed to provide literally the exact same high-quality educational and research outputs at exactly zero cost, they would drop to around #20 in the rankings. In contrast, suppose the College of William and Mary, ranked #32, somehow was able to provide the same-quality education and research at fifty times its current expense; it would jump to about #27 in the rankings.[42]

U.S. News and World Report uses expenses as a proxy for quality. It uses inputs as a proxy for outputs. But in doing so, it inadvertently incentivizes colleges to be inefficient in their spending. In a normal market, the firm that can produce the same output at lower cost is the *better* firm. In academia, the university that produces the same output at *higher cost* is, according to the most important ranking, the better school.

Over the past forty years, federal and state governments have imposed more regulations on universities, which, in turn, require universities to hire more staff to monitor and ensure compliance. At least some of the spending growth results from that. However, as Ginsberg documents repeatedly in *The Fall of the Faculty*, administrators frequently *invite* external accreditation requirements and frequently *lobby* for increased regulation.[43] Doing so both gives the staff (1) a pretext for hiring *more* staff and increasing their budget, and (2) additional power over the faculty. For instance, Ginsberg comments as follows on why administrators pushed for the external accountability and measurement of faculty teaching even before the Department of Education implemented any regulations:

> For several years, some administrators have been aware of the potential value of externally mandated performance criteria as instruments through which to wrest control of the curriculum from the faculty. Accountability measures allow administrators to require the faculty to "teach to the test," rather than devise the curriculum according to its own judgment. In this way, college professors can be reduced to the same subordinate status to which elementary and secondary school teachers have already been reduced.[44]

Now, we're not automatically taking the side of faculty here. As you'll see in Chapter 3, we're worried that students don't actually learn much in college. Still, it's far from obvious that the solution is to have lay-people with no knowledge of physics, economics, or political science (or teaching!) tell experts in physics, economics, and political science what and how to teach.

Most universities now require students to complete course evaluations after every class, and at many universities, student evaluations of their instructors count heavily in consideration for tenure and promotion. But the research overwhelmingly shows that course evaluations are, well, garbage.[45] Indeed, the empirical work on course evaluations is so damning that using them is, frankly, morally irresponsible. (See Chapter 4.) They do not track objective measures of learning or skill development, but they do track students' preference for fun classes, easy grading, and charismatic and attractive faculty members, and may reflect prejudice against female or black professors.[46]

If administrators genuinely cared about improving teaching quality, they would examine the empirical evidence showing that course evaluations don't work, and either get rid of them or reform them radically. But if we recognize that the point of student evaluations is *not* to evaluate teaching effectiveness, but instead to help administrators further their own goals (the appearance of objectivity, increased power over faculty, increased funds for themselves), then it makes sense that they continue to use them. (Again, we'll expand on this point further in Chapter 4.)

Previously, we discussed how faculty want freedom. They want freedom to teach courses how they see fit and do whatever research they see fit, no matter how controversial. To some degree, administrators want the opposite: They want to restrict faculty freedom.

That's not because they are malicious gremlins, but because they face different incentives. Consider the fact that administrators, not faculty, have to recruit and retain students, appease legislators and credentialing boards, handle university public relations, soothe and assure parents, raise outside money for buildings and toilet paper, create class schedules and assign classes to rooms, assign departments to buildings and allocate office and laboratory space, monitor and demonstrate regulatory and accreditation board compliance, induce alumni to donate, and so on. In general, these activities are easier when the faculty are quiet, predictable, and uncontroversial, and when classes and faculty are largely interchangeable with each other. A chef may want to experiment with new food creations every day, but an Applebee's franchise owner wants line cooks who grill the steak the same way every day.

Security

Administrators, like anyone, want job security. But unlike faculty, they cannot win tenure. This puts administrators at a disadvantage—if a university faces serious financial problems, the university is supposed to fire administrators and professional staff before it cuts tenured and tenure-track faculty.

Accordingly, this gives administrators a few strange incentives, including these:

1. *To be seen as busy and therefore essential.* While faculty can be measured by their discrete outputs (articles published, classes taught), it's harder to measure what administrators are doing or whether they add more value. But busier administrators inherently seem more important, significant, or "essential" than administrators who aren't busy. As Ginsberg finds, though, there often isn't objectively much work for them to do. Administrators respond by filling their schedules with meeting after meeting, with a large percentage of those meetings being little more than administrators reporting to each other about

what happened at other meetings.[47] Anecdotally, we've noticed that whenever we've had to serve on joint faculty–administrator initiatives, the faculty always want to do things via email, while the administrators always want to schedule meetings.

2. *To replace tenure-track faculty with non-tenure-track faculty*. As we'll discuss in Chapter 6, it's simply a myth that full-time faculty are being replaced by adjuncts. However, there is some evidence that, over the past forty years, full-time tenure-track faculty are being replaced by full-time but not tenure-track faculty. Between 1993 and 2015, the percentage of full-time faculty with tenure dropped from 59 to 49 percent at public four-year institutions and from 50 to 43 percent at private institutions.[48] The number of full-time faculty off the tenure track has risen in both cases. Administrators have two reasons to push for this shift: (1) Faculty without tenure are easier to control and push around, because they can be fired more easily. (2) In the event of any financial problem, tenure-track faculty take strong priority over administrators in keeping their jobs. But administrators have less of a chance of losing their jobs when they are competing with non-tenure-track faculty.

CONCLUSION

The university is a political environment, one in which different groups and individuals compete for power and resources. Individuals have strong incentives to promote their self-interest at the expense of others, and in some cases to promote their political team's interest at the expense of others. It's not that the university is full of gremlins or beset by poltergeists, but that individual professors, students, and administrators face incentives that put them in conflict with the core values of the university.

Over the next few chapters, we'll go into more depth. Each chapter will be a case study in bad behavior as explained by bad incentives.

3

Why Most Academic Advertising
Is Immoral Bullshit

. . . Education on Your Terms
Your Education. Your Way.
Personal Education. Lifetime Success.
Personal Education, Extraordinary Success
Where Success Begins
Where Success Is a Tradition
Your Success. Our Tradition.
Experience Tradition. Expect Success.
Real Tradition, Real Success
Real Education. Above All.
Real Education. Real Results.
Real Life. Real Knowledge. Real People.
Real People Start Here
A Great Place to Start
It All Begins Here. . . .

> —Steve Kolowich, "88 College Taglines, Arranged as a Poem,"
> *The Chronicle of Higher Education*[1]

UNIVERSITIES ADVERTISE, BUILD BRANDS, and market themselves, just
like most other businesses and non-profits.

Some universities and colleges are "enrollment dependent." They receive most of their operating funds from student tuition fees, including
fees paid by subsidized federal loans and grants. These colleges must

maintain a sufficiently large student body or face a financial emergency. They are like regular businesses; they can't survive without customers.

Many colleges and universities that are not enrollment dependent still advertise special programs that generate extra revenue. For instance, Wharton, Harvard Business School, Stanford Graduate School of Business, Georgetown's McDonough School of Business, and so on, each offer "executive MBA" programs. Senior executives take intensive weekend classes and earn an MBA on an accelerated, part-time schedule. But—here's the open secret—EMBA programs are highly profitable. They're expensive, but the students' employers often pay their tuition. Faculty usually teach "off-load" for extra money, often for more than $1,000 per contact-hour in the classroom. An EMBA program can generate 40 to 50 percent margins.

Universities and colleges also make additional profits through their continuing education programs. For instance, Harvard's "Extension School" offers classes for "every type of adult learner."[2] Although Harvard College—the real undergraduate school—has about a 5.4 percent acceptance rate, the Extension School has open enrollment, like a community college. It also charges $1,550 per class,[3] and courses are generally taught by low-paid adjuncts rather than actual Harvard professors.[4] People enroll in the extension school and then brag about being Harvard students.

Many universities advertise to enhance their prestige. As an analogy, you might be surprised to see BMW, Mercedes Benz, or Rolex advertise to audiences that cannot afford their products. They advertise to the lower and middle classes in order to maintain their cachet and desirability among the upper middle classes. Harvard, Yale, and Princeton do the same. They want *everyone*, not just their potential students and potential employers of their students, to think Harvard = Fancy, Elite, High Quality.

But there's more. All things equal, the lower a university's acceptance rate, the more prestigious it is. The *U.S. News and World Report* rankings explicitly reward universities for having low acceptance rates.[5] This partly explains why Harvard and Yale will send admissions brochures to and encourage applications from mediocre high school students who have no chance of getting in. They want to trick the students into applying, so they can reject them, thus ensuring that the schools maintain a lower acceptance rate. Harvard's undergraduate admissions office declares, "You belong here. Wherever your life may have started, and whatever its destination, there is a place for you at Harvard."[6] Well, maybe there's a place for you as a janitor, but almost certainly not as a student.

In this chapter, we criticize how universities and colleges market themselves to potential students. In particular, we'll examine how they promise (or at least strongly insinuate) that they will transform students, teach them to think, and turn them into leaders. The problem, we'll argue, is that little evidence exists that universities succeed in doing any of these things. Thus, universities engage in, if not quite false advertising, what we might instead call *negligent advertising*. They are not exactly lying, but selling snake oil.

This chapter may be the most damning in the entire book. As we'll show in our discussion, there is no proof that universities do deliver, or are capable of making good, on most of their promises. Universities do not just engage in unethical marketing. Rather, they seem to not even do much educating, period.

A TRANSFORMATIVE EXPERIENCE!

Colleges routinely promise big and beautiful things. Let's take a look.

Harvard University offers a "transformative education."[7] Harvard Business School's MBA program offers "an intense period of personal and professional transformation that prepares you for challenges in any functional area—anywhere in the world."[8]

Georgetown University is committed to "helping students grow intellectually, spiritually and emotionally as well as encouraging them to become thoughtful and caring members of society who contribute to the greater good."[9] Between 2011 and 2016, the McDonough School of Business at Georgetown University advertised that it "develops principled leaders committed to serving both business and society."[10]

Yale University:

> is committed to the idea of a liberal arts education through which students think and learn across disciplines, literally liberating or freeing the mind to its fullest potential. The essence of such an

education is not what you study but the result—gaining the ability to think critically and independently and to write, reason, and communicate clearly—the foundation for all professions.[11]

Not to be outdone, Princeton University makes the same promise:

By exploring issues, ideas and methods across the humanities and the arts, and the natural and social sciences, you will learn to read critically, write cogently and think broadly. These skills will elevate your conversations in the classroom and strengthen your social and cultural analysis; they will cultivate the tools necessary to allow you to navigate the world's most complex issues.[12]

Amherst College says the same:

A liberal-arts education develops an individual's potential for understanding possibilities, perceiving consequences, creating novel connections and making life-altering choices. It fosters innovative and critical thinking as well as strong writing and speaking skills. The liberal arts prepare students for many possible careers, meaningful lives and service to society.[13]

Smith College, located in middle of nowhere Massachusetts, nevertheless declares, "At Smith, the world is your campus. You'll be ready to live, work, and lead across global borders."[14] Nearby sister college Mount Holyoke also claims that since 1837 its mission has been to "prepare women to face the future. To take the lead. To make a difference."[15]

Well, maybe, but those are some of the most elite universities and colleges in the United States. Their graduates do become presidents, CEOs, and cultural leaders. What about less prestigious places?

Apparently, they *also* offer transformative experiences and crank out world-changing leaders. For instance,

At Northwood University, leadership isn't simply taught, it's instilled. The DeVos Graduate School degree programs will transform you— personally and professionally. Accelerated, Traditional, Working

Professional or Online students are welcome to explore our dynamic learning environments. Discover your leadership potential and begin your personal transformation today![16]

Or, at the "edge of possible . . . also known as the University of New Hampshire . . . there's a new opportunity around every corner, a new project starting every minute, and an always-expanding, always-inspiring sense of possibility."[17]

George Mason University offers "a college experience like no other." Their "top priority is to provide students with a transformational learning experience that helps them grow as individuals, scholars, and professionals."[18] Two hours away, competitor James Madison University offers "A Better You."[19] They go on:

Engaged learning happens everywhere at JMU. Every discussion. Every lab. Every study group. Every team project. Every interaction with a professor.

Wow! By the way, JMU defines engaged learning as "developing deep, purposeful and reflective learning, while uniting campus and community in the pursuit, creation, application and dissemination of knowledge."[20]

Amazing! JMU's marketing team claims literally every single interaction with a professor and every study group involve deep, purposeful, and reflective learning, which unites the campus and community in the pursuit of knowledge. When we the authors were in college, study groups were for scoping out potential girlfriends. But then we didn't attend JMU.

Southern Methodist University proclaims, "World Changers Shaped Here."[21] They offer "unbridled experiences." They go on:

SMU's singular approach to integrating rigorous learning with hands-on experience will prepare you to achieve your educational goals and expand your world in ways you never imagined. Ours is a community of people forging their own paths. We'd like to help you shape yours.

Hillsdale College "offers an education designed to equip human beings for self-government."[22] They continue:

> Think about the people you want to be around. Think about everything that's the opposite of shallow and trendy. Think about four years of conversations you'll never forget. That's Hillsdale College. In and out of class, people here are on a journey together—one where intellectual enthusiasm is valued, friendships are genuine, and honest discourse is unflinching.
>
> When you come to Hillsdale, you also become part of something bigger. For more than 170 years, Hillsdale has promoted "the diffusion of sound learning" as the best way to preserve the blessings of civil and religious liberty. Learn more about the pursuit of the good, the true, and the beautiful at Hillsdale College.[23]

They conclude that Hillsdale College is what college is meant to be.

Not every school makes hyperbolic claims. Some just provide plain statistics about students, classes, and professors. But, see for yourself. Check out the admissions webpages of the colleges and universities near you, or if you're an academic, check out your own. You'll probably find grandiose promises.

These promises aren't simply filler text on websites either. They're usually the product of elaborate and expensive marketing campaigns the colleges undertake. To give you an example, a marketing industry trade survey estimated that the average US college spends about $472,000 a year on marketing advertisements. There's also a sizable range in marketing expenses, with the largest budget in the sample reaching $3.5 million.[24] These numbers are usually in *addition* to standard admissions office materials and don't include staff salaries. Some of the more extravagant expenses include a college that spent $100,000 on Facebook ads, another that invested $400,000 in Google ads, and a third that reported doing the same on Bing.[25] The average college in the same survey sent out 65,000 pieces of direct mail per year, and more than half spent money on broadcast media (typically radio).[26] While most colleges handle these expenses in-house, a growing minority have started outsourcing their marketing to public relations firms, giving rise to an entire industry that openly touts its own specialties in connecting colleges to prospective students.[27]

Remember: While some marketing may be necessary to sustain recruitment, every dollar spent on marketing has any number of other potential uses: a new faculty hire, scholarships or tuition cuts for students, facilities upgrades, or even refunds to the taxpayers who support public institutions. We take no stance on which is appropriate, but at minimum a sizable expenditure on a flimsy or even deceptive marketing claim raises ethical issues about the trade-offs.

Now ask: Can the college back up its extravagant claims about transformative experiences and world-opening opportunities? Can it back up even its most basic and mundane promises?

THE WONDER OF THE LIBERAL ARTS!

Four-year universities and colleges do not provide much vocational training. Even engineering and business schools require students to spend far more time learning theory and abstract concepts than practicing vocational skills. Instead, most four-year schools, even professional schools, focus on the liberal arts. But this presses them to justify their curriculum: *Why* study the liberal arts? Insert joke here about art history majors flipping burgers.

If you google "Why study the liberal arts?," you'll find many colleges and universities answer with a number of bold *empirical* claims. For instance, Montclair State University says,

> Study of the liberal arts prepares you for a career by instilling those attributes that employers repeatedly say they want when they hire college graduates—the intellectual skills of critical thinking, analysis of information, and effective expression of ideas. In this sense, the liberal arts provide the ultimate job training. The liberal arts prepare you not just for landing that first job, but for your promotion in a few years . . . and for your second and third jobs.[28]

Wheaton College claims a liberal arts education imparts six benefits:

1. It teaches students how to think.
2. It teaches students how to learn.

3. It allows students to see things whole.
4. It enhances students' wisdom and faith.
5. It makes students better teachers.
6. It contributes to the students' happiness.[29]

The University of California, Berkeley, explains,

> To be liberally educated is to be transformed. A liberal arts education
> frees your mind and helps you connect dots you never noticed be-
> fore, so you can put your own field of study into a broader context.
> It enables you to form opinions and judgments, rather than defer to
> an outside authority.[30]

The University of Iowa says,

> The liberal arts and sciences teach what today's employers say they
> value most: how to communicate your ideas; find and analyze infor-
> mation and data; adapt to new technology and professional trends;
> work with others to solve problems; and make confident, knowl-
> edgeable decisions.
> A liberal arts and sciences education does more than teach you
> the skills you need for a successful career—it provides you with the
> experiences and understanding you need for a fulfilling life.
> . . . The liberal arts and sciences are more important than ever in
> today's job marketplace. Employers can train you on the specifics of
> a job—but they can't teach you the ability to communicate ideas,
> obtain and analyze information and data, work in teams, and solve
> problems.
> These are the essential career skills and qualities that a liberal arts
> and sciences education will bring you.[31]

Park University advertises,

> Liberal studies can, in fact, free a person from ignorance, prejudice
> and apathy. A liberal arts education equips students with an appreci-
> ation for critical inquiry and independent thought and reasoning.[32]

Arizona State University declares,

Our redefined liberal arts and sciences education will help transform you into a socially aware, critically thinking global citizen who strives to bring about positive change.[33]

St. Lawrence University asserts,

St. Lawrence University inspires students and prepares them to be critical and creative thinkers, to find a compass for their lives and careers, and to pursue knowledge and understanding for the benefit of themselves, humanity, and the planet. Through its focus on active engagement with ideas in and beyond the classroom, a St. Lawrence education leads students to make connections that transform lives and communities, from the local to the global.

Drawing on the best of the liberal arts tradition, we provide an education that is personally and intellectually challenging. We push our students to ask deep, even unsettling questions from multiple perspectives and to be responsible for the ways they move through the world. At the same time, we surround them with a supportive community as they engage in complex processes of personal and intellectual discovery. By cultivating an atmosphere that is both intellectually rigorous and attentive to the whole person, we excel at helping students reach their full potential.[34]

And so on. Almost every college and university we examined said the same thing. They admit that liberal arts education does not directly teach the specific hard skills needed for most jobs. But they claim— even better!—that it provides a range of soft skills that allow students to adapt to any job; help students write and communicate clearly; assist students in thinking through hard problems; and make students morally better and more aware, with a wider perspective. The word "transform" appears again and again.[35] Some schools merely say that they are going to "help" improve students' writing, communication, and reasoning skills, or merely "help" prepare them to be leaders and catalysts of change; they don't specify *how much* help they will provide. Others declare they will *instill* these skills.

WHY STUDY PHILOSOPHY?

What happens if we get even more narrow and focus on how individual departments market themselves? Take, for instance, philosophy. To parents, philosophy may sound useless: 2,500 years of asking the same abstract questions with no progress in finding answers.[36]

To counter that, many philosophy department websites include a page or two defending the study of philosophy. They make the same argument for philosophy that liberal arts schools make for liberal arts in general: Studying philosophy improves your writing, communication, thinking, finding connections, evaluating ideas, and so on. It prepares you for *everything*.[37] In addition, they claim that philosophy itself brings unique benefits, especially in terms of standardized test preparation. It's liberal arts education on steroids.

For instance, the Daily Nous blog offers a series of webpages on "the value of philosophy." One such page contains a number of graphs showing that:

A. Philosophy majors have the fourth highest overall GMAT scores of any major, after physics, mathematics, and engineering.
B. Philosophy majors have the highest average LSAT scores of any major.
C. Philosophy majors have the highest average GRE verbal and analytic writing scores of any major, plus better GRE quantitative reasoning scores than all other humanities and social science majors except economics. They have the highest overall GRE scores.
D. Philosophy majors have the highest midcareer salaries of all non-STEM majors, with an average midcareer salary of just under $85,000.[38]

Now, to be clear, claims A–D are all true. The Daily Nous blog simply points out these well-documented and persistent facts. Philosophy majors have been outperforming everyone else for a long time. So far, nothing dishonest is afoot.

However, things get fishy when we ask whether this indicates anyone should major in philosophy. The University of Washington's philosophy department asserts:

Philosophy students learn how to write clearly, and to read closely, with a critical eye; they are taught to spot bad reasoning, and how to avoid it in their writing and in their work. It is therefore not surprising that philosophy students have historically scored more highly on tests like the LSAT and GRE, on average, than almost any other discipline.[39]

The University of Wisconsin's department further states:

Studying philosophy can also help you get into graduate school. Philosophy majors excel on standardized tests like the GRE, GMAT, and LSAT. They rank first among all majors on the verbal and the analytical section of the GRE. Philosophy majors also tend to do better than just about any other major on the LSAT. With a mean score of just over 157, they are second only to physics majors. When it comes to the GMAT, philosophy majors rank in the top five of all majors, and they consistently have higher scores than business majors (including management, finance, accounting, and marketing majors).[40]

Similarly, Louisiana State University's philosophy department argues:

It's well known that a BA in philosophy provides excellent preparation for study in a philosophy graduate program as well as in law school. The superior performance of intended philosophy graduate students on the GRE and philosophy majors on the LSAT [is] . . . evidence of this.[41]

Washington and Lee University's department poses the "why major in philosophy?" question and then answers it with a list:

- Philosophy majors outperform all other majors except math/physics, and perform equally well as economics majors, on the LSAT.
- Philosophy majors are admitted to law school at a higher percent than any other major.
- Philosophy majors outperform all business and accounting majors on the GMAT.

- Philosophy majors outperform all other majors on the GRE Verbal and Analytic.
- Philosophy majors outperform all other humanities majors on the GRE Quantitative.
- Prospective philosophy graduate students earn the highest mean scores of students heading into any arts or humanities in all three areas of the GRE.
- Philosophy majors have the third highest acceptance rate to medical school.
- Midcareer salaries for philosophy majors are the highest in the humanities and higher than those of accounting, business management, and marketing majors.[42]

DePauw University argues:

> The study of philosophy develops one's abilities to read and understand difficult material, to think critically, to distinguish good and bad reasoning, and to develop and defend one's own ideas. These skills are invaluable in any academic field and, we submit, are often quite useful even in the real world. Of course, proponents of many fields would claim that their disciplines hone these very same skills. Perhaps; but we claim that the study of philosophy is not just one way of developing these skills; rather, it is one of the most effective ways. One sort of evidence for this is the data concerning the performance of students with various undergraduate majors on standardized tests like the LSAT, the GMAT, and the GRE. This data is relevant because these tests are not tests of knowledge but rather tests of certain intellectual skills—indeed, they are supposed to test for the very skills mentioned above. The numbers don't lie; the performance of philosophy majors on these tests when compared to the performance of students with other majors is telling.[43]

See for yourself. Google "Why Study Philosophy?" and see what various philosophy departments have to say. Over and over, you'll find they claim that studying philosophy makes you not only better at, well, doing philosophy, but also it trains you to be good at critical thinking in *any* and *every* walk of life. They do not just claim that the skills *could* be transferred to any area, but that studying philosophy, in fact, *will* induce you to transfer and apply those skills elsewhere. Furthermore, they cite the facts about philosophy majors' superior midcareer salaries and standardized test results as *reasons* to study philosophy. Most go on to claim that studying philosophy *causes* you to get better test results.

But, as we'll discuss here, these are all deeply problematic claims. We'll argue that philosophy departments making such arguments have bad business ethics; they violate basic norms of ethical advertising. Indeed, from a moral perspective, they are much *worse* than used car salespeople who "forget" to mention problems with their cars.

So, having now shown how universities and particular departments market themselves, let's turn to explaining why it's mostly immoral bullshit.

SELECTION VERSUS TREATMENT EFFECTS

Years ago, Jason had a cold. Aunt Bonnie noticed and offered a cure: "Drink this tea concoction every day for seven to ten days, and the cold is certain to go away."[44] Jason suppressed a good laugh when he realized she wasn't kidding.

The problem with Aunt Bonnie's prescription is that colds generally disappear after seven to ten days anyway. So, if you follow Aunt Bonnie's advice, your cold will indeed go away, but not *because* you followed her advice.

A similar story: When Jason's older son Aiden "graduated" from his Montessori School's primary program, Aiden's teacher said, "We know we're doing great work when we see them like this. They're so much more mature now than they were three years ago." Once again, Jason bit his tongue, but later said to his wife: "Yes, of course, they're more mature. They started the program at age 3, and now they're 6." Three-year-olds who begin instruction at the Montessori School of Northern Virginia (MSNV) almost invariably emerge in three years as more mature 6-year-olds, but it doesn't follow that MSNV *made* them more mature. Perhaps, for all we know, MSNV even *stunted* their maturation, but MSNV's possibly pernicious effects were outweighed by natural intellectual and emotional development.

Maybe something similar happens to college students. College students generally begin college at 18 and graduate when they are 22. If they're "better" in certain ways when they depart, we'd want to know how much of that resulted from their chronological age, other events that occurred in their lives during those four years of college, or the mere fact of *attending college*. Notice the "if" here: Before we start exploring what explains their improvement, we should also check to see *if* they have actually improved.

Some people have tried to answer this question. The results are, in general, quite depressing for colleges. In fact, there's good evidence that students for the most part do not much improve in their writing, mathematical, or critical reasoning skills over the course of four years. We'll return to this point in more depth later on.

Such a lack of improvement is not the only problem, however. Suppose we know the following facts to be true:

1. People with bachelor's degrees are generally smarter and more successful than people without bachelor's degrees.
2. Philosophy majors tend to be smarter and more successful than other majors.

Even if claims 1 and 2 are true (and, yes, they are true), it does not follow that getting a bachelor's degree or that majoring in philosophy *makes* you smarter or more successful.

From the fact that "students declaring an intention to go to graduate school in philosophy have the highest mean scores on the Verbal section of the GRE (mean: 589) of any major," we cannot conclude that "philosophy prepares students for the Graduate Record Exam."[45] Instead, we would need to determine if A) *philosophy makes people smarter*, B) *the people who study philosophy are, on average, smarter*, or C) both statements are true.

When laypeople see graphs showing that philosophy majors have high GRE and LSAT scores, they tend to assume, "Wow, philosophy must make you smart, or at least teach you how to do well on such tests." But social scientists know better than to make such assumptions. Rather, their first reaction is, "Treatment effect, selection effect, or both?"

Here's the difference:

- *Treatment Effect*: People who study philosophy *become* smarter as a result of studying philosophy. Philosophy *creates* smart students.
- *Selection Effect*: The people who choose to major in philosophy and who obtain a degree in philosophy are already smarter than those students who choose to major in other fields. Philosophy *attracts* smart students.

Similarly:

- *Treatment Effect*: People who finish a bachelor's degree *become* smarter and more successful as a result of getting their degree.
- *Selection Effect*: The kinds of people who manage to complete a bachelor's degree are already smarter, more conscientious, and more likely to be more successful, on average, than those who don't.

Let's illustrate with some clear examples. Consider the following:

1. US Marines tend to be tough, in excellent shape, and skilled warriors.
2. Models at IMG tend to be thin, tall, and beautiful.[46]

The first is mostly a treatment effect. Marine training makes you tough, gets you in shape, and you spend weeks learning how to fight. (It's not *entirely* treatment; Marine training, amazing as it is, can't fix everybody. They won't enlist paraplegics.) The second is clearly a selection effect. As Malcolm Gladwell explains:

> Social scientists distinguish between what are known as treatment effects and selection effects. The Marine Corps, for instance, is largely a treatment-effect institution. It doesn't have an enormous admissions office grading applicants along four separate dimensions of toughness and intelligence. It's confident that the experience of undergoing Marine Corps basic training will turn you into a formidable soldier. A modelling agency, by contrast, is a selection-effect institution. You don't become beautiful by signing up with an agency. You get signed up by an agency because you're beautiful.[47]

Similarly, we know that Harvard graduates are smarter and more successful, on average, than graduates of, say, Keene State College in New Hampshire. But we want to know, how much of that is *treatment*, and how much is *selection*?

Obviously, a great deal of it is selection. After all, Harvard is exceptionally selective. They reject 95% of applicants and nearly everyone it admits is *already* extremely impressive. Keene State is unselective. The average admitted applicant has less than a B average in high school and low SAT scores.[48]

Suppose, the day *before* classes begin, you randomly select 100 freshman students from Harvard University, and compare then to 100 randomly selected freshmen from Keene State College. Although some overlap would exist and some Keene State students might be smarter than some Harvard students, you'd expect that, on average, the Harvard students are smarter, more skilled, and more accomplished than the Keene State students. You'd also expect that twenty years down the road, the 100 Harvard freshmen you selected would be, on average, more successful than the 100 Keene State freshmen, not just because of the doors Harvard opened for them or the skills Harvard taught, but in large part because these students were sufficiently impressive to *get into* Harvard to begin with.

As a college freshman, Jason considered going to medical school. He read an article at the time indicating that classics majors had the highest success rates when applying to medical school. The article was careful, though, to explain why. It didn't say there was any evidence that the classics better *prepared* one for medical school. It's not like studying Greek and Latin makes you medical doctor material. (Maybe it helps one memorize anatomical terms, but that would be it.) Rather, the article made clear, the classics are *hard* and require a lot of work and effort. You can't bullshit and half-ass your way through a classics degree the way you can a communications degree. You actually have to learn Latin and Greek, and that's *really, really hard*. Accordingly, the article suggested, the kind of people who choose to major in the classics and actually complete such a rigorous academic program are (1) smart, (2) diligent, and (3) studious. They are the kind of people who will get into medical school, more or less regardless of what they major in. In short, the article argued, the success of classics

majors in being admitted to medical school was predominantly a selection effect.

Now imagine the classics department, after reading the same article
as Jason, tried to sell the discipline by saying, "Hey, everyone, major
in classics! We'll get you into medical school!" It would be a dishonest
form of advertising. The classics don't *make* you a good candidate for
medical school. Instead, the people who choose to major in the classics
are also students who are good candidates for medical school. If you do
not already possess the characteristics previous classics majors had, then
majoring in the classics probably won't help you.

So, this brings us to the big question posed in this chapter.
Universities, liberal arts colleges, and philosophy departments do not
simply claim that their graduates tend to be better than nongraduates
along some dimensions. They don't simply say, "Our graduates are, on
average, better at critical thinking than 22-year-olds who did not go
to college." They don't simply advertise themselves as excellent *sorting*
mechanisms. Rather, as the earlier quotations from marketing materials
illustrate, they claim that they *cause* their students to become better.

But here's the problem: Universities, liberal arts divisions, and philosophy departments generally aren't in a position to justifiably make
such claims. They don't *know* if these claims are true. Thus, we'll argue,
they're engaging in what we'll call "negligent advertising."

NEGLIGENT ADVERTISING: THE PFIZER ANALOGY

Imagine if the pharmaceutical giant Pfizer placed the following
advertisement:

> Introducing Collegra! Collegra is a drug unlike any other. If you take
> Collegra 256 times a year for four years, Collegra will improve your
> critical reasoning, moral reasoning, analytic, and quantitative skills.
> It will transform you into a better person with a global mindset. It
> will make you able to face any challenge. It will prepare you for any
> job. It will dramatically improve your cognitive skills. It will make
> you score higher on standardized tests, such as the LSAT or GMAT.
> Furthermore, it will help you make more money! Indeed, Collegra

users, on average, earn an extra million dollars of lifetime income compared to nonusers.

The cost of Collegra varies from person to person. Collegra is not covered by your insurance. Pfizer charges rich kids and foreign students on government grants $60,000 a year. But if you can't afford Collegra, Pfizer may be able to help. Some satisfied previous Collegra users have generously provided us with funds to help new users.

Warning: Taking Collegra is more like undergoing chemotherapy than taking a pill. Users need to spend at least thirty hours a week for thirty weeks a year over four years for it to be effective. Most users will be unable to work at a job while taking Collegra.

Side effects include increased tendency to engage in binge drinking and to acquire tens of thousands of dollars in debt.

If you want, imagine that as a narrator makes all these proclamations, we see smiling and attractive 20-year-olds squeezing chemicals into test tubes, then later reading poetry, then later looking spellbound at math equations, then watching a Nepalese dance troupe, then finally walking down the aisle in black robes and mortarboards.

Now imagine that Pfizer sincerely believes everything it says. But suppose Pfizer has not engaged in *any* of the standard testing that drug companies must conduct in order to sell drugs in the US or Europe. They have conducted *no* clinical trials. They have done *no* randomized controlled experiments. They haven't even examined any natural experiments. All they have, at most, are various statistics showing that drug users outperform nondrug users. Suppose, also, that they have good reason to suspect that their "findings" are the result of a selection effect, because Pfizer itself has explicitly chosen to only administer their drug to smart, conscientious, perseverant, and already successful people.

Now ask, would Pfizer's advertisement be unethical?

The US government would say so. Indeed, Pfizer would not be allowed to legally sell or advertise Collegra in the United States unless the corporation conducted extensive testing proving that Collegra was both safe and effective. The sincerity of Pfizer's beliefs would make no difference whatsoever.

In this (hypothetical) case, Pfizer engages in, if not *false* advertising per se, what we might instead call *negligent advertising*.

Negligent advertising: Selling a product based on the claim that the product delivers certain benefits, despite *lacking* evidence that the product, in fact, delivers those benefits.

Here, Pfizer isn't lying—they believe what they say. The problem isn't that they're sincere but mistaken. It's *possible* their claims are true, but they don't know for sure. Instead, the problem is that they're claiming their drug produces certain results, but they haven't done even the most basic due diligence to prove that it does. Given the evidence available to them, they aren't in a position to assert causation. They may sincerely believe in their product, but they aren't *entitled* to that belief.

It's bad business ethics to sell something by claiming it is responsible for some good effect unless you have sufficiently strong evidence that it, *in fact*, causes such an effect. It's even worse business ethics if good evidence is out there that the product does not result in the supposed evidence, and you just ignore and evade the proof. As we'll see, when it comes to selling higher education, there is indeed strong evidence *against* many of its claimed benefits. In other cases, evidence exists that higher education does produce some of its putative benefits, but *not* for the reason colleges affirm it does.

Negligent advertising is bad, but just how bad depends, in part, on the cost of the product. To illustrate, consider two different cases:

1. Pfizer offers Collegra, as previously described, on the marketplace. On average, it costs consumers—after income-based price discrimination—$100,000 to take the drug, while governments kick in another $100,000 or so on the drug user's behalf. The drug requires about 4,000 to 6,000 hours of treatment over a thousand days across four years. Most drug users leave with tens of thousands of dollars of debt. Pfizer again obtains no real evidence that the drug works.
2. Rival drug company Eli Lilly and Co. offers Universitalis. They claim that Universitalis will provide the same benefits as Collegra. Eli Lilly also lacks evidence for their claims. However, their drug only costs a total of $1 and requires one minute to administer.

Although both Pfizer and Eli Lilly have engaged in negligent advertising, Pfizer's behavior is much worse. After all, when patients buy and use the Pfizer's product, they "pay" not just tens or hundreds of thousands of dollars more, they also pay in terms of time and lost wages. The full cost of Collegra is staggering, while Universitalis costs almost nothing. This doesn't excuse Eli Lilly's (hypothetical) behavior, but Pfizer's behavior is far worse than Eli Lilly's.

So, what makes negligent advertising wrong in the Collegra case is at least the following two features:

1. *A failure of due diligence.* In many cases, sellers owe it to potential buyers to do due diligence. They may not claim a product has a benefit unless they have sufficient evidence to substantiate that claim. But Pfizer lacks this evidence.
2. *Harm.* Collegra is extremely costly, so Collegra users give up a great deal to take it.

If Pfizer engaged in any of this behavior, our academic colleagues would be up in arms. Our business ethics colleagues would write case studies about their negligent actions. If an auto company claimed that their cars were the safest in the world, but had done no testing and possessed little if any evidence to support such a claim, both groups would view the company as dishonest and immoral in how they conduct business.

But, perhaps not surprisingly, we college professors hold ourselves and our employers to far lower moral standards than we hold others. Although Pfizer doesn't sell Collegra, universities do sell a similar product—the *degree*—and make the same promises. As we'll now show, they are engaging in negligent advertising.

PROBLEM I: UNIVERSITIES DO NOT TEST THEIR PRODUCTS

In real life, Pfizer tests drugs before they bring them to market. They do randomized controlled trials, collect data, and demonstrate statistically that their drug produces certain effects over and above a placebo. They also collect and measure side effects. They have to go through an extensive review process with the FDA, a process that can cost well over a billion dollars.

Similarly, automobile manufacturers also engage in extensive testing before they sell their vehicles. BMW claims their 340i can go from 0 to 60 mph in 4.6 seconds.[49] It does not merely *assert* that without evidence. BMW puts its vehicles on a track and tests them under a number of conditions.

The basic model of higher education developed in medieval Europe nearly a thousand years ago and has endured since then with slight modifications. Back in 1088, when the University of Bologna opened, no one knew how to test cause and effect in a scientific way. Since then, with the development of statistics, we've learned how.

However, unlike Pfizer or BMW, the universities and colleges we earlier quoted from have not tested, and have no plans to test, any of the extravagant claims they make about the efficacy of their product. Unlike Pfizer, they do not randomly select 1,000 students for a particular treatment and then compare them to a randomly selected control group, all while measuring and controlling for confounding variables.

Suppose Pfizer tried to sell Collegra, and we pointed out that they hadn't tested the product. Imagine they respond, "Sure, we haven't tested Collegra to prove that it works, but you also haven't shown us that it doesn't. So there!" No one would accept that response. After all, it's a basic norm of argument and scientific reasoning that the person asserting the novel positive claim bears the burden of proof. In the first instance, Pfizer would have the burden of proving that its product worked. We would then have the burden of *disproving* their claim only *after* they had collected a great deal of evidence supporting it.

Similar remarks apply to universities and colleges. They promise many wonderful and beautiful things. They claim they will transform students (for the better), improve their cognitive skills, prepare them for any job, teach them to think, and so on. *They* bear a burden of proof, just as Pfizer does. But they make almost no effort to discharge that duty.

That's already enough to condemn pretty much every university and college as engaging in negligent advertising. But the situation gets worse.

Universities and colleges might be justified in making their grandiose claims if preexisting research was out there showing that they do indeed deliver the supposed benefits of an education at their institution. However, the problem is that educational psychologists, economists, sociologists, and others have already investigated how colleges work, what they do and fail to do, and why they make the choices they do. The results are not good for the universities. There's solid evidence that colleges do not, and in many instances cannot, deliver on some of their promises. In some other cases, colleges *do* deliver—for instance, getting a bachelor's degree really does tend to help people earn more money—but *not for the reasons* colleges claim.

PROBLEM 2: EVIDENCE OF SELECTION EFFECTS

On average, a person who graduates from college is smarter, more conscientious, more successful financially, healthier, happier, and more likely to maintain a satisfying marriage than a mere high school graduate.[50] Compared to high school graduates, college graduates are far less likely to get divorced, go to jail, become unemployed, or get hurt on their jobs.[51] On a wide range of factors, college graduates are, on average, superior to high school graduates. These are well-documented facts.

But, again, none of this by itself *proves*, pace researchers who assert otherwise, that the "total value of a college education is thus considerably greater than just the higher earnings."[52] After all, *nonrandom* selection is at play in determining who goes to college versus who doesn't, and who finishes college versus who doesn't. Even lower-tier schools like Keene State admit students who already have superior credentials, family backgrounds, conscientiousness, and so on, when compared to students who don't even apply and who never go to college. Furthermore, to finish college, even at Keene State, requires perseverance, and so only the more conscientious students will actually finish.

Thus, we would, of course, expect people with college degrees to have happier marriages, lower incarceration rates, higher rates of saving, and so on. The personal qualities that make you able to *get into* and *finish* college are roughly the same personal qualities that help you build a good marriage, avoid jail, find and keep a job, become a good parent, and save for retirement.

Now, in principle, savvy researchers can measure such qualities and find ways to estimate college's *value added*, while controlling for these selection effects. But when colleges announce how wonderful their graduates' lives are, they almost never do so. Even researchers who should know better often don't bother. In 2015, the Lumina Foundation produced a gushing report—"It's Not Just the Money"—that chronicles all the advantages college grads have over others, but the authors made no attempt at all to control for selection bias. Accordingly, we can say here, quite frankly, that the foundation's report is garbage, because controlling for selection bias is an elementary and basic requirement for such research. (For what it's worth, the report was published by an advocacy group, rather than in a peer-reviewed outlet.)

Previously, we noted that as a matter of fact, philosophy majors receive the best overall scores on the GRE, and some of the best scores on the LSAT, the MCAT, and GMAT.[53] Philosophy majors tend to be smart. But we worry that by themselves these test results provide no evidence philosophy makes anyone smarter. They do not show that any randomly selected student will benefit from studying philosophy, or that studying philosophy will help improve the test scores of some random student.

The problem is that students choose their majors; the majors aren't chosen for them. Students tend to major in the subjects they find interesting and are good at. So, it's both possible and plausible that philosophy students excel at these standardized tests in significant part because those who choose to major in philosophy are already good at logic, mathematics, and critical reasoning—precisely the subjects these standardized tests assess. We need to investigate whether philosophy majors' high scores result from a treatment effect (philosophy makes you smart), or a selection effect (smart people tend to major in philosophy), or both.

In fact, we already have strong evidence of a selection effect. High school students who say they intend to major in philosophy have significantly higher than average SAT scores. Most high school students have never taken a philosophy class.[54] Many of them will later discover that philosophy is more demanding and logic-intensive than they might have presumed. Philosophy will tend to weed out the worst students; at most schools, it's not an "easy major."

Still, it's possible that there is a treatment effect on top of the selection effect, that is, that philosophy majors start off smart, but studying philosophy makes them even smarter. The people making such a claim bear the burden of proof in establishing it.

So far, they've made very few attempts to do so. We located one paper that found philosophy students improved their critical thinking skills slightly over the course of a semester, but the paper didn't show that such skills persisted after the class ended.[55] In general, studies on the positive benefits of philosophy are inconclusive; some show no effect, some show a negative effect, and some find a weak positive effect.[56] A few studies also exist on whether studying philosophical ethics improves students' moral behavior, but such studies are largely inconclusive.[57]

College graduates generally make more money than nongraduates, and graduates from elite schools generally make more money than graduates from nonelite schools. Why? Fortunately, this issue has been studied rigorously by world-class researchers. But the results aren't encouraging for university marketers.

Previously, we asked you to imagine how one hundred randomly selected Harvard freshmen would compare to one hundred randomly selected Keene State freshmen on the day before classes begin. We know that Harvard has much more stringent admissions requirements than Keene State. You'd expect that the Harvard students would be more successful than the Keene State students, not just because they got the superior Harvard education, but because they were already gifted, talented people, good enough to get into Harvard in the first place.

What value does Harvard add? What value does any college add? These are not mere imponderables. Social scientists can and do study these questions rigorously. One way to do so—one way to compare the value-added of Harvard versus Keene State—goes roughly as follows. First, we have to operationalize what we mean by "success." Sure, success means different things to everybody. But we can just select specific factors to measure: writing skills, lifetime income, employment rates, marital satisfaction, health, and whatnot. We can then independently measure a number of other variables (such as race, sex, gender identity, parental income, IQ, SAT scores, parental education level, high school rank, ACT scores, etc.) and see if these correlate with success, as we defined it. These correlations give us a baseline, and they allow us to isolate the effects of going to college while statistically correcting for the effect of these other variables. Now it's just a matter of finding the right data. We can start asking questions such as, "If 1,000 people with an IQ of 130, identical socioeconomic backgrounds, etc., go to Harvard, and 1,000 otherwise identical people go to a no-name school, how much better, on average, will the Harvard graduates do in life, if at all?"

In fact, economists Stacy Dale and Alan Krueger have attempted to answer a very similar question. They've produced a series of papers that estimate what value going to an *elite* college actually has, while correcting for the fact that elite students are already, well, elite.[58] Economist Bill Easterly offers an excellent summary of their research:

> [W]hat if the basis for all this stress and disappointment—the idea that getting into an elite college makes a big difference in life—is wrong? What if it turns out that going to the "highest ranked" school hardly matters at all?
>
> The researchers Alan Krueger and Stacy Berg Dale began investigating this question, and in 1999 produced a study that dropped a bomb on the notion of elite-college attendance as essential to success later in life. Krueger, a Princeton economist, and Dale, affiliated with the Andrew Mellon Foundation, began by comparing students who entered Ivy League and similar schools in 1976 with students who entered less prestigious colleges the same year. They found, for instance, that by 1995 Yale graduates were earning 30 percent more than Tulane graduates, which seemed to support the assumption that attending an elite college smoothes one's path in life.
>
> But maybe the kids who got into Yale were simply more talented or hardworking than those who got into Tulane. To adjust for this, Krueger and Dale studied what happened to students who were accepted at an Ivy or a similar institution, but chose instead to attend a less sexy, "moderately selective" school. It turned out that such students had, on average, the same income twenty years later as graduates of the elite colleges. Krueger and Dale found that for students bright enough to win admission to a top school, later

income "varied little, no matter which type of college they attended." In other words, the student, not the school, was responsible for the success.[59]

That's not to say that which college a student attends doesn't matter at all. Getting a four-year degree really does help students earn more money. But the particular college they go to has very little independent effect on their future earnings. Harvard students do better than Tulane students not because Harvard is better than Tulane, but because Harvard students are, on average, better than Tulane students.

PROBLEM 3: EVIDENCE OF SIGNALING

Dale and Krueger's studies asked, in effect, do Harvard students make more money because they were good enough to get into Harvard, because they went to Harvard, or both? And, unfortunately for Harvard and its peers, Dale and Krueger found the answer was mostly the first half of the preceding statement: Harvard students make more money because the personal qualities that got them into Harvard also tend to generate higher income. The "Harvard" name adds a little in the short run, but not much in the long run. Going to college, period, matters, although the particular college doesn't matter much.

Still, getting a four-year degree really does help you earn more money, on average. But now we need to ask, why, in general, college students make more money than others? There are two basic theories that could explain this:

- *Human capital theory*: Wages are determined by productivity, and productivity is determined by skills. Colleges teach students a number of soft and hard skills, for example, how to reason critically and how to do double-entry bookkeeping, which improve students' productivity. As a result, college students make more money. In short, colleges make students more productive and thus help them earn more.
- *Signaling theory*: It's difficult and costly for employers to sort good potential employees from bad ones. However, to complete a college degree, especially from an "elite" school or with a "difficult" major,

requires students to pass a lengthy and difficult admission process, and then survive four years of jumping through hoops, pass mentally difficult (even if useless) classes, and so on. Thus, having a college degree tends to *demonstrate* to employers that the potential employee has a combination of three desirable traits: intelligence, perseverance/conscientiousness, and conformity/willingness to play along with social expectations. In short, colleges are sorting mechanisms that separate the wheat from the chaff.

Academic marketing pushes the human capital theory. But it's possible that the signaling theory explains some, most, or even *all* of the gains college graduates receive. The only way to know is to rigorously test each theory.

Colleges, of course, don't test these theories; they just presume everything results from human capital development. That in itself is a cardinal sin in advertising—it's an instance of negligent advertising. Colleges shouldn't be making such promises unless they have strong evidence their institution, in fact, develops students' human capital.

The most rigorous and thorough investigation of the signaling theory to date has been Bryan Caplan's *The Case Against Education*. Caplan carefully lays out exactly what the human capital and signaling theories would predict, then carefully tests each prediction using a variety of public data sets. He finds that, in general, students forget almost everything they learn in college and high school, skills and learning are generally compartmentalized and nontransferable, gains in skill are at best modest, and gains to earnings are largely explained by preexisting abilities. Furthermore, college degrees have a sheepskin effect: That is, if you drop out of college a few weeks before graduation, you would have more or less the same skills as a person who actually finished college. If the human capital model were true, you'd both make the same earnings. But, in fact, drop-outs get almost *no* boost; what matters is that you actually obtain the degree. In the end, he estimates that most of the earnings increase from a college diploma may be explained by signaling rather than human capital development.[60]

It gets worse for colleges. The human capital theory says that students develop various skills, these skills make them more productive, and, as a result, they earn more money. But what if it turns out students *don't* develop more skills, or don't develop them much? Then the theory is in deep trouble. We turn to that problem now.

PROBLEM 4: EVIDENCE MOST STUDENTS DON'T LEARN SOFT SKILLS

Testing whether individual college majors improve various skills is difficult, because nonrandom selection is at play in who majors in what. A priori, we expect students bad at math to avoid economics, engineering, and physics. We expect students good at logic and analysis to major in philosophy. We expect classics majors to be more conscientious and perseverant than communications majors.

In principle, we could test majors by testing students' skills before college, randomly assigning thousands of students to different majors, and then test them again after they complete their majors. We'd then know what value the majors add while controlling for selection effects. But, alas, we can't do these kinds of experiments.

However, it's easier to measure whether college *as a whole* adds value. Researchers can test first-year undergraduates' critical reasoning, writing, and quantitative skills at the outset of college. They can test those same students again later in their academic careers and see if these skills have improved. Now, if they get positive results, that would not quite prove college works—after all, it's possible these skills fade away after students leave college. Researchers could determine whether or not this happens by testing the students again, say, five, ten, and then twenty years after graduation. But if they find *no* gains or only *weak* ones in their initial tests, that sure would be damning.

Now for some damnation: In 2013, Richard Arum and Josipa Roksa published *Academically Adrift: Limited Learning on College Campuses*. This book is a treasure trove of depressing statistics. For instance, they found that over the past forty years, colleges have assigned students progressively less demanding work, and students spend progressively less time studying and more time on leisure. In 1960, studying was a full-time, forty-hour-a-week job; now, the average student in the University of California system spends roughly three hours of leisure for each hour of study.[61]

Arum and Roksa studied 2,300 college students of all different socioeconomic backgrounds, levels of college preparation, and so on. They asked students to take the Collegiate Learning Assessment multiple times over their college careers:

> The Collegiate Learning Assessment (CLA) consists of three open-ended, as opposed to multiple choice, assessment components: a performance task and two analytical writing tasks (i.e., to make an argument and to break an argument). According to its developers, the CLA was designed to assess "core outcomes espoused by all of higher education—critical thinking, analytical reasoning, problem solving, and writing." These *general skills* are the "broad competences that are mentioned in college" and university mission statements.[62]

In short, the CLA tests the soft skills that liberal arts curricula are supposed to "instill," the very skills liberal arts colleges brag about in their marketing. So, how do colleges fare?

Not well. Arum and Roksa found, "At least 45 percent of students in our sample did not demonstrate any statistically significant improvement in CLA performance during the first two years of college."[63] At least 36 percent walk away with no measured gains after four years of college.[64] More conservative and cautious approaches to testing statistical significance yield worse results: At least 53 percent showed no gains after two years.[65] Worse, the students who did improve their CLA scores generally had only *modest* gains. And, again, we don't know if or how long those gains endure beyond college. For all we know, about half of students see mild improvement during college, but a year after they graduate, those skills fade away from lack of use. Arum and Roksa summarized their findings as follows:

> [M]any students are not only failing to complete educational credentials, they are also not learning much, even when they persist through higher education. In general, as we have shown, undergraduates are barely improving their CLA-measured skills in critical thinking, complex reasoning, and writing during their first two years of college. Even more disturbingly, almost half are demonstrating no appreciable gain in these skills between the beginning of their freshman year and the end of their sophomore year.

In addition to limited growth, learning in higher education is also unequal. Students from less educated families and racial/ethnic minority groups have low levels of skills in critical thinking, complex reasoning, and writing (as measured by the CLA) when they enter college. These inequalities are largely preserved—or in the case of African-American students, exacerbated—as students progress on their journey though higher education.[66]

In general, Arum and Roksa determined that about half of students gained no general reasoning and writing skills in college, about 40 percent gained very modest skills, and only the top 10 percent of students gained significant skills.[67] That's what $500 billion a year in higher ed spending on students appears to have gotten us.

Now, maybe this study was flawed. Perhaps students knew the exam didn't affect their grades and so put in no effort. Maybe they would have done better if something were at stake. We don't have good evidence nevertheless that they learned the soft skills colleges say they do, and our best available long-term, comprehensive study found no evidence that most students learn much.

PROBLEM 5: STUDENTS DON'T SEEM TO TRANSFER SOFT SKILLS

Liberal arts education is grounded on an assumption—on a particular *psychological* theory—about how we learn. The assumption goes as follows:

The Psychological Assumption of the Liberal Arts

Liberal arts classes—in philosophy, classics, literature, and so on—are not useless. On the contrary, these classes teach students *how to think*. They teach students to develop their skills in logic, analysis, conceptual clarification, and interpretation. They teach students to find patterns, to isolate cause and effect, to assess reasons, and to evaluate arguments. They train students to be enterprising and creative. These are skills useful for almost any job. A liberal arts major can learn "hard skills" specific to this or that job in a few weeks, but the real value of the liberal arts is that it builds students' mental muscles. When we teach students to read Joyce or dissect Plato's arguments, they can and will use those same skills in whatever jobs they ultimate get.

Professors started teaching liberal arts–style classes on the basis of this assumption long before anyone knew how to test whether the underlying premise is true. They just took the assumption for granted. Most professors continue to take it for granted; they show little interest in learning about learning. (That's not surprising: See Chapter 2.)

In the last section, we already arrived at a reason to believe this assumption is false. We can measure students in such soft skills before, during, and after college, and see whether they improve. It looks like a large percent of students make no statistically significant gains, the majority make only small gains, and a mere 10 percent make large gains. College doesn't appear to build students' mental muscles much at all. So, college marketing is—unbeknownst to the marketers—mostly false and colleges have bad business ethics. QED?

Liberal arts schools do not merely claim that their students will be interpreting Shakespeare, reading difficult historical texts, or finding holes in philosophical arguments. They assert that students *can* and *will* use those "skills" to interpret the stock market, devise better marketing methods, read difficult corporate memos, or find holes in a strategic business plan. But what if that assumption is false?

Educational psychologists used the term "transfer of learning" to describe when a student applies skills or abilities learned in one context or domain to a different context or domain. For instance, if you learn how to write essays about Shakespeare, and you then somehow use that skill to be a better financial analyst, that's transfer of learning. But whether students, in fact, engage in a transfer of learning, or *could* even do so, is a psychological question. It depends on how our brains work, on how we learn.

The only way to know whether transfer regularly occurs is to check. College marketing professionals and admissions officers, of course, never do. They just *assume* it does. But that's bad business ethics—it's the equivalent of Pfizer assuming Collegra works without evidence. For all they know, we might be throwing away $500 billion a year on the basis of a mistaken theory of learning.

Unfortunately for academic marketers, many educational psychologists have studied transfer of learning. Once again, the results look bad for higher ed. As Caplan summarizes:

> Can believers in the power of learning-how-to-think back up teachers' boasts with hard evidence? For the most part, no. Educational psychologists who specialize in "transfer of learning" have measured the hidden intellectual benefits of education for over a century. Their chief discovery: Education is narrow. As a rule, students only learn the material you specifically teach them . . . if you're lucky.[68]

Psychologist Richard Haskell summarizes as follows:

> Despite the importance of transfer of learning, research findings over the past nine decades clearly show that as individuals, and as educational institutions, we have failed to achieve transfer of learning on any significant level.[69]

Douglas Detterman says:

> Transfer has been studied since the turn of the [twentieth] century. Still, there is very little empirical evidence showing meaningful transfer to occur and much less evidence for showing it under experimental control.[70]

Terry Hyland and Steve Johnson assert:

> On the basis of the available evidence, however, drawn from many very different disciplines, we believe that the pursuit of [general transferable] skills is a chimera-hunt, an expensive and disastrous exercise in futility.[71]

How do educational psychologists know? One way is to run experiments. For instance, they might teach students how to solve a problem. Then they assign some students a similar problem with a similar solution right away. Even then, under ideal conditions, the majority *fail* to see the connection between the two problems and fail to solve the second problem. Failure rates become even higher if the psychologists introduce a time delay between the first and second problem, or if they distract students with an unrelated problem, or if the problems are introduced by a different professor in a different context.[72] In short, under ideal conditions, most students don't transfer learning, and under realistic conditions, hardly any do.

Another investigative strategy is to ask students to apply their classroom skills outside the classroom, and then see if they're any good at it. In general, they're not. For instance, Barry Leshowitz took hundreds of Arizona State University science students and tested whether they would apply the scientific reason skills they learned in the classroom to problems they might read about in a newspaper.

As an example, he asked them, if the majority of students needing psychological counseling have poor dietary habits, does it follow that these same students should eat better? This is a softball question. The correct answer is no, not necessarily. It could be that a poor diet *causes* psychological problems. But, alternatively, it could be that suffering from a psychological problem causes people to eat badly. It could be that psychological issues and poor eating habits have a common cause. A good science student should know that correlation does not imply causation and should be able to think of natural and artificial experiments to test these various hypotheses. But almost none of the students could do so. In Leshowitz's own words:

> Of the several hundred students tested, many of whom had taken more than six years of laboratory science in high school and college and advanced mathematics through calculus, almost none demonstrated even a semblance of acceptable methodological reasoning about everyday-life events described in ordinary newspaper and magazine articles. The overwhelming majority of responses received a score of 0. Fewer than 1% obtained the score of 2 that corresponded to a "good scientific response." Totally ignoring the need for comparison groups and control of third variables, subjects responded to the "diet" example with statements such as "It can't hurt to eat well."[73]

Leshowitz gave students an *easy* question. These students had spent years training to answer questions *like* this, but couldn't do it. At most, they were only good at using scientific reasoning about the narrow range of issues they had previously discussed in class. They couldn't extend that reasoning to novel but analogous cases. Physics and chemistry students can solve a problem in physics and chemistry, but can't reason about the structurally equivalent problem in nutrition or psychology. Transfer of learning *sometimes* occurs. Students who take heavy doses of statistics become somewhat better at statistical reasoning outside class. Some science students are slightly better at certain forms of conditional reasoning.[74] Still, overall, the available results are fairly grim. In general, learning is highly specific. People acquire skills in narrow domains and apply those skills to only those same narrow domains. Studying philosophy will make you a better philosopher, perhaps, but there's not a lot of evidence it makes you a better person, romantic partner, business leader, or much else.

SUMMARY

Let's be clear: The people who write college admissions brochures are probably sincere. They make grandiose promises. They probably believe what they say, though they have no evidence for their claims, and even so, if they bothered to look, they'd find quite a bit of disconfirming evidence.

College marketers are slimy, but it's a different kind of slimy from the stereotypical used car salesperson. Shifty Shane at Buy Here, Pay Here Auto knows he's lying through his teeth. Rather, college marketers are more like true believer psychics, TV evangelists, or cult leaders. They believe in what they do. They just aren't *entitled* to that belief.

Academia is expensive. It costs tremendous amounts of time and, for many students, tremendous amounts of money. Since students could instead work full-time or pursue other activities, it also has serious opportunity costs. When we sell academia, we'd better have good evidence it delivers the goods we say it does, for the reasons we say it does. But we don't. Academic markets don't have the evidence they need to back up their claims. Worse, insofar as researchers have rigorously tested those claims, the claims appear to be false or at least highly misleading. College advertising isn't exactly a *lie*, but it isn't true. It's *negligent advertising*.

WHAT SHOULD WE DO ABOUT IT?

On the whole, academics have a strong vested interest in ignoring everything we've said in this chapter. Academia makes money through pompous marketing. Students, wealthy alumni donors, corporations, and governments must be made to believe they're investing in a noble, world-changing institution.

It's comforting for faculty to believe, without evidence, that what they do *must* work. We know that getting an undergraduate degree in philosophy trains you to be a graduate student in philosophy. We don't know whether it accomplishes anything more than that. But it certainly is comforting to believe that somehow this trains you to do anything. This belief relieves philosophy professors of the burden of actually testing their claims. It lets them sleep comfortably at night, convinced they're serving the world.

All things considered, traditional college lecturing is quite easy. In contrast, experimenting and discovering what methods of teaching actually deliver the goods are expensive and time-consuming processes, and there's no guarantee of success. But as we saw in Chapter 2, professors are rewarded for minimizing their teaching in order to maximize their research output. We can't expect faculty to lead the charge. It's not in their self-interest to acknowledge the problem or do anything about it.

College marketers are no different. While drug companies are subject to FDA regulations and can be sued for fraudulent claims, there's no body of case law in which buyers successfully sued established universities for failing to teach them how to think. Colleges make grand, almost hyperbolic claims, but also carefully shy away from offering easily verifiable or easily refuted promises. No one is going to sue Northwood University for failing to turn them into a leader.

So, what would it take to actually improve the bad business ethics of collegiate marketing? There are no obvious solutions. But here are three approaches that might work:

1. Regulate academic marketing the way we regulate other forms of marketing, in particular, that related to drug companies.
2. Launch and succeed in a class-action lawsuit against four-year colleges for failing to deliver on their promises.
3. Face competition from alternative forms of education that better deliver the goods.

We don't have much confidence that any of these will succeed. But until the incentives change, the behavior won't. Universities and colleges can and do get away with unethical forms of marketing and advertising that pharmaceutical, automobile, or banking companies would not dare try.

The title of this chapter understates just how bad all of this is for universities. It's not *just* that they engage in unethical advertising. Rather, look at the content of what they advertise—they say they develop students' skills, knowledge, and character. But the evidence makes clear that for the most part, universities *don't* do that—or they do so only in narrow ways and only for the top 10 percent of students. One of the main missions of the university system is to educate students, and our discussion here suggests that we're spending half a trillion a year on a failed mission.

4

On Reading Entrails and Student Evaluations

For the king of Babylon will stop at the fork in the road, at the junction of the two roads, to seek an omen: He will cast lots with arrows, he will consult his idols, he will examine the liver.

—*Ezekiel 21:21*

HOW DIVINATION RITUALS DO AND DON'T WORK

The haruspex slices open the bleating lamb's abdomen. His expert hands remove the liver in one swift motion. The lamb lies still. He throws the pulsing purple mass on the sacred stone and waits, his eyes fixed. A pattern emerges that only his eyes can see. He sighs with relief and proclaims, "The king will survive."

The augur turns his eyes to the sky. For twenty minutes, he watches as flocks of birds sweep overhead. He closes his eyes and listens to their songs. A pattern emerges that only his eyes and ears can detect. He sighs and mutters, "The gods do not support our invasion. I fear the battle will be lost."

Many ancient cultures practiced—and some current ones still practice—divination rituals. Certain people, including witch doctors, augurs, haruspices, heptomancers, and oracles, would "read" the movement and sounds of birds, patterns in smoke, images in fire or the entrails of sacrificial animals, or messages hidden in the stars. Often such "seers" occupied high positions in society. They served as advisers to kings, queens, and generals, who made important, sometimes life-or-death, decisions on the basis of their visions.

But here's the problem: Taken at face value, the nearly universal practice of divination is bullshit. A sheep's liver cannot tell you whether Julius Caesar is in danger. The flight of birds cannot tell you whether nonexistent gods will aid or hinder your battle. The way tea leaves float tells you nothing about whether an illness will pass or whether your child will be born healthy. Eating black and white impepho does not allow you to speak with dead ancestors. Divination does not work, in the sense that divination practices fail to provide any evidence for the claims the seers later make. The cultures and individual people who practice divination may be sincere—they often genuinely believe that their rituals allow them to predict the future or communicate with gods and spirits—but they are wrong.

We say "taken at face value" because there is a way in which these divination rituals are *not* bullshit. They are invalid as methods of generating knowledge. But these rituals also serve secondary *social* purposes and may be quite effective in this regard.[1]

For instance, shared sacred rituals and shared beliefs in the divine help to bind a community together; they facilitate trust and mutual cooperation.[2] (The mechanism: That you adopt an "expensive" belief and practice expensive prayer rituals is evidence you're one of us and committed to the group, and we can trust you.) Sometimes certain people know the rituals are nonsense, but they enable better-positioned, more knowledgeable people to influence or placate the superstitious masses. Sometimes, thanks to the placebo effect, fake medicine cures psychosomatic illness. Sometimes the purpose of the rituals is straightforward: to allow the powerful to control the less powerful. Possessing sacred knowledge means you know more and have higher status than others, which thereby entitles you to additional power.

Finally, sometimes the reason cultures continue such practices is simple inertia. People just do what their ancestors did, because it's what they grew up with, and so a practice continues year after year.

STUDENT EVALUATIONS OF FACULTY TEACHING EFFECTIVENESS

This chapter examines how colleges routinely make faculty hiring, retention, and promotion decisions on the basis of what they *ought to know* are invalid tests.

Most universities and colleges in the United States ask students to complete course evaluations at the end of each semester. They ask students how much they think they've learned, how much they studied, whether the instructor seemed well-prepared, and how valuable the class was overall.

Colleges and universities use these surveys to make decisions about whom to hire, whom to reward with a raise (and how much), whom to tenure, and whom to promote. Some colleges—especially small liberal arts colleges where faculty focus almost exclusively on teaching—rely heavily on these results. They may even request past teaching evaluations from new job applicants along with the usual materials, such as a cover letter and CV, or academic résumé. At some schools, student course evaluations make or break faculty careers. In contrast, tenure-track faculty research-heavy RIs are evaluated mostly on their research output. But even at RIs, student evaluations affect promotion, tenure, and salary decisions. Furthermore, many RIs employ a large number of permanent/long-term but non-tenure-track teaching faculty (lecturers, teaching professors, professors of the practice, clinical professors, etc.), and they often evaluate such faculty heavily on the basis of course evaluations.

It's clear that nearly all universities and colleges use student course evaluations.[3] But we could not find good information quantifying just *how* universities use the data.

That isn't important for our argument here, though. Our argument is simple: Student course evaluations do not track teacher effectiveness. Thus, the more you rely on them, the more irresponsible and blameworthy you are in moral terms. In this chapter, we'll argue that teaching evaluations are largely invalid. Using student evaluations to hire, promote, tenure, or determine raises for faculty is roughly on a par with reading entrails or tea leaves to make such decisions. (Actually, reading tea leaves would be *better*; it's equally bullshit but faster and cheaper.)

Here, we'll recite the rather damning evidence about course evaluations. However, given how damning the evidence is—and given that the evidence has been accumulating steadily for forty years—one might wonder why universities continue to use student course evaluations. We'll end by discussing a number of the reasons why: Using student evaluations gives some people (administrators) power over others. Student evaluations may placate students and make students believe (in some cases, falsely) that they have control over the university and share in university governance. Administrators may use course evaluations because they believe they must produce *something* that evaluates teaching, and more effective and reliable methods of evaluation are just too expensive and time-consuming. Finally, it may just be that universities continue to use student evaluations because it's what they've been doing for forty years, and change is hard. Student evals are like other divination rituals: They fail to serve their putative information-gathering purpose, but fulfill secondary social purposes.

AN ASIDE: THIS IS NOT SPECIAL PLEADING ON OUR PART

A significant portion of this chapter simply summarizes others' research. Writing this chapter required us to dig through hundreds of papers. Rather than summarize all of them, we will rely heavily on recent meta-analyses of past research.

It's reasonable for you, the reader, to worry that we might have read this material incorrectly. It's especially reasonable for you to worry that we may have a *stake* in misrepresenting it—after all, didn't we argue in the early chapters that professors are not saints? Haven't we made it clear that we the authors are not especially noble or good compared to other academics? The philosopher David Hume argued centuries ago that the reliability of testimony depends, in part, on the self-interest of the speaker. If you know it's in someone's self-interest to make a claim, that should reduce your confidence in his testimony; if you know it's *against* someone's self-interest to make a claim, that should increase your confidence in her testimony.

We the authors are faculty. Our students evaluate us, and this has some effect on our raises, our job prospects if we decide to apply elsewhere, and tenure and promotion decisions.

You might be concerned that we're bashing student evaluations because we received bad reviews and have a stake in attacking student evaluations overall. So, let's set that worry aside.

Here are Jason's evaluations over the past few years (Table 4.1), for the time between his receiving tenure and being promoted to an associate professor with an endowed chair in 2015, to his promotion to full

TABLE 4.1 Brennan's Course Evaluations

Semester	Course	"Mean" Overall Evalution
Fall 2018	Moral Foundations of Market Society	4.82
Spring 2017	Moral Foundations of Market Society	4.77
Fall 2016	Moral Foundations of Market Society	4.96
Fall 2016	Political Economy of Entrepreneurship	4.64
Spring 2016	Moral Foundations of Market Society	4.75
Fall 2015	Moral Foundations of Market Society	4.52
Fall 2015	Political Economy of Entrepreneurship	4.15

TABLE 4.2 Magness's Course Evaluations

Semester	Course	"Mean" Overall Evalution
Fall 2017	Markets and Society	4.50
Fall 2017	Markets and Society	4.60
Fall 2017	Markets and Society	4.50
Fall 2016	Methods of International Commerce	5.00
Fall 2015	Methods of International Commerce	4.42
Fall 2014	Methods of International Commerce	4.73
Fall 2013	Methods of International Commerce	4.16

professor with the same endowed chair in 2018. (He went on a sabbatical in the spring of 2018.)

And here also are Phil's course evaluations over the past few years (Table 4.2). Initially during this period, he taught part-time in a graduate program while working in an administrative role and then switched to a regular faculty position teaching undergraduates in 2017.

The highest score a professor can receive is a 5. While a few professors in our departments and schools routinely get higher scores, most faculty do about the same or worse, and overall, we're rated significantly above average compared to most professors. Accordingly, we have a vested interest in *using* student evaluations, not dispensing with them.

RELIABILITY AND VALIDITY

Before we get to the research on course evaluations, we'll need to review some important definitions. In day-to-day talk, we often use terms like "reliability" and "validity" interchangeably. But in scientific or statistical talk, they have more specialized meanings.

A measurement device, instrument, or test is said to be *reliable* if it obtains consistent results. Suppose you measure pots of boiling pure water at sea level fifty times. The thermometer registers readings between 100 and 100.01 degrees Celcius each time. The measured results under the same conditions are always the same, so the thermometer is highly reliable.

But to say a measurement device, instrument, or test is reliable doesn't necessarily mean the results are accurate or correct. Suppose you measure the temperature of a pot of boiling water at sea level fifty times. Your thermometer reads between 94 and 94.1 degrees each time. Here, the thermometer is reliable, but it is miscalibrated—it's off by 6 degrees.

A purported measurement device could be completely reliable but also completely fail to measure the very thing it's supposed to measure. For instance, suppose you ask the character Hodor from *Game of Thrones* to read a bunch of flash cards. He's reliable—no matter how many times you show him a card, he'll always indicate that the card says "Hodor"—but he's not accurately reporting what the cards say.

Or, suppose we tried to use your bathroom scale to measure your *height*, not your weight. The bathroom scale will give consistent readings—it's a reliable device. But although its readings are perfectly reliable, the resulting data are fairly close to useless, because they don't track your height well.[4]

When we measure faculty teaching effectiveness, we want a reliable test—we plan a test that gets the same readings under the same conditions, rather than one that varies wildly even when we know the conditions are the same. But reliability, even perfect reliability, isn't enough. We also want a test that accurately tracks the thing to be measured.

That brings us to our second definition. A measurement device, instrument, or test is said to be *valid* when it, in fact, tracks the thing it's supposed to measure. The bathroom scale is an invalid measure of height.

A good test of teacher effectiveness should be *both* reliable and valid. It should generally yield similar results under similar conditions, and it should actually track the thing being measured.

As we'll see in the discussion that follows, student evaluations appear to be *reliable* but not *valid*.[5] Instructors tend to get the same results in the same courses year after year, but the evaluations do not track something we could reasonably call teaching effectiveness. Using student evaluations to measure teaching skill is like using a bathroom scale to measure your height.

THE ETHICS OF PERFORMANCE EVALUATIONS

Our goal here isn't just to argue that evaluations are invalid. Rather, we want to argue that it's *immoral* for universities and colleges to use them *because* they are invalid. Using course evaluations in hiring and promotion decisions is bad, and administrators should feel badly about doing so. By using invalid measures, they (to the extent they rely on them) violate two major obligations:

1. An obligation to faculty to evaluate them on the basis of fair and reasonable criteria.
2. An obligation to students to use fair and reasonable criteria in determining who their teachers will be.

To illustrate: Imagine Joe the Plumber is an excellent plumber. Whatever the job is, he gets it done correctly and on time. He quickly diagnoses and fixes customers' problems. His repairs and installations last as long as they should. He never overcharges his customers or does unnecessary repairs. He comes to work on time, volunteers to cover for coworkers when they're sick, and treats his boss and other fellow employees with respect.

Now suppose it's time for Joe's annual evaluation. Suppose Joe's boss Mike did any of the following:

1. He says, "Joe, time to determine whether you get a raise. Let's shake my Magic 8 Ball. Alas, it says no."
2. He says, "Joe, time to determine whether you get a raise. Stand on this bathroom scale, and I'll make your raise dependent on whether you have an ideal BMI."

3. He says, "Joe, you were a model plumber, employee, and friend. However, you're a Republican and I'm a Democrat, so you're not getting a raise."
4. He says, "Joe, you were an excellent plumber, but I'm planning to replace you with Sally, because she's so hot."

And so on. In each case, Mike acts badly. Mike owes it to Joe to evaluate him on the basis of whatever factors determine excellence in plumbing.

Of course, being a good employee requires more than just being a good plumber: Joe's personal appearance matters somewhat—he should probably be neat and clean and dress appropriately. He should get along well with customers and employees. He should show up on time and exhibit some willingness to lend a hand. He shouldn't be recalcitrant or hard-headed, but he shouldn't be a pushover either. It's also not enough that Joe has the skills to do the job; he needs to use them.

What counts as relevant in assessing someone's performance or worthiness for a job depends on the job. For certain jobs—actor, model, in some cases even waiter or store sales clerk—appearance does and should matter. In other cases, it shouldn't. In some cases—priest, economist, physicist—one's beliefs about certain issues (theology, economics, physics) do and should matter; in others, they should not.

But in general, a good manager owes it to her employees to evaluate them according to the correct standards of excellence for that particular job. The standards will vary from job to job, and there is reasonable disagreement about how to weigh these standards or just what the standards are. But while there are hard questions about how to evaluate employees, there are also easy questions. It's clear Manager Mike acts badly in cases 1–4. When Mike relies on a Magic 8 Ball, he's using a completely unreliable and invalid decision-making device. In case 2, Mike relies on a reliable but invalid measure. In cases 1–4, Mike relies on irrelevant and invalid factors.

In general, products are bought and sold with tacit prior expectations. When you sit down at a restaurant and order food, it's understood that you must pay for it, even though you never explicitly agree to do so. When someone hires you to be a plumber, it's understood that certain tasks are part of the job and will be a component of any performance review, just as certain things are not.

In some cases, you can opt out of these expectations. Suppose you approach the hostess at a restaurant and say, "I'd like to order five things from the menu, but to be clear, I have no intention of paying and I'd like the food for free." If she then seats and feeds you, it's plausible that she's agreed not to require payment. If you work for a small family business, the owner might make it clear that his son, not you, will become the assistant manager if the son wants the job, even if you're more deserving. Perhaps in a small, private business like this one, that practice is fine, and as long as the owner is upfront, you don't have a complaint.

All of this applies to academia as well. Professors are hired with a host of background expectations and mutual understandings. Faculty know they will be evaluated on the basis of research, teaching, and service. They understand that expectations—what counts as a good publication, what counts as the right *number* of publications, how much and what kind of teaching they should do, and so on—will vary from school to school. Harvard has different expectations from UMass Boston or Bunker Hill Community College.

Nevertheless, unless there is a morally proper explicit or implicit agreement to the contrary, managers should evaluate employees on the basis of *valid* measures of *relevant* aspects of employee excellence. Academic managers should evaluate faculty on the basis of relevant measures (such as publication output) rather than an irrelevant measure (such as the person's sexiness or golf game). They should also use measures that reliably and accurately track the skill, rather than measures that fail to do so.

In addition, academic managers should avoid using measures that heavily correlate with irrelevant factors—or, at least, if they do so, they should correct for such polluting factors. For instance, suppose Mike sends a survey to each of his customers. He notices that Joe consistently gets slightly worse evaluations than his other plumbers. Perhaps this means that Joe is actually a somewhat worse plumber. However, suppose Mike's Plumbing serves a largely white community, but Joe is Mike's only black employee. In that case, it's possible Joe is getting dinged because he's black and the customers are prejudiced against him. Mike owes it to Joe to check out the poor evaluations, rather than to just take them at face value. Now, suppose Joe follows up and discovers that yes, indeed, customers rate black plumbers consistently lower, regardless of the actual quality of their services. In that case, Mike should find a different way to evaluate Joe, or otherwise adjust Joe's evaluations to correct for his customers' prejudice.

Let's bring this scenario back to faculty. The majority of professors in the US, Canada, and English-speaking world more broadly are teachers first and researchers second, while a minority (especially tenure-track faculty at Rɪs) are researchers first and teachers second. It's perfectly reasonable—indeed, laudatory—for administrators to demand that faculty teach *well*. The previous chapter of this book casts strong doubt on the idea that faculty as a whole do much to improve students' skills, and we think faculty should find such results upsetting—in a very real sense, they are failing to do their jobs. We therefore think it's perfectly reasonable, in principle, for administrators to measure and quantify teaching quality, and to use such measurements in decisions about hiring, retention, promotion, and compensation.

But it's unreasonable and immoral to use invalid measurements. The university owes it to the faculty to treat them in the way they deserve, which includes evaluating them on the basis of valid measures of teaching effectiveness. If the university fails to do so, it doesn't just mistreat faculty, but violates a duty to its students, too. Students reasonably expect that the university will take proper care in selecting adequate instructors. If students learned their university had hired some teachers on the basis of tesseography or Magic 8 Balls, they'd have a legitimate complaint that the university failed to act with sufficient care.

That's the main normative half of our argument. (We'll consider some objections later on.) Now for the empirical half.

THE BIG PROBLEM: HOW DO WE OPERATIONALIZE AND MEASURE TEACHING EFFECTIVENESS?

To measure something, we need a clear idea of what we're trying to measure and some clear unit with which to measure it.

Some things are easy to measure. We all know what is meant by "height." We can then pick an arbitrary measure, such as a meter, as a standard unit by which to quantify height. We know exactly what it means to express the height of a thing—a person, an elephant, or a building—in terms of meters.

Now, even when we have a clear and meaningful unit, some things are harder to measure than others. It's easier to measure the height of a toddler than a newborn, because one stands up straight and the other has squirmy, bent legs. It's easier to measure the height of a building than the length of a giant squid. It's easier to measure the height of a building than the distance of a supernova from the earth's surface. The list goes on. But at least we know what it is we're measuring, and so measuring a particular height or distance becomes a technical problem.

There are, of course, some difficult cases where it's not clear what we mean by "height." For example, the boundary between the atmosphere and outer space is fuzzy, so stating how high the atmosphere extends is a bit arbitrary.

How about teaching effectiveness? What does it even *mean* for someone to be a good versus a bad teacher? Here, one common complaint in the research on student evaluations is that administrators began using such evaluations without having a clear idea of just what it is they were trying to measure. Are we measuring how technically impressive a professor's PowerPoint presentation is? Are we measuring what the professor knows? Are we measuring whether the students *enjoy* her class, *feel* stimulated, and are *inclined* to take more classes with her or in the department? Are we measuring whether the professor induces students to feel good about the school, so they'll donate more money to future fundraising events? Are we measuring whether the professor is sexy, energetic, or amiable?

A priori, we know that A) whether students enjoy class and like the professor and B) whether a professor successfully helps them learn could come apart. After all, a professor could be excellent at imparting, say, math skills, even if his students hate him and find his class boring. A professor could be entertaining and students might love his class, even if they learn nothing.

Here's an anecdote to illustrate the principle. One of Jason's colleagues—let's call him Bob—regularly teaches business ethics classes to the entering MBA cohort during their intensive summer session. He asks them to assess their own sense of how moral they are. Students believe themselves to be morally good and not easily corrupted; they claim that stress, lack of preparation, or simple unawareness would not induce good people like them to act dishonestly. Bob then gives the students a journal assignment. In the end, the overwhelming majority end up "cheating" on it, not because they have bad character, but because of stress, lack of preparation, or lack of attention. The students learn an important lesson: They are indeed vulnerable to moral traps, the very traps they can expect to encounter at work. And although Bob may well have taught the MBAs the most important piece of learning they'll ever receive, they don't reward him for that. Instead, they get angry and give him low evaluation scores. In much the same way, Jason's kids, when young, would become angry when they got their immunity shots. Maybe MBA students are like toddlers: They reward what they like, not what's good for them.

Perhaps the most obvious gauge of teacher effectiveness would be to measure how much the students actually learn. That is the purest and most obvious measure of teaching effectiveness. But this is more difficult than it seems.

Suppose we know that students learn a great deal during a course. Even then, we can't automatically attribute this to the skill of the instructor. Part of it depends on the students themselves or on factors other than the instructor's skill. Suppose a bad teacher instructs 100 randomly selected MIT freshmen, while a good teacher instructs 100 random Keene State College freshmen, on multivariable calculus. We'd expect the MIT students to learn more than the Keene State students, because MIT students generally have higher IQs, higher levels of conscientiousness, higher mathematical aptitude, and better study skills. So, we cannot just operationalize "effective teaching" in terms of how much students learn over a semester.

Now, in principle, we can correct for such confounding variables. We could give students the final exam on the first and last day of class, to see how much they learned in-between. We could independently measure students' cognitive abilities, study habits, and the like in order to correct for students' own capabilities on learning and to thus isolate the independent effect of the professor. We could randomly assign students to different sections of the same course, taught by different professors, but that use a common textbook, tests, and other learning materials.[6] With controls like this, we could then start to determine what value the professor herself adds. (Though, of course, part of what it means to teach well is to select good materials.) As far as we know, no university does anything like this to try to measure their faculty's effectiveness.

Now, it might turn out, fortuitously, that these confounding variables have very little effect, and so failing to control for them doesn't impact the value of the student evaluations. However, as we'll soon explain, when we examine empirical work on student evaluations, these variables, in fact, have a huge effect. Of course, to some degree this is all irrelevant, because most universities do not measure student learning at all. At best, they ask students how much they think they've learned, but as we'll see, these reports are not valid.

Mathematician Philip Stark and education researcher Richard Freishtat have raised another concern about student evaluations. Nearly every university asks students to rate their professors' effectiveness, class preparation, helpfulness, and so on, on a 1–5 or 1–7 scale. These numbers are not cardinal values. Each number instead corresponds to a verbal description. For example, 5 just means "extremely effective," while 3 just means "somewhat effective." You could replace the numbers with these descriptions with no loss of information.

But here's the problem: Universities then "calculate" and report professors' *average* scores using these numbers. As Stark and Freishtat point out, though, you cannot meaningfully average *verbal descriptions*, nor can you meaningfully average ordinal numbers. We don't know whether students interpret the gap between a score of 1 and 2 and a score of 4 and 5 as meaning the same jump in quality.[7] When fifty students each rate you from 1 to 5, it's mathematically incoherent to average their ratings together.

So, take a look back at Table 4.1 and Table 4.2, again reviewing Brennan's and Magness's *mean* overall student evaluation scores. You might think these numbers are meaningful in some way. But, as far as we know, the concept of a "mean" score is simply incoherent.[8]

In the next section, we'll review the rather damning empirical evidence on student evaluations. But in some sense, we could stop here. Universities use student evaluations as evidence of teaching quality. They owe their employees and their students to take proper care in determining whether these measurements actually mean anything and whether they track what they are supposed to. However, universities started using them without taking any such care. Their use has exploded in scope and importance, but university administrators have done effectively nothing to answer these basic questions about them or to study their meaningfulness.

Note also that defenders and users of student evaluations bear the burden of proof. They make the positive claim that such measures are in some way *good*. They thus bear the argumentative burden of proving their case. Skeptics need but cast strong doubt.

You might complain: Well, we don't know how to measure faculty effectiveness, but surely we should do something.

That's not a good argument for student evaluations, though. If we don't know how to measure teaching skill, then we should admit we don't know how. We shouldn't use some fake proxy. Unless we have evidence that student evaluations are reliable and valid, then this "we have to use *something*" argument is just as good an argument for evaluating professors by their batting averages, their weight, their chess rankings, their height, their physical appearance, or their skill with regard to death metal trivia. We might as well read tea leaves.

EMPIRICAL WORK ON STUDENT EVALUATIONS

Course Evaluations Are Invalid

As we previously stated, perhaps the purest and most important way to determine the validity of student evaluations would be to show they reliably and validly track independently measured student learning. (Furthermore, even if the two turn out to be correlated, we'd need to correct for students' independent contributions.) In general, though, attempts to do so find either *no* correlation, a very small positive correlation with a weak effect size, or in some cases a very strong *negative* correlation.

In perhaps the most recent and state-of-the-art meta-analysis of research on this question, researchers Bob Uttl, Carmela White, and Daniel Wong Gonzalez conclude, "[S]tudents do not learn more from professors with higher student evaluation of teaching (SET) ratings."[9] They summarize their research as follows:

> [W]hen [previous analyses that apparently showed a large effect size] include both multisection studies with and without prior learning/ ability controls, the estimate SET/learning correlations are very weak

with SET ratings accounting for up to 1% of variance in learning/
achievement measures. . . . [W]hen only those multisection studies
that controlled for prior learning/achievement are included in the
analyses, the SET/learning correlations are not significantly different
from zero.[10]

In short, the most comprehensive research shows that whatever student
evaluations (SETs) measure, it isn't *learning caused by the professor*. SET
scores and student learning are simply *unrelated*.

Previous studies that seemed to find significant correlations between
high SET scores and what students learn had methodological errors,
such as failing to control for student's prior aptitude, or failing to do a
multisection study:

> An ideal multisection study design includes the following features: a
> course has many equivalent sections following the same outline and
> having the same assessments, students are randomly assigned to
> sections, each section is taught by a different instructor, all instructors
> are evaluated using SETs at the same time and before a final exam,
> and student learning is assessed using the same final exam. If students
> learn more from more highly rated professors, sections' average SET
> ratings and sections' average final exam scores should be positively
> correlated. [11]

In brief, the reason some earlier studies seemed to validate SETs is that
these studies failed to include the necessary controls we discussed in the
previous section.

An earlier though perhaps less rigorous meta-analysis yields similarly depressing results. In a comprehensive meta-analysis of forty-two
studies that try to measure the relationship between objective student
learning and SET scores, D. E. Clayson finds at best a small positive
correlation, but with an effective size/magnitude not statistically different from zero.[12] Clayson further claims that most studies find a *negative* relationship between SET and class rigor.[13] He also determines
that rigorous or stringent grading improves students' achievement in
follow-up courses, but students punish their professors by giving them
lower SET scores.[14]

Clayson notices the same trend that Uttl and his coauthors observe about the research on SET scores:

> As statistical sophistication has increased over time, the reported learning/SET relationship has generally become more negative. Almost 40 years have passed since the positive result in Sullivan and Skanes' (1974) study was obtained. No study could be found after 1990 that showed a positive significant relationship between learning and the SET.[15]

That is, as researchers have gotten better and better at controlling for confounding variables, the evidence that the SET is connected to learning vanishes before our eyes. Early studies were not particularly positive, but these early positive results were almost certainly due to methodological errors. That's not a slight against those early researchers—they were the first to try and figure out how to test the hypothesis that the SET is a valid measure of how well faculty facilitate learning. We stand on their shoulders and thus can see farther. But as we learn from their mistakes, we learn they were mistaken.

Stark and Freishtat say,

> The best way to reduce confounding is to assign students randomly to classes. That tends to mix students with different abilities and from easy and hard sections of the prequel across sections of sequels. This experiment has been done at the U.S. Air Force Academy and Bocconi University in Milan, Italy.
>
> These experiments found that teaching effectiveness, as measured by subsequent performance and career success, is *negatively* associated with SET scores. While these two student populations might not be representative of all students, the studies are the best we have seen. And their findings are concordant.[16]

In general, the more carefully controlled the experiment, the more negative the results for the SET. There is no good evidence that good SET scores validly track teaching effectiveness, where teaching effectiveness is defined as how well professors help students learn.

But Course Evaluations Are Reliable

So, the SET tells us nothing about how well faculty promote learning. But many researchers find that the SET is reliable, if not valid.[17] (Of course, many disagree that the SET is even reliable.) What, then, is the SET measuring, if not how well faculty help students learn? It does not appear to measure *other* scholarly traits of college professors. Even early studies find that other traits, such as how much a professor publishes, how prestigious the professor's research is, and so on, are largely unrelated to student evaluations.[18]

Course evaluations do appear to measure how likable and fun a professor is. In the famous "Dr. Fox" experiment, researchers had an attractive, charismatic lecturer deliver an energetic but nonsensical lecture on "Mathematical Game Theory and Its Application to Physical Education." Though the talk was nonsensical, participants rated the lecture highly.[19] Audiences easily mistake charming bullshitters for the real McCoy.

Subsequent research corroborates these early results. Professors who tell jokes and use other entertaining lecture methods receive much higher marks than those who do not.[20] Charismatic personality traits greatly influence student evaluation scores.[21]

Indeed, the effect of personality is so strong on the SET that some researchers worry the SET *simply is* a personality test.[22] For instance, one major study asked students to evaluate professors on their "Big 5" personality scores—Openness, Conscientiousness, Extraversion, Agreeableness, and Neuroticism—on the first day of class, after only five minutes of exposure. The researchers then asked students to evaluate professors again on weeks 10 and 16 of class. They also asked them to rate the professors' teaching effectiveness. In the end, there were extremely high correlations between the professors' personality traits and their SET scores, such that at the end of the term, "global personality perception accounted for fully 64% to 73% of the variance of the evaluation."[23]

Michael Huemer summarizes a similar study that received similar results:

> [In] . . . another study, . . . students were asked to rate instructors
> on a number of personality traits (e.g., "confident," "dominant,"

"optimistic," etc.), on the basis of 30-second video clips, without audio, of the instructors lecturing. These ratings were found to be very good predictors of end-of-semester evaluations given by the instructors' actual students. A composite of the personality trait ratings correlated .76 with end-of-term course evaluations; ratings of instructors' "optimism" showed an impressive .84 correlation with end-of-term course evaluations. Thus, in order to predict with fair accuracy the ratings an instructor would get, it was not necessary to know anything of what the instructor said in class, the material the course covered, the readings, the assignments, the tests, etc.[24]

SET scores very closely track how open, agreeable, and extroverted professors are; in general, they closely track professors' charisma. They also track how "hot" professors are; attractive professors get about a 0.8 bonus on the 5-point SET scale.[25]

Now, by themselves, such strong correlations and effect sizes are not necessarily damning. After all, teaching is a social discipline. It's possible that attractive professors with engaging personalities are better at getting students to come to class, to pay attention, to care about the issues discussed, and to thus learn. However, as we have already discussed, the most up-to-date and rigorous meta-analyses of the existing studies find *no* real relationship between how much students learn and professors' SET scores. So, while it's logically possible that the SET tracks personality and that personality, in turn, tracks learning, our evidence shows the SET tracks personality but not learning. The SET is a valid personality test, but not a valid test of how well professors help students learn.

One study tried to test the external validity of SET scores by comparing student evaluations of professors to the teaching evaluations they receive from other professors or deans. Deans and peer reviewers' evaluations turned out to be highly correlated and very similar, with correlations on total teaching of about 0.91 for peers and 0.79 for deans. So, fellow professors and deans largely agree with each other about how well other professors teach. But the correlation between what peers/deans think of professors' teaching aptitude on a wide range of factors and what students believe is quite low; for total teaching, about 0.43 for the deans and only 0.17 for the peers.[26] Again, this doesn't prove by itself that student evaluations are worthless. In fact, research on peer evaluation tends to show that peer evaluations are *also* invalid.[27] Perhaps students better know what makes for a good teacher than fellow teachers or deans do. But, as we just saw, SET scores do not track student learning.

WHAT IF WE CAN'T DO BETTER?

J. V. Adams summarizes what extant research on student evaluations shows:

> The implication of the above research is clear. While student evaluations of faculty performance are a valid measure of student satisfaction with instruction, they are not by themselves a valid measure of teaching effectiveness. If student evaluations of faculty are included in the evaluation process of faculty members, then they should represent only one of many measures that are used.[28]

Let's be clear: We don't know how to measure teaching effectiveness in a way that is A) valid and reliable but also B) inexpensive and easy to do on a large scale. We have valid and reliable ways of measuring how much an individual teacher contributes to individual student learning, but these methods require accumulating massive amounts of data both before and after students take a class, and may also require us to randomly assign students to classes rather than allow them the freedom to choose which professor's class they take. At any rate, these methods cannot easily be scaled up and would eliminate student choice.

But that's not much of an argument for continuing to use student evaluations. Student evaluations *do not* measure teacher effectiveness or quality. In a world where no one had invented the ruler and no one thus knew how to measure height, it would still be stupid to "measure" it with a bathroom scale or a personality test. And it would be immoral for employers to use an invalid measurement device, fraudulently portraying it as a good device, simply because they cannot think of or are unwilling to use a better one. Administrators owe it to their students and faculty to use a valid test or otherwise do nothing at all.

ATTEMPTS TO DEFEND THE SET

Adams says that student evaluations *are* a valid measure of student satisfaction. For the sake of argument, let's just assume he and others that say this are correct. One might then try to defend student evaluations on the grounds that it's reasonable to base hiring, retention, and promotion decisions at least partly on student satisfaction.

Now, we could spend an entire chapter assessing that proposal. Here, though, we'll note that whatever the merits of that proposal might be, it doesn't let current universities and colleges off the hook. If universities intend for professors to be evaluated on student satisfaction, instead of teaching competence, they should be clear and upfront about that. Administrators could just say, "We want satisfied students. We'll use the SET to measure satisfaction. We do not base hiring, retention, and promotion decisions on teaching effectiveness. What we want are happy students who don't complain." But to our knowledge, aside from a few anecdotes of deans shamefully admitting the same to their faculty, universities and college fraudulently or mistakenly represent the SET to students and faculty as if it were a veritable measure of teaching effectiveness.

Note also that SET scores are inversely related to rigor—students generally punish professors for making a class difficult. Furthermore, it's clear professors *believe* this. As Mary Gray and Barbara Bergmann write,

> [T]he use of student evaluations against faculty members appears to adversely effect the educational experience of students. In one survey of faculty, 72 percent said that administrative reliance on student evaluations encourages faculty to water down course content. And a careful study at Duke University by statistician Valen Johnson demonstrated that students' expectations of grades influence their ratings of teachers. His finding provides a powerful incentive for faculty to raise grades. Johnson argues that "the ultimate consequences

of such manipulation is the degradation of the quality of education in the United States."[29]

Faculty respond to incentives. The SET rewards lax grading policies and easy assignments. When deans reward "good" SET scores, they thereby encourage professors to dumb down their classes.[30]

D. A. Dowell and J. A. Neal offer a strange defense of student evaluations:

> The confusion in the literature does not justify abolition of student ratings. Few university policies have a truly "scientific" basis. For example, where are the studies of the validity of the faculty peer evaluation process? As a form of consumer control, student ratings have a useful place.[31]

Now, their main intention here is to argue that SET scores could be useful as a way of placating students and measuring their satisfaction. We've already discussed such an argument. However, they also argue that "few university policies have a truly 'scientific' basis." But even if so, that doesn't *justify* the SET; rather, it instead shows these other university policies are unjustified. Suppose we complained that bloodletting in the 1790s was unscientific. It would be strange for someone to defend bloodletting by saying most medicine back then was also unscientific. That's a *critique* of medicine as a whole, not a *defense* of bloodletting in particular.

One final defense of student evaluations goes as follows:

> Sure, the SET is not a valid measure of learning. However, if a professor continually receives very low average scores, say 1s and 2s, that probably means something bad is going on. So, the SET should be used as part of the evaluation process. But deans and fellow faculty just need to use the scores the *right way*.[32]

We see two major problems with this argument. First, it's far from clear that the literature establishes consistently "low" SET scores reflect bad teaching. As far as we can tell, the existing papers and meta-analyses do not support this claim.

Second, the argument relies on a sort of "ideal theory" of dean behavior. Suppose we established that while, in general, SET scores have no valid correlation with teaching effectiveness, very low scores do validly indicate bad teaching. This would not justify the current practice, where deans continue to use "mean" SET scores from "high-scoring" faculty to make illicit fine-grained distinctions between them, or where schools routinely publish faculty's SET scores as if they were meaningful. At most, it would justify a sort of pass/fail system. Rather than calculating and reporting "mean" SET scores or the distribution of scores, schools should—by the lights of this argument—just report whether a particular professor was above or below the supposed informative cutoff line. If a low average SET score of 1 is meaningful but averages between 2 and 5 are not, then we should not report or use these higher scores.

The general point is that it's not enough to state, "SET scores can be good, as long as universities know their limits and use them the right way." That reads perilously close to saying there's no problem with giving guns to toddlers, as long as toddlers recognize their limits and use the guns in the correct manner. It's nearly a tautology to say that almost any measure is fine as long as you use it the right way. The real question is whether people will use any given measure "the right way." As we'll see in the next section, deans generally don't seem to know their limits and have plenty of incentive to use SETs the wrong way.

WHY UNIVERSITIES WON'T FIX THE PROBLEM

The research on student evaluations is quite damning and becomes more damning over time. Why, then, do universities persist in using these bullshit measures?

Donald Morgan, John Sneed, and Laurie Swinney surveyed a number of accounting faculty and business school deans and administrators, asking them questions such as whether they believed student evaluations were valid measures of learning, the evaluations were mostly personality tests, and the evaluations really tracked the course's difficulty rather than learning. While few administrators had glowing responses, in general, administrators thought SET scores were more valid and less biased than faculty. As Morgan, Sneed, and Swinney summarize:

> The statistical analysis showed that the administrator's perception is significantly greater ($p = .004$) than the faculty's perception that student evaluations are an accurate indication of teacher's effectiveness. Further, the perception that factors exist which bias the student evaluation is significantly stronger ($p = <.001$) for the faculty group than the administrator group in all biases investigated. These results indicate that although administrators believe that student evaluations are good indicators of teacher effectiveness, faculty do not share this belief. Further, faculty recognise that factors exist which bias the evaluations to a greater degree than their administrative counterparts.[33]

Other studies we looked at discerned a similar pattern: Administrators are generally more confident about student evaluations than faculty are.[34] For instance, in one study, D. Larry Crumbley and Eugene Fliedner asked administrators overseeing business school accounting departments what factors they believed determined SET scores. In all, 14.3 percent said they strongly agreed, while another 36.8 percent said they agreed, that student learning determined SET scores; 30.5 percent were neutral; only about 18 percent disagreed or strongly disagreed.[35] Administrators also heavily discounted biased factors; while most agreed that instructors' "niceness" improved their scores, they generally disagreed or at least failed to agree that inflating grades, holding parties, giving students power over grades, and other ways of dumbing down courses tend to improve SET scores.[36]

The best available research shows that student evaluations are not valid measures of student learning but are heavily influenced by an instructor's personality. The research also tends to confirm professors' suspicions that they can improve their scores by dumbing down their classes. But administrators' beliefs about the SET do not conform to the evidence. Administrators are far more confident in the SET than the research allows. Why?

To be frank, we don't know. In principle, someone could do an experiment in which they survey administrators about their attitudes toward the SET, next require them to read a number of papers on its validity, and then survey them again. If their attitudes change, that would suggest administrators are simply *ignorant* of the research.

Administrators might even be *rationally ignorant* of the research. A person is said to be rationally ignorant about X when the reason she fails to know X is that knowing X is not in her self-interest. For instance, we the authors don't know where the next American Anthropological Association (AAA) annual meeting will be held (or if that group even holds an annual meeting). It's not that we're dumb, but rather, we have no stake in knowing this fact. We do not teach in an anthropology department and don't publish in anthropology journals, so we have no reason to determine where the AAA meetings will take place.

Similarly, perhaps administrators have no stake in knowing the truth about SET scores. All the stronger a reason, they seem to have a stake in *remaining* ignorant. To illustrate the idea: One of Jason's colleagues— let's call him Steve—once said to Jason, "I refuse to read the philosophical papers on the ethics of meat-eating. I'm worried I'll discover meat-eating is wrong, but I want to keep eating meat. So as long as I don't read, I won't know." By his own admission, Steve actively avoids learning something because he's afraid he will uncover an unpleasant truth, one that would require him to change his behavior.

It turns out such behavior is rampant. Most of us suffer from confirmation and disconfirmation bias. We tend to read things we agree with and avoid reading things we know will present evidence contrary to our existing views. We try not to learn truths we'd rather not believe.[37]

Administrators have a stake in continuing to use SET scores for each of the following reasons:

1. The SET is relatively cheap and easy to implement.
2. Valid measures of faculty effectiveness are expensive and difficult to implement.
3. As a corollary of 1 and 2: Since nearly every American university and college already uses SET scores, the framework for collecting these scores is already in place. Replacing the SET would require finding and implementing a new system.

4. Some people's jobs—including those of certain administrators, staff members, and software developers—*depend* on universities continuing to use SET scores. So, these individuals will actively lobby schools to keep using them.

5. Perhaps students generally do not know the SET is invalid, and so using the SET helps the university trick students into thinking the university cares about teaching and is trying to improve it.

6. Even though the SET is invalid, so long as administrators continue to collectively behave as if it were valid, they can use SET scores to wield power over and control faculty.

We won't belabor each of these points, as we suspect you get the idea. The point is that the SET doesn't have to work to work, that is, it doesn't have to be a valid measure of faculty effectiveness for administrators to have a stake in using it. They might be using it for *other* purposes.

As we discussed in Chapter 2, faculty and administrators are supposed to complement each others' work. Faculty are the prize capital assets of the university,[38] while administrators do the upkeep. But in reality, faculty and administrators have strong incentives to try to control each other, to get that group to *serve* them. They also know that a dollar going to administration is not a dollar going to faculty, and vice versa. If administrators did not try to measure faculty teaching effectiveness, then they would, to their own detriment, cede too much control over course structure, faculty retention, student happiness, and so on, to the school's professors. But institutionalizing the SET gives administrators significant power over who teaches, what gets taught, how faculty teach, who gets money, and who doesn't. Never mind that the SET is invalid. From the standpoint of administrators, it works. As sociologist Thomas Cushman says,

> [Defending student evaluations] is quite functional for the administrators. To argue otherwise would be to acknowledge that the instruments are problematic and practically useless for measuring actual learning. But administrators are aware that, if the evaluations were abandoned, they would be deprived of their principal means of power over tenured faculty, who have no other significant restraints

on their behavior. In this case, the old sociological adage applies to the relationship between grading practices and evaluations: if people define situations as real, it does not matter whether they are real or not, they have real consequences.[39]

Thus, part of the reason universities continue to use student evaluations, even though they do not "work," is that doing so serves administrators' self-interest by giving them power over faculty. In much the same way, divination rituals gave certain groups of privileged people power over others—the priestly or shaman class gained power over kings, lords, and peasants alike.

But that's not the whole story. Divination doesn't need to "work" in order to work. For instance, the economist Pete Leeson, in his book *WTF?!*, explains how in certain parts of Africa, people try to settle who is at fault for slights and insults through a bizarre ritual in which they poison two chickens, ask each chicken a question, and then wait to see if the chickens die. At first glance, the ritual seems absurd—obviously, whether a chicken dies from poison has nothing to do with whether your neighbor used witchcraft to bring harm to you. But, as Leeson demonstrates, the practice works in a different way—in effect, it randomly assigns blame to one of the two people involved, who is required by custom to apologize, and the other party is then required to accept the apology and move on. The practice reduces violence and facilitates cooperation by quickly forcing people on bad terms to make amends.[40] Indeed, the practice works so well we might wish a similar custom was followed in the United States.

Perhaps something similar is true of student evaluations. Student evaluations do not appear to track professors' teaching ability, but instead track a number of other factors not obviously relevant to teaching. However, perhaps—and this is an empirical speculation in principle open to testing—student evaluations serve some other useful but hidden purpose, and will continue to do so as long as this chapter is not widely read. Maybe student evaluations placate students by making them believe—mistakenly, perhaps—that they have input on teaching and some power over the classroom. The complaints department needn't fix problems to make complainants feel better—maybe they just need to let the complainants vent.

Perhaps student evaluations make students feel better about and more invested in the university. Or, maybe they serve some other unknown purpose. Again, these are just hypotheses, and in principle a social scientist could test them.

Regardless, student evaluations are not a proper measure of teaching effectiveness, but deans don't and won't care.

5

Grades: Communication Breakdown

IN THE LAST CHAPTER, we complained about how students "grade" professors. Course evaluations are invalid as measures of student learning or teaching effectiveness; using them in hiring and promotion is immoral. In this chapter, we turn the tables and argue that we professors aren't much better. There's something fishy about the way we calculate GPA.

At first glance, grading students seems unproblematic. Although students are not experts at evaluating teaching effectiveness, professors are, in fact, experts on the topics they teach and at identifying quality work in their fields.[1] Indeed, elite professors at R1 universities are often the most expert people in the world on certain narrow topics. While student evaluations of professors fail to measure or track professors' teaching effectiveness, professors' evaluations of students do track something like the quality of the students' writing and their (current but fleeting) understanding of certain material.[2]

Nevertheless, we'll argue, the practice of grading is replete with problems. Grades are a kind of language. They are meant to be a form of communication. They are sometimes meant to communicate to students how well they've mastered a set of material. Most colleges calculate grade point averages (GPAs) and compare students to one another. Some, such as Georgetown's business school, even select valedictorians on the basis of their GPA. Grades are thus also meant to communicate to students how they compare to one another. In addition, they are sometimes meant to communicate to outsiders something about how good a student is, and how he or she compares to other students from other universities.

But, we'll argue, the grading and GPA systems are such a mess that they largely fail to accomplish these goals. In some cases, the mathematics used to calculate an average final grade in a class are incoherent. In nearly all cases, the mathematics used to calculate students' GPAs are incoherent. It's often not meaningful to compare two students' GPAs.

When we grade our students, we faculty act as if we are all speaking the same language, using the same symbols and words. In reality, we're speaking nine or more different, incommensurate languages. In North American universities and colleges, we have almost universally coordinated on using the same grading symbols (A, A–, B+, . . . F), but we have not coordinated on ascribing the same *meaning* to those symbols.

As a collective, we faculty fail our students. After fifteen weeks of classes, the main and most important form of feedback we give students are grades. After four years of classes, the main and most important form of feedback we give students is their final GPA. But both forms of feedback are a conceptual mess. It's as if our students asked us to advise and evaluate them, but we responded with gibberish.

Everyone is so accustomed to grades that this seems hyperbolic. But bear with us.

INDIVIDUAL GRADES ON INDIVIDUAL ASSIGNMENTS

Philosophy professor Smith sits down, red pen in hand, to grade thirty political philosophy essays. In his head, he has criteria for what he regards as worthy of an A, an A–, a B+, and so on. For instance, an A paper will have a well-stated and interesting thesis, will be written in a clear and engaging way, will present an argument original to the class and that goes beyond any articles the class may have read, will make a strong case, and will consider and respond to major objections to its thesis and argument. A C might sort of summarize a reading and include random half-relevant thoughts.

It's easy for Professor Smith to judge which papers are better or worse than others and which are approximately equal. Given his internal standards—which might be quite different from his colleagues' standards or from his own standards two years ago—it's surprisingly easy to judge which papers get an A and which get a C. Grading undergraduate papers isn't difficult; it's just time-consuming and boring.

He returns the marked papers. Perhaps he's written extensive comments; perhaps not. But at least students in the class can meaningfully compare their individual marks on that assignment to one another's. The student with an A most likely wrote a much better paper than the student with a B. So far, so good.

Sally, one of Professor Smith's students, receives a B on her essay. She might wonder whether a different professor with a reputation for "easy grading" would have given her a B+. Suppose Sally has read the empirical literature on how extraneous factors can bias people's judgments. She might reasonably worry that had Professor Smith graded her paper right after breakfast rather than right before lunch, her grade would have been higher.[3] She might worry that Professor Smith would have given her a higher grade if she shared his political views.

Indeed, she might wonder whether Professor Smith's or any professors' grading is reliable. (Remember the definition of reliability from the last chapter: A measure is reliable when it yields consistent results.) She might be distraught to learn that educational psychologists have found all sorts of biases and inconsistencies in grading. As Jeffrey Schinske and Kimberly Tanner summarize:

> [Educational psychologist W. C.] Eells investigated the consistency of individual teachers' grading by asking 61 teachers to grade the same history and geography papers twice—the second time 11 wk after the first. He concluded that "variability of grading is about as great in the same individual as in groups of different individuals" and that, after analysis of reliability coefficients, assignment of scores amounted to "little better than sheer guesses." Similar problems in marking reliability have been observed in higher education environments, although the degree of reliability varies dramatically, likely due to differences in instructor training, assessment type, grading system, and specific topic assessed. Factors that occasionally influence an instructor's scoring of written work include the penmanship of the author, sex of the author, ethnicity of the author, level of experience of the instructor, order in which the papers are reviewed, and even the attractiveness of the author.[4]

Nevertheless, the thirty students in Sally's class can presume that the A papers are *usually* better than the B papers, although perhaps they can't tell by how much.

ON CALCULATING FINAL GRADES WITHIN ONE CLASS

Things start to unravel when we average the semester's assignments to calculate a student's final class grade. In some classes, this involves incoherent math.

Recall the problem Philip Stark and Richard Freishtat raised about so-called mean student evaluation scores: Students rate faculty on a 1–5 or 1–7 scale. These numbers are ordinal, not cardinal, numbers. They correspond to verbal descriptions rather than to cardinal degrees or constant mathematical units. For example, on the 1–5 scale, 5 just means "extremely effective." It does not mean "5 effectiveness points." We could drop the numbers with *no* loss of information.

However, we cannot meaningfully average verbal descriptions to- gether, nor can we meaningfully average ordinal numbers. We don't know whether students interpret the gap between a score of 1 and 2 as being the same distance as the gap between 4 and 5. When we "average" students' evaluations, we pretend the numerical scores rep- resent constant units, even though they do not. Accordingly, mean fac- ulty evaluations are literally meaningless.[5] When we average students' evaluations, we *insert* information into their individual ratings that was never there.

The same worry applies to students' final grades in individual classes. In some classes, the concept of an average grade is coherent. In others, it's not. It depends on what the professor intends her grades to mean. As we'll see next, there are at least nine different "languages" a professor could be speaking with her grades, but only some of these allow us to calculate average final grades.

Suppose you get three 60-question multiple-choice tests in BIO 101. Each question is worth 2 points out of 120. Even here, it may be arbitrary or implausible for the professor to treat each question on each test, and each test as a whole, as the equal of every other. But, given these possibly arbitrary weights, one can meaningfully compute a class average. In this case, grades represent cardinal numbers. Cardinal numbers can be averaged, just like we all learned in second grade. A B just means "The student got 85 percent of the questions correct."

But now consider a typical writing-intensive introductory composition or introductory philosophy class, such as the political philosophy class Sally took. The professor assigns letter grades to each paper. For this professor (as for most liberal arts professors), grades are shorthand and stand in for verbal descriptions of students' work. An A just means "excellent, exemplary work." A B just means "good." A C just means "adequate" or something like that. A D just means "passing but poor." An F means "So deficient that it fails the assignment" or something like that.

Here, there's no obvious way in which the difference between an A and a B is equivalent to the difference between a C and a D, or between a D and an F. (That's why we said the students in Sally's class might know that an A paper is better than a B paper; they just don't know *by how much*.) The letter grades A, B, C, D, and F are *not* consecutive units along a constant cardinal scale. Indeed, when we grade papers, we often judge that the best student papers—the ones we give perfect scores—are many *times* better than the fairly good student papers. An essay that gets an A is not really 5 percentage points better than a paper that gets an A–; rather, they are in entirely different leagues. My colleagues and I have each had classes where the best student paper is really worth more, and contains more insight, than all the other papers *combined*. In the same way, a single Nobel Prize–winning chemistry paper contributes more to knowledge than, say, sixty issues of some second-rate chemistry journal.[6]

Yet when professors calculate "final" grades in a class, they assign weights to each assignment a student has completed and then "calculate" the "average" grade across each assignment. Except in special cases, it's unclear we can meaningfully compute such averages. When we convert letter grades to percentages, we are frequently inserting meaning that wasn't there to begin with, or we distort and misrepresent the qualitative differences between papers, usually by downplaying the gaps between them.

So, suppose Sally has written three papers, each worth one-third of her final grade. Her first paper is exceptional, nearly worthy of peer-reviewed publication. So the professor gives her an A. The second is mediocre, so the professor gives her a B. The third is something she cobbled together an hour before it was due, so the professor, in disappointment, gives her a C. It's not obvious her "average" is therefore a B, because that presupposes the professor treats the gaps between an A and B and B and the C the same way, as representing consecutive units along a cardinal scale. The letters A, B, and C are shorthand for verbal descriptions, and you cannot average verbal descriptions. That's not to say the professor cannot assign her a meaningful final grade, but he'd have to judge her overall performance, rather than do impossible math.

Let's get a bit technical. (Skip this and the next two paragraphs if you'd prefer to avoid that sort of discussion.) We are not complaining that the gaps between grades might be nonlinear.

Suppose the truth is that each letter grade is better than the next on some meaningful exponential scale. In this case, the gaps between grades still represent cardinal units. In principle, then, we could use a logarithmic equation to translate these gaps into a linear curve, just as, say, the decibel or Richter scales allow us to represent exponentially different magnitudes of energy on a linear scale.

To illustrate, consider that many faculty use the following percentile scale: A = 93, B = 83, and C = 73. Suppose Sally writes three equally weighted essays and gets a C, B, and then an A. Her average is an 83, a B. However, suppose that by her professor's standards, an A paper is twice as good as a B, a B twice as a good as a C, a C twice as good as a D, and so on. Thus, a more exact cardinal scoring would be A = 8, B = 4, C = 2, D = 1. According to this system, if Sally gets a C, B, and then an A, her average is a 4.667, which is still a B on this curve. (A B+ would be a 5.32.)[7] So far, so good. Since the professor is using a constant formula, she can convert her grades onto a linear scale. For her, the gap between an A and B is a logarithmic unit, just as the gap between an 8 and 9 on the Richter scale is a logarithmic rather than linear unit. However, even in our hypothetical example, the conversion isn't perfect: At the margins, a few students may get unfairly pushed up or down a third of a letter grade.

Still, this mathematical point will save individual faculty from complaint only if they carefully fit their letter grades to some meaningful equation or curve in the first place. We suspect many do not. Instead, for many, the gaps between a C– and C versus, say, a B+ and an A–, do not fit into any meaningful nonlinear function. The professor is just using the letter grades as stand-ins or shorthand for qualitative differences, and these qualitative differences do not fit any well-defined mathematical curve.

When we professors average the grades of our students' papers, projects, presentations, and so on, we often make the very same mistake. We replace meaningful verbal, qualitative descriptions with artificial cardinal units.

COMPARING AND AVERAGING GRADES ACROSS CLASSES

Even for a single student inside a single class, it's an open question whether the student's "final grade"—or the "average" of all her work over the semester—is meaningful. But for the sake of argument, let's put these worries aside. Individual professors can easily correct the problem by instituting more coherent grading scales or weighing projects in a more sensible way.

The real problem arises when we try to calculate a student's GPA by "averaging" her grades across classes. Often, there is no meaningful way to do this, even in principle.

To a significant extent, professors set their own standards of what different letter grades mean. A Russian literature professor might give almost everyone in his class an A, regardless of how competent they are. The chemistry professor might reserve As only for exceptional students. A different professor teaching the same class might be far more lenient in her grading policies.

In fact, we're understating the problem. The problem isn't just that some professors are "easier" graders than others. This suggests their grades represent the same fundamental *kind* of standard with their grades, but some apply these standards more loosely. In fact, grades can and do represent many completely different and incommensurate kinds of standards. Consider the following.

Some courses have mandatory curves. For instance, all classes at Georgetown University's McDonough School of Business are curved. The business school's curriculum committee, not an individual professor, set the maximum average grade for each class. Here, grades have a stipulated meaning—they are *rankings* rather than some measure of absolute levels of quality.

But this again creates a number of different problems. One problem arises because different classes have different maxima. Certain accounting and finance core classes have 3.0 mandatory averages. Most classes have a 3.33 average. Electives outside of finance and accounting generally have 3.5 averages.

Now, although individual grades for individual McDonough School of Business classes are meaningful—a grade is by definition an abbreviation for a students' class rank—it's generally meaningless to *average* two or more class grades together. Suppose we removed students' grades and just reported their rank in each class. We wouldn't *lose* information, but rather gain information from doing so. Suppose Sally is ranked 1st out of forty-five in STRT 101, but 21st out of forty-five in ACCT 101. Is it meaningful to say that she is, on average, ranked 11th in those two classes? We could say that only if we knew the gaps between the rankings in both classes were always the same. But even inside one class, it's not necessarily true—and indeed almost never is true—that the distance between being ranked 1st and 2nd is the same as the distance between being ranked 2nd and 3rd, and so on. When we start averaging curved classes together, we're inadvertently acting as if we can average ordinal numbers in a meaningful way.

Averaging Sally's business classes together introduces incoherence. But the situation gets even worse once Sally starts taking uncurved classes outside the business school. Suppose she also takes PHIL 101, ENGL 101, and CHEM 101. The philosophy and English professors, let's suppose, use letter grades as stand-ins for qualitative descriptions. The chemistry professor only uses multiple-choice tests. In CHEM 101, final grades literally stand in for and correspond to the percentage of questions a student got right on various exams. Finally, remember that Sally's other strategy and accounting grades represent rankings, not qualitative descriptions or absolute percentages.

When we "average" her grades in PHIL 101, ENGL 101, CHEM 101, STRT101, and ACCT 101 to calculate her semester GPA, we thereby pretend that we can meaningfully average two verbal descriptions, two ordinal rankings, and one score signifying the the percentage of questions she answered correctly on various tests. The equation for her final GPA would look something like this:

Sally's GPA in Fall 2017

$$= \left[\frac{Good\ +\ Excellent\ +\ 100(249/320)\ +\ ranked}{1\ out\ of\ 45\ +\ ranked\ 19\ out\ of\ 38} \right] \div 5$$

$$= [3.00\ +\ 4.00\ +\ 2.66\ +\ 4.00\ +\ 3.33] \div 5$$

$$= 3.398$$

The second step in this equation is nonsense. When we replace "good" with "3.00" and "ranked 19 out of 38" with "3.33," we're *inserting* information that was not there to begin with. Sally's GPA thus results from voodoo, magic math. In principle, if all her classes used genuine percentage point grades, we could meaningfully average her grades together to calculate a GPA. But in reality, for most students, the GPA results from nonsense calculations, from illicitly converting verbal descriptions and ordinal rankings to cardinal numbers. When we calculate a GPA, we pretend we can "average" a mix of verbal descriptions, ordinal rankings, and cardinal percentages. We can't.

COMPARING DIFFERENT STUDENTS

Yet another complication surfaces when we try to compare two different students' GPAs. Suppose Harry and Sally have had identical schedules for four years: They've taken exactly the same classes with the same professors at the same time. If Sally literally gets a better grade than Harry in every class, we can meaningfully say she was the better student, although (except in exceptional circumstances) we cannot meaningfully use their GPAs to estimate *how much better* Sally was overall.

But suppose instead that Harry and Sally both get As in half their classes and Bs in the other half. Suppose that whenever Harry got an A, Sally received a B, and vice versa. Harry and Sally would graduate with the same GPA: 3.5. But even here, we don't really know whether Harry and Sally have done equally well overall, because their GPAs represent the "average" of a collection of verbal descriptions, percentages, and rankings.

Suppose also that Sally and Joe have identical GPAs after four years at the same university, but there's been no overlap in their classes. In this instance, it becomes even more questionable to say their GPAs show they are equally good students.

Both their GPAs represent artificial, voodoo math. The registrar illicitly converts letter grades—which sometimes stand in for percentages, sometimes for verbal descriptions, and sometimes for rankings—into cardinal numbers on a 0.00–4.00 scale, and then averages these numbers together. Sally's own class grades are not commensurate with one another, and neither are Sally's and Joe's different grades from different classes.

Of course, things become even more problematic once we compare students across universities. Some universities, such as Chicago, are reputed to be "hard"; others, such as Brown, are reputed to be soft and easy. If—and this is a big "if"—the stereotypes are correct, then a potential employer or graduate school admissions officer looking at student transcripts might reasonably presume a student with a 3.0 average from Chicago is probably more studious and a harder worker than a student with a 3.0 from Brown. But, otherwise, employers remain largely in the dark.

Let's take a step back. Notice that our complaints here are not the kind you are likely to hear from hippies at Hampshire College.[8] We're not saying, "You can't reduce people to a number, man." Personally, we're perfectly happy to reduce people to numbers when we can. (Jason even wrote a book arguing you can meaningfully put a dollar value on individual human lives.[9]) Our complaint isn't with math or numbers or measuring per se; it's that grading is done so haphazardly, erratically, and arbitrarily that the math is incoherent.

WHAT WE HAVE HERE IS A FAILURE TO COMMUNICATE

The reason GPA calculations are incoherent (in most cases) is that grades mean different, incommensurate things in different classes. When a professor assigns a class grade, she might intend her grades to mean any of the following:[10]

What Grades Could Mean

1. *Grades as rankings*:
   a. A letter grade ranks a student against other students in the same section of the same class that semester.
   b. A letter grade ranks a student against all other students in any section of a given class in a semester.
   c. We can expand the rankings outward to go across professors, years, or even universities. At the limit, a letter grade in introductory microeconomics could rank a student against all other students who have ever taken that class at any university anywhere.

2. *Grades as qualitative evaluations*:
   a. A letter grade reports a qualitative description of how well a student mastered material according to the professor's absolute standards, although different professors might have different standards.
   b. A letter grade reports a qualitative description of how well a student mastered material according to the university's absolute standards, consistent among all professors, but the standards might vary from university to university.
   c. A letter grade reports a qualitative description of how well a student mastered a given set of material according to what is meant to be a universal absolute standard, for example, such that a B in ECON 101 at Boise State equals a B in ECON 101 at Cornell.

3. *Grades as quantitative scores/percentages*:
   a. A letter grade reports what percent of questions and problems a student got correct, according to the professor's standards, but the standards might vary from professor to professor.
   b. A letter grade reports what percent of questions and problems a student mastered according to the university's internal standards, consistent among all professors, although the standards might vary from university to university.

c. A letter grade reports what percent of questions and problems a student mastered, according to what is meant to be a universal standard, for example, such that a B in ECON 101 at Boise State equals a B in ECON 101 at Princeton.

This is an incomplete list. With a bit of reflection, you can think of new subcategories or main categories. For instance, we might imagine grades to reflect not a ranking per se, but distribution along a bell curve. And, again, the comparison groups for that distribution could be broader or narrower.

So, grades *could* mean any number of things. This gives rise to a normative question: What *ought* grades signify? Frankly, we don't have any strong intuitions. Of the nine or more possible meanings delineated in the prior list, it's not obvious which meaning grades ought to have. You could probably make a case for each of them.

Instead of asking what grades ought to signify, let's ask what they *do* signify. In fact, individual professors pick and choose from the list given here, or insert their own meanings, largely at will. Different faculty grade differently, and they have different models in their minds about what grades mean when they assign them. Some professors ask themselves, "What's good by Providence College standards for sophomores?" Others might ask themselves, "What do I think any first-year undergraduate anywhere should know about microeconomics?" Others question, "How well does Sally rank against her peers in this class?" Some are ranking students, some are reporting genuine percentages, and some are assigning qualitative descriptions.

For the most part, it's up to professors to decide what grades mean. Thus, when Professor Smith says Sally got an A in ECON 101, while Professor Thompson indicates Sally got an A in PHIL 101, they may be speaking radically different languages.

Over 100 years ago, in the preface of a book critiquing the practice of grading, Guy Montrose Whipple complained,

When we consider the practically universal use in all educational institutions of a system of marks, whether numbers or letters, to indicate scholastic attainment of the pupils or students in these institutions, and when we remember how very great stress is laid by teachers and pupils alike upon these marks as real measures or indicators of attainment, we can but be astonished at the blind faith that has been felt in the reliability of the marking system. School administrators have been using with confidence an absolutely uncalibrated instrument. . . .

What we know to know is: What are the traits, qualities or capacities we are actually trying to measure in our marking systems? How are these capacities distributed in the body of pupils or students? What method ought we to follow in measuring these capacities? What faults appear in the marking systems that we are now using, and how can these be avoided or minimized?[11]

One hundred years later, we still can't answer these questions. Instead, we chug along, doing what we always do, with little to no concern about why we do it or what it means.

THE ETHICAL PROBLEM

In the last chapter, we argued that universities owe it to professors and to students to assess professors' teaching performance by reasonable, coherent, and valid standards. For the same reasons, professors and universities owe it to students to assess them by reasonable, coherent, and valid standards. If universities are going to "calculate" and report GPAs, they owe it to students to ensure such a calculation is coherent rather than nonsensical.

We make students jump through hoops to achieve higher GPAs. We pressure them to earn high grades. We act *as if* grades communicate some sort of universal standard of meaning when they really don't. At their request, we send these grades on to potential future employers or to graduate admissions committees, where these largely incoherent numbers can have a huge effect on students' futures.

But as we saw, the practice of grading is plagued with inconsistent, incompatible, and incommensurate meanings. Student GPAs result from voodoo math: from illicitly converting a mix of rankings, verbal descriptions, and cardinal percentages to cardinal numbers on a 0.00–4.00 scale. Yet in many cases students' future success—whether they get into grad, law, or medical school, or whether they land a good, bad, or no job—is determined by these voodoo calculations.

Students could reasonably complain that they don't know what their individual grades in individual classes actually mean. The strength of this complaint varies from class to class. After all, some professors provide ample feedback and others don't. Some professors clearly explain which meaning they assign to grades, while others don't. Some professors make it clear what the difference between an A and A– versus B and B– means, while others don't. Some professors use letter grades to reflect meaningful (linear or logarithmic) units; others don't.

But the GPA is the real problem. Calculating Sally's GPA is like calculating the "average" of her height, weight, 40-meter dash, vocal range, and max one-rep bench press.

We don't want to overstate our worries. The good news is that employers and admissions committees are aware of some of these problems, and so discount GPA quite a bit.[12] But that's a weird defense of our collective behavior: "Oh, our failure to communicate clearly isn't so bad, because others don't take what we say too seriously."

Furthermore, it's possible, as an empirical matter, that high GPAs are positively correlated with various outcomes, and thus predict future success in a variety of ways. Even though the math is incoherent, nevertheless, high GPAs might turn out to be positively correlated with conscientiousness, perseverance, good time management skills, or whatnot.[13]

However, to our surprise, literature on this question does not appear to have developed. There are many papers showing that adverse life events negatively affect GPA, but few papers testing what a college GPA itself predicts. And, the few empirical papers on this question largely fail to save the concept of a college GPA. One major paper claims the relationship between GPA and future job success is weak.[14] In contrast, Frank Schmidt and John Hunter, in a comprehensive meta-analysis of previous papers, claim that the correlation between the college GPA and future job success is 0.34.[15] One major paper argued that the high school (not college) GPA was a strong predictor of future income, but this may be because high school students with high GPAs are more likely to get bachelor's degrees and thus secure the premium college wage.[16] In the end, as far as we can tell in doing a literature search, there is mixed evidence about whether a high college GPA predicts future success. However, this also seems to be an underinvestigated area. For instance, it seems reasonable to hypothesize that people with high college GPAs are less likely to get divorced than those with low GPAs, but we couldn't find any research testing this. So, GPA is a conceptual mess, but the empirical papers at least somewhat rescue the practice.

Suppose we want to clear up the mess. Who should do it? Individual professors can communicate to students clearly what they want grades to mean, but they cannot control how the university then manipulates these grades into meaningless averages. Individual professors cannot, except in special circumstances, induce other professors to adopt the same standards and meanings. With their grades, professors speak different languages. There's no obvious way to induce professors to speak the same language, and there's no obvious language that's better than others. It's a coordination problem no one can solve.

It's not just a coordination problem inside individual universities, but among them all. Any given university could, in principle, get its professors to adopt a common standard whereby grades between classes might be averaged meaningfully. It could then explain this meaning on its transcripts. (Of course, that won't necessarily help students, as there's no guarantee employers will read or understand the explanation.) However, it's infeasible to induce all universities to coordinate on some fixed, coherent meaning.

Rather than trying to reform GPA, it's probably best to dispense with it altogether, perhaps while simultaneously dispensing with class final grades. Instead, it would be more informative/less distortionary to report some or all of the following information:

1. Short qualitative descriptions of students' work in different aspects of the course, for example, excellent writing skills, good creativity, poor time management.
2. What percent of students received these different evaluations. (For instance, 10 percent of Sally's class had excellent writing skills.)
3. The students' ranking in class, or (when meaningful) how many standard deviations below or above average the student is.

4. What percentile the professor estimates a student falls in, with regard to different skills, compared to other students the professor has taught over her career.

Of course, reporting such information would make grading difficult—it would take professors far longer to submit final evaluations than it currently does. Furthermore, it would give students more issues to protest and complain about. As we discussed in Chapter 2, professors generally have strong financial and reputational incentives to minimize teaching in order to increase research, and they have a disincentive to push for or endorse such reforms.

Indeed, we selfishly hope our own universities do not follow our advice. If we have to spend more time evaluating students, that would reduce our lifetime earnings.

DO GRADES "WORK"?

It's not written into the fabric of the universe that we must assign our students letter grades of any sort, even for individual assignments. Many countries around the world do not use the A–F grading system common in North America. Even in the US, the A–F grading system is a fairly recent invention, becoming widespread only in the early 1900s. Before that, many universities gave their students written feedback and evaluations, but did not assign students grades for individual papers, projects, and exams, or for their "final class average."[17]

Why not dispense with grades altogether? We've already seen that there is significant incommensurability between grades and thus incoherence in calculating grade point averages. But it's worth asking whether the practice of grading has positive effects, enough to justify continuing the practice. Perhaps grades end up being useful forms of feedback that help students improve their work. Or, perhaps it turns out that the desire to earn good grades and avoid bad grades causes students to learn more. These are empirical claims, so we don't know unless we investigate them.

Experimental data suggest grades do little to help students improve their work. R. Butler and M. Nisan ran an experiment in which students completed a task, received either no feedback or one of two different types, and then had to complete the task again.[18] The researchers could then measure the value-added, if any, of the feedback. They gave the experimental groups either what they called evaluative or descriptive feedback. Evaluative feedback—such as a letter grade—tells students how good or bad their work is. Descriptive feedback gives students advice about how to do better. They generally found that giving grades and evaluative feedback was better than giving no feedback, but offering descriptive feedback by itself was better than giving evaluative feedback and grades.

Furthermore, grades do not appear to have a positive effect on students' motivation. Here's how Jeffrey Schinske and Kimberly Tanner summarize the extant research:

> It would not be surprising to most faculty members that, rather than stimulating an interest in learning, grades primarily enhance students' motivation to avoid receiving bad grades. Grades appear to play on students' fears of punishment or shame, or their desires to outcompete peers, as opposed to stimulating interest and enjoyment in learning tasks. Grades can dampen existing intrinsic motivation, give rise to extrinsic motivation, enhance fear of failure, reduce interest, decrease enjoyment in class work, increase anxiety, hamper performance on follow-up tasks, stimulate avoidance of challenging tasks, and heighten competitiveness. Even providing encouraging, written notes on graded work does not appear to reduce the negative impacts grading exerts on motivation. Rather than seeing low grades as an opportunity to improve themselves, students receiving low scores generally withdraw from class work. While students often express a desire to be graded, surveys indicate they would prefer descriptive comments to grades as a form of feedback.[19]

When we read that same literature, this summary seemed apt. Grades seem to cause a great deal of stress and anxiety, but there was little evidence in favor of the view that they help or motivate students to learn. We're not claiming strong evidence exists that grades backfire and undermine learning or love of learning—though some of that does occur. Rather, our point is that there isn't strong evidence justifying the practice of grading.

WHAT ABOUT GRADE INFLATION?

When we first conceived of this book, we planned to write a chapter on "grade inflation." We expected to report overwhelming empirical evidence of grade inflation. We planned to push the contrarian argument that even if 90 percent of the grades at Ivy League universities are an A, that's not necessarily a problem, because it depends on what grades are supposed to mean. We planned to outline the 9+ different meanings grades could have and point out that inflation is a problem only if someone can show grades are supposed to have certain meanings rather than others. This was our original plan. But, to our surprise, once we started digging in, we discovered that there is flimsy evidence grade inflation exists in the first place.

The theory of grade inflation claims that in the good old days, an A used to mean something, but now it doesn't. In the good old days—say, the 1920s or the 1950s—the average college grade was a C (where a C is supposed to just mean "average"). Back then, an A signified truly outstanding and exceptional work. However, for various reasons, average class grades and GPAs have crept up. Supposedly, students now get As for what in the past would have been B or C work.

As far as we can tell, most people who write about this issue believe grade inflation exists. Indeed, we found many more scholarly and news articles hypothesizing about *why* inflations occurs or how to fix it than papers actually trying to prove it's real.

So, is the problem real?

Before we talk about the empirics, let's discuss the conceptual issue. We have to start by asking what it would even mean for grades to be "inflated."

Suppose for the sake of argument that the average college GPA has increased over time. Suppose for the sake of argument that, in 1950, the average GPA among all students at all universities was a 2.0, but now, in 2017, it's a 3.0. (Again, this is just a hypothetical.)

By itself, this doesn't show inflation has occurred. What we'd need to show, to borrow Alfie Kohn's formulation, is that there is "an upward shift in students' grade point average *without* a corresponding rise in achievement."[20] Or, to use Clifford Adelman's formulation, we'd need to show that teachers are "*paying* a higher and higher *price* for the same product from students."[21] That is, to know whether inflation has occurred, it's not enough to prove that raw GPAs have increased over time. We need to also show that the quality of student work has not kept pace with the increase in GPA.

To illustrate, consider four cases:[22]

1. The average GPA has increased from 2.0 to 3.0 since 1950. However, student work has gotten objectively *worse* over time, such that a C student today is worse than a C student of 1950, and so on.

2. The average GPA has increased from 2.0 to 3.0 since 1950. However, student work has not improved at all over that period, and students are handing in the same-quality work now as they did in 1950. A B student of today is only as good as a C student in 1950.

3. The average GPA has increased from 2.0 to 3.0 since 1950. However, at the same time, thanks to a combination of better teaching, more support for student learning, students having more freedom to drop classes they are doing poorly in, and better-quality students in general, the quality of work has gone up by a full grade point such that average students today really are B students compared to the students of yesterday. A B student today is equivalent to a B student in 1950; there is just a higher percentage of A and B students today than in the past.

4. The average GPA has increased from 2.0 to 3.0 since 1950, but at the same time, thanks to a combination of better teaching, more support for student learning, students having more freedom to drop classes they are doing poorly in, and better-quality students in general, the quality of work has gone up by one and a third grade points such that B students today are the quality equivalent of B+ students of yesterday.

And so on.

If all we know is that raw GPAs have increased, we don't yet know enough to identify *which* situation we are in. In cases 1 and 2, something we could call "grade inflation" has indeed taken place. In case 3, there has been no grade inflation—the increase in GPA perfectly reflects the increase in student output. Grades meant the same thing in 1950 that they do now. In case 3, raw GPA has gone up because students are doing better work. In case 4, there has been grade *deflation*—even though average grades and GPAs are higher, students are actually getting "paid" lower grades than their peers in 1950. The quality of work has gone up faster than the grades. In case 4, a C grade today is *better* than a C was in 1950.

So, again, even if we discover that students' average GPA has increased over time, we would not yet know whether inflation has occurred. To know that, we would also have to somehow measure the quality of students' work over time, grade all that work according to some universal standard, and then see whether grades over time match that work or not. Of course, no one has performed such research.

Furthermore, we do know that students generally have more freedom to choose and drop classes now than in the past. Perhaps students get better grades because they are better at sorting themselves into classes in which they will do well. We know that universities tend to offer more tutoring and support services now than in the past. We aren't sure how well those services work. We don't know whether college professors are better teachers now than in the past, although we do know colleges have pushed for more innovative forms of teaching, and they tend to have more teaching centers and teacher training programs than they used to. We know that the Ivy League schools and their peers have gotten much more selective over time: The median student in Harvard's freshman class of 1950 would have been in the bottom 10 percent by 1960.[23] We know that average SAT scores have gotten somewhat lower over time, because a higher percentage of high school students take the test now than in the past, and high schools currently push lower-quality students to attend college, students who in the past would have gone to trade schools or just found jobs.

But we don't have objective measurements of the quality of student work over time. When we want to know whether market prices have become inflated, we find identical products, for example, identical grocery lists from 1950 and now, and then determine whether their nominal prices have increased over time. We aren't in a position to do that with student grades.

So, to prove grade inflation has occurred, you'd need to show A) that GPAs have increased over time at a faster rate than B) the quality of student work. No one's done such research. So, even if you know GPAs have increased, you don't know whether inflation has occurred.

However, we can at least check to see whether raw GPA has increased. To our surprise, the grade inflation story falls apart here. Many reports that appear to show a raw GPA increase use student-reported GPAs. These are unreliable: Students might lie, misreport, or forget their GPAs; there might be selection problems in who answers the surveys; and so on.

It would be better if we just looked at students' transcripts. Clifford Adelman, a researcher with the US Department of Education, did just that. He examined over 30,000 college transcripts over a number of years. He reports his methods:

> The large-scale evidence comes from the postsecondary transcripts of three national longitudinal studies conducted by the National Center for Education Statistics of the U.S. Department of Education. These studies followed members of the scheduled high school graduating classes of 1972, 1982, and 1992 for a minimum of twelve years. For those students who entered the postsecondary system, transcripts were collected at the end of the student period, with a response rate of over 90 percent from over 2,500 institutions of all kinds (research universities, community colleges, trade schools). Whatever the occasional problems with transcripts, they neither lie, exaggerate, nor forget, particularly when gathered in a way that does not allow anyone to screen out undesirable cases. The data they present are more reliable and valid than those derived from the questionable source of student self-reported grades one finds in [other studies].[24]

Adelman's findings are complex and would take us many pages to report in detail. But the short version is that the cohort of 1972 had an average GPA of 2.70, the cohort of 1982 had an average GPA of 2.66, and the cohort of 1992 had an average GPA of 2.74.[25] (Remember, schools were using SETs back then, so the "SETs induce professors to inflate grades" story looks fishy.)

In contrast, the popular website gradeinflation.com seems to offer strong evidence that GPAs have increased steadily over the past forty years. But Adelman warns us that this website uses problematic data, and that it summarizes some of these data problematically:

> [T]he eighty-three institutions on gradeinflation.com as of July 2005 present seventy-nine different reporting periods, ranging from four years to forty years. In less than thirty of those eighty-three cases can the data be traced back to an unassailable source—an institutional research office or a registrar's office (other sources include local newspapers, student newspapers, the national trade press and in one case, a report from school A that tattles on school B). The gatekeeper for gradeinflation.com says only one school reported a declining average undergraduate GPA, but when one clicks through the links to the underlying reports and examines the rest of the data, there are seven prima facie cases of no change and another dozen in which change is doubtful.[26]

Adelman points out that many of the changes are tiny, and there isn't sufficient data to determine whether many of the purported changes are *statistically significant* rather than random noise. Furthermore, often no information is given about who the students are, what percentage of grades are reported, whether these grades are for graduates or for full- or part-time students, and so on. We didn't just take Adelman's word for all of this. We clicked through the links on gradeinflation.com and found the same problems.

In a few cases, there is clear evidence that certain institutions have seen raw GPA increases over time. For instance, Brown University seems to have experienced genuine raw GPA increases since 2003, though not by very significant amounts.[27] However, during that same period, Brown's admissions rate dropped from 16.9 to 9 percent,[28] and it admitted ever more talented and competitive students.

Should we be alarmed that as Brown became more selective, slightly more students received As? That's far from obvious. If the purpose of grades is to rank students, then raw grade increases would be a problem. But if the purpose of grades is to indicate objective quality, then we'd expect the more talented Brunonians of today to get better grades than the less talented students of yesteryear.

Adelman's study is the best available one, but its data are out of date. Perhaps newer data on a par with Adelman's would reveal that in the past twenty years raw GPA scores have indeed increased dramatically. Even if so, remember, we'd still need more information in order to assess whether this reflects genuine inflation, rather than students getting better, teaching getting better, students getting better at sorting themselves into classes where they will do well, and so on. As of right now, though, we just don't have sufficient information to determine whether grade inflation is real.

HOW EVEN THE ILLUSION OF GRADE INFLATION COULD SCREW OVER STUDENTS

So, we don't have strong evidence that grade inflation is real, but we do have good reason to doubt it. No harm, no foul, right?

Not so fast. Even if the best research fails to substantiate the grade inflation story, it appears most laypeople and newspaper reporters nonetheless believe it. As of August 2017, the phrase "grade inflation" returns about 334,000 hits on Google, including about 16,300 scholarly articles and many thousands of news articles. Most of these articles, as far as we can tell, take it for granted that grade inflation exists. The widespread *belief* in grade inflation, even if it's a mistaken belief, could have real and detrimental effects on students.

To illustrate: Imagine that the distribution of GPA has remained constant over time. However, suppose potential employers or graduate and professional school admissions officers mistakenly believe rampant grade inflation has occurred. This means that the perceived value of a given GPA will drop over time. If BigData Company cares about grades but falsely believes today's B is worth yesterday's C, then it won't be much impressed by your B average, even though they *should* be. This means that you, the student, must do more and more to distinguish yourself from your fellow students. You'll have to earn *even higher* grades. You might have to participate in more extracurricular activities, rack up extra awards, double major or complete additional minors and certificates, do extra internships, or perhaps even pursue additional degrees, all to signal how awesome you are, and all to combat the mistaken perception that your GPA is unimpressive. Furthermore, you'd have a strong incentive to lobby, beg, or cajole your professors for higher grades.

In the end, the value of the GPA depends, in part, on what others think of it. And a widespread but mistaken belief in grade inflation devalues the currency of grades. Students are engaged in a status competition. The less grades distinguish you, the more you must seek out other forms of distinction. Admittedly, this view is speculative. In principle, we could test this hypothesis by collecting data (1) about the perception of grade inflation over time and (2) on the "extra" stuff students do to counter this perception. But this approach would be confounded by the problem that we don't really know how to test whether inflation is real. Alternatively, we could run experiments in which we tell experimental groups of first-year students that employers believe grade inflation is widespread and then ask students what plan they will devise to become more competitive for jobs. We could compare those results to the findings for a control group that is told employers do not believe in grade inflation. We haven't conducted such studies ourselves (we aren't trained in psychology), although we may opt to do so in the future.

CONCLUSION

Professors offer students feedback in many forms, including written or spoken comments and corrections. But the main currency of undergraduate education is a grade, which serves as the final, overall assessment of a student's performance.

We professors have largely coordinated on using the same sounds and symbols. We act as if we're speaking a common language, even though we're not—we're speaking at least three different *kinds* of languages, each of which has at least three dialects, through grades. Often the very act of calculating a final grade in one class involves incoherent mathematics. But, even when that's not the case, university registrars routinely engage in the mathematically incoherent act of calculating and reporting "grade point averages" as if these were real numbers, rather than some oddball attempt to "average" disparate and incommensurate meanings. Beyond that, it's unclear how much GPAs predict future success.

Colleges could revise transcripts and instead include more informative and mathematically valid forms of feedback. However, doing so would require far more work from faculty. It would cost research-oriented professors research time, and thus income and prestige. It would also increase the potential for student complaints—instead of students protesting grades, they could protest qualitative evaluations, rankings, percentiles, and the like. We professors continue to use an uncalibrated and sometimes incoherent instrument not simply because of inertia, but because the costs of change aren't worth it to us. For the most part, students, not we professors, bear the costs of our behavior.

Colleges should do more to combat the appearance of grade inflation, even if grade inflation is a myth or an unsubstantiated hypothesis. The widespread belief in grade inflation probably hurts students. Our collective inability to dispel the grade inflation rumor most likely wastes our students' time.

6

When Moral Language Disguises Self-Interest

AT FIRST GLANCE, THE website Who's Driving You? is all about safety.[1] It tracks every known safety incident involving Uber and Lyft drivers. It mocks ride-sharing services with dank memes. You might think the website's creators are morally motivated, public-spirited people, who— out of a selfless concern for others—took it upon themselves to expose a public menace.

Nope.

In fact, the website is "an initiative of the Taxicab, Limousine, & Paratransit Association (TLPA)."[2] Taxi lobbyists built the website to attack their competitors. Perhaps this explains why the website offers *no* comparative statistics establishing whether taxis are any safer than Uber and Lyft. (Also, Uber and Lyft together average about 7 million rides per day, but the website lists fewer than 500 incidents. Hardly an indictment.)

The website isn't about protecting the public; it's about protecting taxi drivers' profits from competition. TLPA is trying to trick you into supporting regulations that harm its competitor, but it disguises its self-ishness with moral language.

A related story: A few years ago, Jason debated Alfred Apps, former president of the Liberal Party of Canada, on the topic of compulsory voting.[3] During the public debate, Apps offered plenty of public-spirited arguments on behalf of compulsory voting. He claimed com-pulsory voting enhanced democracy and helped ensure citizens would consent to electoral outcomes.[4] But earlier, in a private speech to fellow

Liberal Party members at the Empire Club in Toronto, Apps revealed *other* reasons for supporting compulsory voting: He believed compulsory voting would help the Liberal Party win more seats.[5] Apps is a cunning politician. He knows he cannot say on TV, "I advocate compulsory voting because it's good for *me*." Instead, he disguises his pursuit of self-interest with moral language.

Another related story: Economists love to criticize the farming firm Archer Daniels Midland (ADM). As Jonathan Adler says, "ADM has perfected the art of rent-seeking as well as . . . any other company in America."[6] "Rent-seeking" is a technical term that refers to when a person, firm, or organization tries to manipulate the legal environment for its own benefit at the expense of everyone else. ADM is a rent-seeking virtuoso. ADM has successfully lobbied for and benefited from a large range of socially destructive tariffs, subsidies, and predatory regulations. You can thank them for the corn syrup in your Coke and the ethanol in your gas. As James Bovard summarized back in 1995:

> Thanks to federal protection of the domestic sugar industry, ethanol subsidies, subsidized grain exports, and various other programs, ADM has cost the American economy billions of dollars since 1980 and has indirectly cost Americans tens of billions of dollars in higher prices and higher taxes over that same period. At least 43 percent of ADM's annual profits are from products heavily subsidized or protected by the American government. Moreover, every $1 of profits earned by ADM's corn sweetener operation costs consumers $10, and every $1 of profits earned by its ethanol operation costs taxpayers $30.[7]

But ADM doesn't admit it's a parasite sucking the public's blood. Rather, ADM claims its "mission" is "turning crops into products that meet the world's growing and vital needs for more food, more energy, and a healthier environment."[8] ADM has a wonderfully detailed social responsibility campaign—*ADM Cares*—dedicated to forming "strong roots," "strong bonds," and "strong communities."[9] The company claims that it wants to "improve the quality of life in our communities today as [it] create[s] a better future tomorrow."[10]

We doubt ADM's lobbyists tell congresspeople, "Give us money. The benefits will be concentrated and the cost diffused. No one other than crusty economists will pay any attention." Instead, they probably insist they need protective subsidies and tariffs because they create food security and good jobs for honest, hard-working, red-blooded Americans.

In democratic politics, the currency is power but the language is morality. People who want power for the sake of power never *admit* that's what they want. People who want to exploit their fellow citizens never say they're out for #1. They put an altruistic spin on it. They say they're trying to save the world, promote justice, and help the children. No one announces from his soapbox, "Hey, everyone, vote for me—because I enjoy power and prestige." Rather, that person declares, "I just want to help all the little people. I'm fighting for others. *Somebody* has to do it, so I guess it has to be me."

There's some evidence that sociopaths—people who lack any genuine concern for others—are overrepresented among politicians. Nevertheless, even sociopathic politicians know not to say "I want to dominate you," but instead "I feel your pain."[11]

Be wary when you hear special interest groups pushing for changes on *moral* grounds. You should ask, "If they get their way, who pays the costs of the changes, and who receives the benefits?" Draw back the curtain of moral posturing and you'll often discover simple self-interest.

All this applies to academia as well. Academics are far from being saints. But professors—especially those in humanities departments—receive specialized training in making morally charged arguments, especially using the language of social justice. ADM is demonstrably a parasite, but it portrays itself as a public benefactor with a just cause. Its executives might even *believe* the spin. If even ADM, the textbook example of a rent-seeking company, can pull off this trick, surely your average English or philosophy professor can do better.

THE ELEPHANT IN THE BRAIN AND HIDDEN MOTIVES

This chapter may seem quite cynical. After all, we're claiming that public-spirited arguments often disguise selfish behavior. But we don't necessarily want to claim that people *know* they're motivated by self-interest. Human behavior is more interesting than this.

Our brains are funny. As Kevin Simler and Robin Hanson show, in their fascinating book *The Elephant in the Brain*, we humans have evolved the capacity and tendency to engage in self-deception about our own motivations. Our brains trick us into believing we have better motives than we, in fact, do.

The reason behind this is simple: We all benefit from living with people who generally play by public-spirited moral rules. We've evolved, in general, to play along with such rules. But we also can benefit from breaking those rules on the margins and taking advantage of others' generosity, fair play, and good will. However, simultaneously other people have evolved to punish the rule-breakers. Furthermore, they've evolved to read our minds; people are good at discerning our conscious motives. Accordingly, our brains have developed a defense mechanism: We often subconsciously pursue our self-interest, but at the same time consciously and sincerely believe we are motivated by altruism. Your brain pursues *selfish behaviors* but *hides* your own motives from you. You think you mean well, so others think you mean well, but often you're really out for yourself.

This is true even of *charity*. For the most part, even charitable giving isn't usually about *helping*. Rather, charity is mostly about conspicuous caring. It's about signaling to other people—potential business partners, coworkers, neighbors, and mates—that we are successful, have a pro-social orientation, are trustworthy, and have empathy. Just as wearing a Rolex screams, "I've made it!," altruistic giving is mostly about signaling to others, "Deal with me! Partner with me! Have sex with me! I'm good!"[12]

How do we know all this? Simler and Hanson suggest we look for the best explanation of people's behavior. For instance, it turns out that when people give away money to charity, almost none of them do any homework to determine how much good they're doing. The amount and rates at which they give turn out to be insensitive to the *amount of good* the charity does—showing them a charity does 100 times as good as another doesn't induce them to give *more*. Fewer than 3 percent of people will actually change their intended donations in order to do measurably more good. Instead, numerous experiments and studies find that the following factors determine when and how much we give:

- *Visibility*. We give more when we're being watched or when others will know how much we give.

- *Peer pressure.* We give more when pressured to give, especially by people we know, or who have high status, or who are in our network.
- *Mating motive.* We give more when we are primed to think about sex or mating opportunities; we give more if the solicitor is sexually attractive.[13]

In short, giving is explained *more* by status-seeking and coalition-building, not so much by the good charity does. But, of course, as they say, it doesn't *feel* as if that's what we're aiming for; we genuinely believe we want to help.

Simler and Hanson aren't saying we're perfectly selfish. If we were all sociopaths, none of this signaling would work. Rather, a better way to think of it is that we're mostly selfish, but most of us (except sociopaths) have *some* genuinely moral motives. We can benefit from tricking others into thinking we have stronger moral motives that we, in fact, do, but in order to trick *them*, we first trick *ourselves*.

If even *charitable behavior*—that is, giving to *others*—is better explained by self-interest than by genuine attempts to help others, it sure would be surprising if politics were any different.

BAPTISTS, BOOTLEGGERS, AND CAMPUS SOCIAL JUSTICE ACTIVISM

Public choice economist Bruce Yandle famously noted that politics creates strange bedfellows or odd alliances between selfishly and morally motivated groups. Take, for instance, dry country laws, or blue laws, prohibiting the sale of alcohol on Sundays. Yandle noted that both Baptists and bootleggers supported such laws. The Baptists believed drinking alcohol was sinful. They formed the morally righteous public face of the movement. Behind the scenes, bootleggers—who sold alcohol for inflated prices on the black market—supported the laws for selfish reasons. For them, blue laws and alcohol prohibition meant less competition, more customers, and more money. Bootleggers often donated to help along the Baptist's teetotaling activism.[14]

Yandle's bigger point is that for many social and political movements, certain morally motivated activist groups form the public face, but behind the scenes you'll find individuals and firms who support the change for selfish reasons. Don't get suckered when you see, for instance, a private firm advocating increased taxes, regulations, or mandatory minimum wages on moral grounds. The firm probably knows such laws would screw its competitors and help it win a bigger market share. For instance, a very high minimum wage hurts Walmart but helps Costco, because Costco has a less labor-intensive business model.[15] Costco lobbies for minimum wage increases not to help workers but to help Costco.[16] And both Walmart and Costco can undermine mom and pop stores by increased regulations and slightly higher minimum wages. Big firms have an easier time paying higher wages and have a lower legal compliance cost per worker.

This kind of thing happens on campus as well. For instance, in the past few years, the campus culture wars reignited, especially over racial issues. Across the nation, at Harvard, Missouri, Yale, Amherst, Ithaca, Oberlin, Berkeley, among many other schools, there have been numerous demonstrations, sit-ins, protests, incidents of vandalism, and waves of violence.[17] Some of these protests were about insensitive Halloween costumes, some about the perceived institutional or explicit racism of academia, some about historical injustice, and some about fighting fascism (where "fascism" means "not far left").

We disclose that we're sympathetic with many of their concerns.[18] For instance, the Georgetown campus used to include buildings named for former university presidents who, as campus leaders recently rediscovered, had sold slaves in the early 1800s to pay the university's debts.[19] Students demanded that the buildings be renamed. The university complied. We agree with the decision; we think it's wrong to celebrate and honor such evildoers. Georgetown also announced it would offer preferential admissions and increased financial aid for descendants of the slaves it had sold. We find the school's response fitting.

Still, many of the campus racial protests have suspicious features. Around the US, in nearly every case, protesting students issued long lists of demands.[20] For instance, Oberlin students wrote a fourteen-page document, insisting that the college:

1. produce a 40 percent increase in black student enrollment from "each of the Americas, the Caribbean, and continent of Africa."
2. produce a 40 percent increase in black student enrollment in the Department of Jazz.

3. hire more black administrators.
4. offer free housing over breaks for international black students who cannot easily travel back to their home countries.
5. create mandatory courses in the "Black Experience" as part of the college's general education requirements.
6. require faculty to attend classes that explain why capitalism is evil and racist; teach faculty to integrate these critical views of capitalism into their courses.
7. increased black faculty members in certain departments.
8. fire a number of professors whom the activists disliked.
9. promote, give salary increases or tenure to, or place on the tenure track other professors whom the activists liked.
10. pay certain black activist students an $8.20 per hour stipend for their activism.

And so on.[21] Oberlin rejected their demands.[22]

However, other activists at other colleges and universities were more successful. Yale launched a $50 million program to increase faculty ethnic diversity.[23] Princeton indicated that it planned to diversify its faculty and hire fifteen to twenty new members.[24] Not to be outdone, in response to student protests over police violence,[25] Brown University recently created a $165 million "Diversity and Inclusion Action Plan":

> The total includes $100 million for endowed faculty positions, $25 million for graduate student fellowships, $20 million to endow research centers focused on race, ethnicity, and social justice, and $20 million to support curricular and co-curricular initiatives. The figures reflect a more detailed final analysis for funding the initiatives, updating a broader $100-million estimate released with the draft of the plan in November.[26]

There's a funny pattern to the student activists' demands. The students usually call for the university's administration to fork over extra money to, fund extra tenure-lines in, and give extra power to . . . wait for it . . . the very departments where the students learned the ideas and slogans they're pushing. These departments—English, comparative literature, various group studies programs—also happen to be among the most tuition-dependent departments with the fewest available sources of outside grants and funding. They are the departments with the strongest financial incentives to gain power in the university.

That's not to say the students or their faculty mentors are insincere or are *merely* seeking to promote their selfish interests at the expense of donors and other students. Nor is to say their complaints are all illegitimate. Some of the complaints and some of their demands, we agree, are good and just. But, nevertheless, it's instructive to imagine what would happen if the students and the faculty behind them—the faculty who taught them the complaints and moral concepts they advance in their protests—were motivated solely by self-interest. In such a case, it's not clear the faculty would behave any differently. We can summarize their position as follows:

> Our college/university is systematically racist, heteronormative, classist, and sexist. The best way to *start* down the long road to fixing these problems would be to increase my department's budget, promote me, let me hire my friends, let me fire my enemies, require students to take my classes, require faculty to push my ideology, make my ideology part of first-year orientation, and give me power over other academic departments. That wouldn't solve our problems, but it sure would help.

Perhaps faculty are sincere in their concerns, though perhaps they've convinced themselves that what's in their self-interest social justice itself just so happens to demand.

Protesting students are right to recognize that even hard left, progressive schools like Brown, Reed, and Oberlin have not yet achieved perfect racial justice. But if students were genuinely concerned first and foremost with fighting racial injustice, these colleges are perhaps the least obvious and plausible places in the US to stage prolonged protests. There are far more serious injustices occurring elsewhere, places far lower on the curves of diminishing marginal returns, places where even small reforms would do far more good. A legal defense fund that provides attorneys for inner-city victims of civil asset forfeiture would almost certainly result in greater benefits for a greater number of marginalized people than creating a newly endowed "social justice" chair for an upper-middle-class professor at an elite liberal arts college. So, it looks to us as if students do not select target schools where protests and demonstrations are most needed or could do the most good. They opt to protest where it's easiest, where they'll face the least resistance, and where they'll be most visible and impressive to their own peers.

Students may be the Baptists and faculty the bootleggers. In stronger terms, students may become pawns in professors' struggle for more money, power, and resources. We don't really know. But it sure smells fishy. When someone says, "Social justice demands you give me cookies!," you don't know whether that person loves social justice or just loves cookies.

MORAL GRANDSTANDING ABOUT TENURE

It's not just protesters who use moral language to cover their self-interest. We all do it. Just ask us professors about tenure.

When a college professor receives tenure, she enjoys tremendous job security. She can then only be fired "for cause" or in case of severe financial emergency. She can hang on to her job for years beyond what should have marked her retirement. At most R1 universities, she can cease publishing without losing her job, even though her primary work responsibility is to publish. At most teaching-centered universities, a tenured professor won't lose her job even if no students want to take her classes.

But in public, when we professors have to explain why tenure should exist, we don't extol the terrific personal benefits of tenure for *us*. Instead, we offer you high-minded, public-spirited, morally charged arguments, such as:

1. *Tenure protects academic freedom.* Tenure makes it harder for administrators and legislators to fire faculty who push controversial ideas. It thus ensures academia can be a genuine marketplace of ideas not beholden to political ideology. Tenure makes certain that academia has the freedom to produce ground-breaking but unpopular new ideas.

2. *Tenure enhances research productivity*, especially in high-stakes research areas. After assistant professors prove their chops and pass probation, they receive the job security to work on risky big ideas that take years to come to fruition. Tenured professors can pursue high-impact, high-value research, rather than having to focus on pumping out as many (possibly low-value) publications as possible per year. Tenure means quality over quantity.

These are the arguments every professor hears as a grad student, and we transmit them to each new generation. But are these good arguments or mere myths? Do we believe them because we have good evidence or because we *want* them to be true? Do we repeat these arguments because it's good for us if the public believes them?

At first glance, it's not clear why tenure per se is necessary for academic freedom. Many colleges and universities write academic freedom guidelines into their contracts. At Georgetown, for instance, non-tenure-track "professors of the practice," teaching professors, clinical professors, and research professors have de jure (by law) as much academic freedom as the tenured and tenure-track professors.

But there might still be a de facto difference. The university can more easily contrive some reason to fire non-tenure-track than tenure-track professors.

These two arguments—that tenure protects freedom and enhances research productivity—are open to empirical testing. Argument 1 predicts that tenured faculty will be fired for political causes at a lower rate than untenured faculty. It plausibly predicts that tenured faculty will tend to produce more radical, extreme, unpopular, or subversive claims than untenured faculty. It predicts tenured faculty will be braver and more likely to take ideological risks or do unpopular things. Argument 2 predicts that tenured faculty will produce bigger and better, more innovative and more paradigm-shifting research than their untenured peers.

Of course, to test these hypotheses, we wouldn't want to compare, say, tenured full professors to teaching-centered lecturers. Of course, a professor with a 2-2 or less teaching load, who gets research funds, and whose raises are based on research will, on average, outpublish someone with a 4-4 teaching load who has no time or funding for research. Instead, we'd want to carefully compare tenured faculty to tenure-track but not yet tenured faculty, or compare research-oriented tenured faculty to research professors with long-term but not tenure-track contracts. We'd also carefully check for various confounding variables. (For example, it's harder to do original mathematics than psychology, so elite math professors publish at a lower rate than average psych professors.)

In fact, an empirical literature exists that tries to test whether tenure "works." The most sophisticated paper we found on this topic offers negative results. Economists Jonathan Brogaard, Joseph Engelberg, and Edward van Wesep summarize their argument as follows:

> Using a sample of all academics who pass through top 50 economics and finance departments from 1996 through 2014, we study whether the granting of tenure leads faculty to pursue riskier ideas. We use the extreme tails of ex-post citations as our measure of risk and find that both the number of publications and the portion consisting of "home runs" peak at tenure and fall steadily for a decade thereafter. Similar patterns hold for faculty at elite (top 10) institutions and for faculty who take differing time to tenure. We find the opposite pattern among poorly-cited publications: their numbers rise steadily both pre- and post-tenure.[27]

They find that in the two years right after faculty receive tenure, publications drop by about 30 percent and then an additional 15 percent through the rest of the decade. Furthermore, the number of "home run" publications drops dramatically.[28]

Brogaard and his coauthors carefully consider whether tenure has other possible benefits; for instance, perhaps it gives faculty the freedom to branch out and do riskier interdisciplinary work. But, on the contrary, they find no evidence of such an effect.[29] They carefully control for whether a drop in productivity results simply from getting tenure or from a natural decline in productivity in the years after receiving a PhD, and they find tenure has an independent effect.[30] Finally, they check to see whether the elite faculty in the very best economics departments (Chicago, Harvard, MIT, etc.) are any different. Even at the most elite schools, most professors peak during the year they receive tenure, with their productivity declining thereafter.[31]

In short, they find that tenure has precisely the perverse incentives a normal person would expect. The tenure game is up or out—either earn tenure, or get fired. So, not surprisingly, faculty work hard, publish a great deal, and further try to publish the most innovative and impressive material they can in order to secure tenure. But, once they have tenure, they become lazier, more risk-averse, and more conservative. Giving them a job for life extinguishes the fire under their asses. Only in academia would anyone find this surprising. Do you think Tom Brady would work better and harder if Belichick guaranteed him another thirty years as quarterback no matter what?

In a similarly rigorous paper, Thomas Goodwin and Raymond Sauer examine 140 economics professors from seven research-oriented departments. They do not try to measure the independent effect of tenure. But they find that the number of publications tends to peak about ten to fifteen years after receipt of a PhD and then declines thereafter. Their picture is compatible with Brogaard's.[32] They don't test whether quality improves as quantity declines. But quantity sure does decline over time, and it seems to peak shortly after most faculty receive tenure.

These studies look at economists. But maybe economists, the very faculty who won't shut up about incentives, are unusually responsive to incentives. Are sociologists any different? Back in 1977, John W. Holley did a similar study to those we previously discussed and obtained similar results. After controlling for a host of confounding variables—such as the type of job a professor had, where she received her PhD, her age, and the like—he found that sociologists become less productive after receiving tenure.[33]

How about everyone else? Lionel Lewis conducted a study comparing how many and what kind of publications professors from a wide range of disciplines tend to publish in when they A) seek tenure (i.e., seek promotion from assistant to associate professor) and B) are under consideration for full professor. In conducting his research, he also read the letters that outside reviewers had written in evaluating the candidates. (At research universities, deans ask five to ten professors from other universities to evaluate the work of candidates for promotion.) Lewis found that the rate of publication dropped after tenure—candidates for full professor did less in their time as associate professors than assistant professors did during their period of probation. But, *worse*, he also determined that the letters evaluating candidates for full professor were more negative: Outside letter writers were less likely to describe candidates' research as excellent and innovative, and more likely to describe it as prosaic, derivative, or minimally competent.[34] (However, Lewis doesn't tell us just *how much* worse the letters for potential full professors are.) Lewis finds no evidence that tenured professors swing for the fence more often, but some proof they simply bat less.

What about the thesis that tenure protects academic freedom? We couldn't find a study directly testing this, for instance, by examining whether untenured or non-tenure-track professors get fired more often for political or doctrinal reasons.

However, Stephen Ceci, Wendy Williams, and Katrin Mueller-Johnson recently surveyed over 1,000 professors, asking them how they believed they would react to a number of "real-world dilemmas involving colleagues who wished to teach courses unpopular with their peers, to investigate unpopular topics, and to publish controversial findings."[35] Now, keep in mind that when you ask people how they *would* behave, the respondents tend to overestimate how well they'd really behave. So, if 40 percent say they'd do something brave, this gives us an upper bound; in reality, fewer than 40 percent would act bravely in the real world.[36] Nevertheless, Williams and Ceci found that tenured professors were, by their own self-reports, risk-averse and timid; they showed no greater interest in pushing or defending controversial ideas.[37]

The best defenses of tenure that we found were largely theoretical rather than empirical. For instance, Richard McKenzie argues that academia is a kind of worker-controlled firm. The workers—that is, the professors—have the most power in hiring and promoting other professors. The "bosses" (the provost and other administrators) are not competent to monitor faculty performance. (After all, how could the university chancellor evaluate whether a given mathematician is doing important work unless she herself is a mathematician?) Professors, McKenzie claims, demand tenure as a form of insurance against the vicissitudes of internal academic politics.

Most importantly, he says, if faculty did not have tenure, they would have strong incentives only to hire their inferiors. To illustrate, imagine a group of professors knew that in a recession, the university might fire the bottom 50 percent of faculty. Now, suppose they ask us to hire new professors in our department. We'd want to hire our inferiors to ensure we keep our jobs come the next round of layoffs. So, McKenzie argues, tenure protects faculty from competition and thus incentivizes them to hire higher-performing colleagues—because they know these new colleagues won't *replace* them.[38]

In reviewing the literature on tenure, we did not find any data-based, empirical articles that validated or confirmed the central justifications for tenure. We found plenty of papers speculating about its effects, examining its history, or looking at current attitudes toward and threats to tenure.[39] The papers we previously discussed cast serious doubt on whether tenure delivers the goods, though they are not quite enough to prove tenure fails. After all, maybe in a world where research-oriented professors all had long-term rolling contracts, their total productivity and tendency to produce "home run" research, especially in the later stages of their career, would be even lower.

Still, ask a typical professor, "Is tenure good?," and he won't say, "I dunno. The empirical research is somewhat negative but inconclusive." Rather, he'll offer several moralistic just-so stories. Since the research doesn't validate those stories, one has to wonder whether deep down academics are just pushing a myth that serves their self-interest. They don't look too closely at the myths because they're worried they won't like what they find.

Marcia Lynn Wicker points out that faculty defenses of tenure are chock-full of inflated moral rhetoric. But, of course, the tenure process creates a barrier to entry in the academic market. Committing to a tenure-track line, and further, actually tenuring someone, are tremendously expensive for the university. Professors rarely suffer pay cuts and usually get raises, so tenuring a professor at, say, age 35 commits the university to paying another thirty-five years of that professor's salary and makes it impossible to replace the professor with someone better. Tenure not only protects professors from external competition by preventing others from taking their jobs, but also pushes universities to hire an underclass of teaching-intensive, easier-to-fire, non-tenure-track professors, who (due to their large teaching loads) can't compete with tenure-line faculty for the best jobs.[40]

THE ADJUNCTS' RIGHTS MOVEMENT

Adjunct faculty—short-term contract workers who are paid a small fee per class—seem to get a raw deal. Adjuncts get low pay, no benefits, no rights, and no job security. Inside Higher Ed reports that adjuncts, on average, receive $2,700 per course.[41] At that rate, an adjunct teaching a 4-4 load would make only $21,600 per year, an amount on par with the living stipend for a typical graduate student, an amount less than Jason and his business school colleagues make per month.

Activists and the press seem convinced this is just plain awful. Al Jazeera describes adjuncts as "indentured servants."[42] Some activists and reports compare adjuncts to sweatshop workers,[43] while others compare them to sharecroppers.[44] A reporter at the *Chronicle of Higher Education*'s ChronicleVitae webpage labels adjuncts "exploited professors."[45] Op-eds in *The Guardian*[46] and *The Boston Globe*[47] concur. An article in *The Observer* exclaims, "Colleges would implode without exploited freelance professors,"[48] while a prominent adjunct activist asserts that she decided to leave academia because she was tired of being exploited.[49] *The American Prospect* celebrates that "exploited faculty members" are "eager to band together" under unions.[50]

In recent years, an adjuncts' rights movement has spread across the US. Activists demand higher status, voting rights, better pay, benefits, and job security. Many activists use offensively hyperbolic moral language: They compare themselves to *slaves*.[51] Their message isn't "We want more money; give it to us or we'll strike." Rather, it's "We are exploited wage slaves. We carry the modern university on our backs. Tenure-track faculty and administrators exploit us. Justice requires we get our due."

Adjuncts' rights activists are probably sincere. But their moral arguments don't stand up to scrutiny. Once again, morality disguises self-interest.

The Easily Falsified Myth of Adjunctification

Newspapers love to claim that in an effort to save costs, universities have been replacing full-time faculty with part-time adjuncts. They call this process "adjunctification."[52] Turns out it's not true.

The ratio of adjuncts to full-time faculty has indeed increased over the past forty years. But that is not because tenure-track or long-term full-time professors are being replaced with temporary adjuncts. US

Department of Education data reveal that in 1970 the ratio of students to full-time faculty at all universities was 23.2 to 1. In 2013, the most recent available data indicate the ratio is 23.7 to 1.[53] Figure 6.1 shows that ratio has remained constant for over forty years, hovering around an average of 24 to 1. In other words, at traditional not-for-profit institutions, the growth of full-time faculty positions has largely kept pace with student enrollments.

Yet the number of adjuncts has also grown dramatically during this same period. Universities are not *replacing* full-time faculty with adjuncts; instead, they are adding adjuncts *on top of* full-time faculty. Adjuncts are supplementing full-time faculty, not replacing them.

Are Adjuncts Underpaid?

Adjunct activists often claim they receive unfairly low pay. They repeat the slogan "equal pay for equal work."[54] They claim adjuncts perform comparable work to full-time professors, but are paid much less.

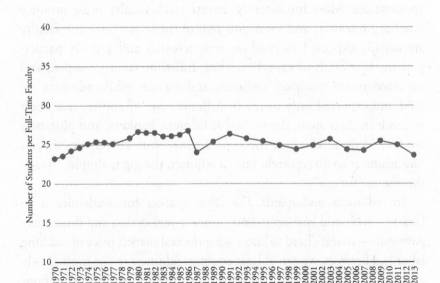

FIGURE 6.1 Ratio of Enrolled Students to Full-Time Faculty, Not-for-Profit Colleges and Universities, 1970–2013

Source: US Department of Education, 2014, *Digest of Education Statistics*, chart derived from Tables 315.10 and 303.10.

Comparing the typical adjunct—the overwhelming majority of whom lack a terminal degree and so are ineligible for higher levels of academic employment—to an endowed chair and full professor at an elite R1 is misleading. That's like comparing a AA baseball player with an all-star MLB pitcher.

One reason it's misleading is that adjuncts are paid *only to teach*; that's it. The university pays them to prepare and deliver lectures, grade, and interact with students via office hours or email. Furthermore, even the "prep" expectations are low; universities usually hire adjuncts to cover courses like intro composition or "101" surveys that anyone in the field should be able to teach with minimal preparation.

In contrast, the typical full-time faculty member of any rank must fulfill extensive university service requirements: committee work, departmental meetings, student advising, applications review, and a multitude of other university functions. Full-time faculty must perform service to the profession and the public: refereeing journal articles, grant proposals, and book manuscripts, presenting at scholarly meetings, and delivering public lectures or making TV or radio appearances. Most importantly, tenure-track faculty must produce scholarly research, and even non-tenure-track but full-time faculty are usually expected to produce *some* research and actively participate in their fields of expertise. Thus, full-time faculty are paid and expected to do teaching, research, and service, while adjuncts are paid and expected only to teach. Adjuncts are, of course, free to do research in their spare time—just as farmers, bankers, and plumbers are free to do research in their spare time—but universities do not *hire* adjuncts to do research. For an adjunct, the gig is simple: "Teach this course for us."

Are adjuncts underpaid? The labor market for academics is so bizarre—with odd barriers to entry, once-a-year-cycles, and third-party payments—that it's hard to know what the real market price of teaching labor is. However, we can at least compare adjuncts to the most closely analogous full-time faculty, to see if they get paid much less per hour spent *teaching* or working on teaching-related activities.

The most plausible comparison class to adjuncts would be an entry-level full-time position with heavy teaching obligations and light research duties at a regional university or small liberal arts college.

Note that even this comparison already entails a number of generous assumptions about the adjuncts. To be eligible for even this low-level teaching appointment, an adjunct would need a terminal degree and probably a few scholarly publications in recognized peer-reviewed journals. (Again, most adjuncts lack a terminal degree and so are ineligible for most full-time academic jobs.[55]) For purposes of comparison, though, we will assume that the adjunct meets the minimum qualification criteria to be hired into an entry-level full-time faculty appointment at a teaching-heavy institution.

Numerous empirical studies have examined how faculty spend their time. A 2014 panel study at a large research university found that the average full-time faculty member spends about 24.5 hours per week on teaching and instruction-related activities.[56] These figures are broadly consistent with a 2003 survey by the US Department of Education, which found the average research university professor spends roughly 24 hours per week on teaching-related activities.[57] In both studies, teaching amounted to about 40 percent of the average research university faculty member's work hours during the regular school semester, inclusive of weekends. The remainder was split between research and university service.

However, note that these figures are for full-time faculty at large *research* universities. These institutions have lighter teaching expectations of their full-time faculty than the average four-year college. Teaching obligations increase dramatically, while research obligations decrease dramatically, at smaller regional universities and liberal arts colleges.[58] Full-time professors at these teaching-intensive institutions work a similar number of total hours per week as research university faculty, but they allocate more time to instruction-related activities. A Department of Education study, for example, finds that private liberal arts college faculty spend an average of almost 36 hours per week, or almost 66 percent of a weekend-inclusive work week, on teaching activities. Regional comprehensive colleges and universities, whether public or private, both report similar time allocations.[59] These numbers reflect the 4-4 course load that is common at such institutions. Yet even faculty at teaching-heavy regional institutions and liberal arts colleges spend an average of 34 percent of their time on a combination of service and research.

Most adjunct respondents to the same survey report spending the vast majority of their time on teaching alone, regardless of the type of institution. Adjuncts at regional comprehensive universities and private liberal arts colleges, on average, allocate over 90 percent of their time to teaching. This number drops to just under 80 percent for large research universities, where some modest service and professional development activities are more common. Remember, though, that while adjuncts at research universities do spend some time on research, they are not expected or paid to do so. Such activities are outside the scope of adjuncts' jobs. Since, it turns out, the overwhelming majority of adjuncts teach two courses or fewer per semester, their average *total* work hours are also significantly less than those of full-time faculty at all types of institutions.[60]

The average full-time faculty member reports working about 53 hours per week during the semester, almost all of it directly for the institution at which she is employed. Most adjuncts work far fewer hours, as they work only part-time. A very small minority of adjuncts string together enough courses to work what we'd consider "full-time" hours, but even the average full-time adjunct reports spending just under 40 hours per week at all jobs, including *other* employment outside of the academy, and just 15 hours per week at a single institution, including both paid and unpaid activities.[61] An adjunct teaching a 4-4 course load split between two campuses is likely working in an academic capacity for a total of between 30 and 40 hours a week based on these estimates, and only during the school semester. Simply using Department of Education data for both paid and unpaid activities, even a "full-time" adjunct teaching a 4-4 load only works about 75 percent of the total weekly hours of the average full-time faculty.[62]

Now, all these numbers rely on surveys. Due to social desirability bias, we expect that surveyed faculty probably inflate the number of hours they work; that is, they probably work fewer hours than they claim to. However, there's no obvious reason to suspect that full-time tenure-track faculty lie *more* to Department of Education surveyors than adjuncts do. After all, full-time faculty are judged on *output*, not input. So, while we should take these numbers with a grain of salt, we don't have reason to discount the numbers provided by full-time faculty more than the numbers of adjuncts.

The overwhelming majority of adjuncts do not teach full course loads and thus work significantly less than full-time, permanent faculty. Although it is certainly true that a small number of adjuncts string together multiple appointments at different universities and a very small number report that they exceed a 4-4 course load, the total number of courses taught in these relatively rare "freeway flyer" adjunct scenarios would still have to reach extraordinary levels to achieve parity with the average number of hours worked by the typical full-time faculty member at any type of institution. A simple comparative calculation illustrates this point.

Suppose Jane holds a PhD and is hired to her first full-time lecturer or assistant professor position in the humanities at a teaching-intensive liberal arts college with low research expectations of faculty. She receives $47,500 per year, a representative salary for a position of this type.[63] Jane is assigned a 4-4 course load with her appointment. As a reasonably efficient instructor, she devotes an average of 10 hours to *each* class per week (3 hours of lecturing and 7 hours of grading, preparation work, and meeting with students per class). This yields a total teaching obligation of 40 hours a week during the regular semester. Her teaching commitments cover two 16-week semesters per year (including the weeks that finals are administered), or 32 weeks total. She therefore allocates about 1,280 hours per year to instruction-related activities.

Suppose that Will is a "full-time adjunct," also in the humanities. For the purposes of reasonable comparison, we assume that Will is among the minority of adjuncts who holds a PhD or other terminal degree. The 2012 Coalition on the Academic Workforce survey found that adjuncts with terminal degrees earn a modest per-class premium in compensation, with per-course pay averaging $3,200.[64] Will similarly works a 4-4 course load, split between two different campuses, and is equally efficient at grading and classroom preparation. At 40 hours per week across two 16-week semesters, he also works 1,280 hours per year on instruction-related activities and receives $26,500 in total earnings.

On the surface, the teachers' individual compensation differs substantially. But our comparison is incomplete. Jane, the full-time hire, is also contractually obliged to perform university service throughout the year. She must also meet basic research expectations to attain tenure or promotion or, in some cases, even contract renewal. She does some of this work during the semester in addition to the 40 hours she devotes to teaching each week—perhaps another 13 hours if she reflects the Department of Education survey. The majority of these hours are logged over the summer and winter breaks when she is not teaching. This period includes an additional two months or more of compensated annual employment. If Jane is indeed fulfilling the normal workload of a full-time private-sector job, she is likely approaching 2,080 hours of compensated work per year.[65] The equivalent hourly wage for her teaching job is therefore $22.84. Jane also receives benefits, likely worth an additional 33 percent of her salary. This brings her effective hourly wage, with nonmonetary benefits, up to about $30.37.

Note that this figure assumes Jane works an average of 40 hours a week, divided between an actual heavier workload during the semester and a lighter workload during summer and winter instructional breaks. Suppose, however, that Jane maintains her 53-hour work week throughout the year, reflecting aggressive research pursuits that might be expected of a faculty member undergoing tenure review. Suppose Jane also takes three weeks off for vacation. If Jane maintains this more active schedule of summer and winter research activities, as her job may expect her to do in order to qualify for academic promotion, her equivalent hourly wage and benefits drop to only $24.33.

Although he earns less than the full-time professor, our adjunct Will has no contractual obligations beyond teaching and is only paid for the 32 weeks of the spring and fall semesters. Will performs what amounts to a part-time job; he's only working 1,280 hours a year.[66] His equivalent hourly wage for the work he is hired to do is actually $20.70, putting him only slightly below the hourly rate for our entry-level, full-time assistant professor. This small divergence increases when we include the estimated value of benefits, with Will receiving about 70 to 85 percent of Jane's total hourly monetary and nonmonetary compensation. However, since Will is teaching a 4-4 load at two different campuses, he may qualify for some health insurance and other benefits, in which case the gap closes.[67]

Remember, we made many charitable assumptions on behalf of adjuncts to draw this comparison. We assumed that both Jane and

Will have comparable qualifications, meaning that adjunct Will, unlike most adjuncts, would stand a chance of being hired full-time at a liberal arts college. We also assumed that both faculty teach with comparable efficiency, and we selected work hours reflecting moderate time management skills and the data in Department of Education surveys. We also assumed an identical teaching load. This is a matter of simply standardizing our units of comparison, as it would be misleading to assert that two faculty with nonidentical teaching loads were performing "equal work" for "unequal pay."

Relaxing any of these assumptions would likely yield different equivalent hourly wages, but they would also weaken adjunct rights activists' grievances about performing equal work. Recall that we seek to make a comparison that matches a highly qualified adjunct with a realistic full-time appointment at a teaching college, not a moderately qualified adjunct with a chaired professor at a top-tier research university. It's not as though, say, Stanford would consider replacing its star researchers with a group of unpublished adjuncts who only hold master's degrees. If adjuncts think they're doing the same job as those professors, then they don't understand academia.

In short: Adjuncts make less total money than comparable teaching-intensive professors because they work less and do less, not because they get paid much less per hour spent teaching. They make much less than research-intensive professors because those professors get paid primarily to *research*, not to teach, and research pays far better than teaching.

CONCLUSION: THE ELEPHANT IN THE BRAIN

Overall, people are fairly selfish, although they do have some genuine moral concerns. In politics, people aren't much different. Sometimes they mean well, but highfalutin moral language, social justice sloganeering, and self-righteous gesticulation frequently conceal selfish behavior.

We can't read people's minds to determine what they really believe. But we can examine whether their moral arguments make any sense. We can follow the money. When we see—as with ADM or the adjuncts' rights movement—that the moral arguments are no good but a lot of money is at stake, we can presume the driving force is self-interest pure and simple.

We're not complete cynics. People sometimes genuinely mean well. But when you hear a person trying to sell you a moral argument that just so happens to imply he or she should be the recipient of more money, power, prestige, and resources, we say, caveat emptor!

7

The Gen Ed Hustle

Monopolists very seldom make good work, and a lecture which a certain number of students must attend, whether they profit by it or no, is certainly not very likely to be a good one.

—Adam Smith, 1774[1]

WHY DO UNIVERSITIES REQUIRE gen eds? If you ask them, they'll offer you a host of nice, public-spirited reasons. The purpose of gen eds is to ensure that students are well rounded, develop a wide breadth of knowledge and skills, and are exposed to multiple fields so they can make an informed decision about their major. But, we suspect, the real reason for gen eds is that they represent a way for certain faculty to capture students' tuition dollars. Faculty exploit students for their own selfish benefit, although they disguise this practice with moralistic arguments. Or, so we argue here.

AN ANALOGY: CALLIGRAPHY AT MED SCHOOL

Let's take a step back and consider an analogy. Medical doctors have notoriously bad handwriting. There's actually a small body of scholarly literature analyzing doctors' handwriting. Poor handwriting often leads to misreported vital statistics and erroneous dosages of drugs on handwritten prescriptions.[2] Bad handwriting kills.

Our goal isn't to rag on doctors or predict an impending handwriting crisis in the medical industry. Instead, their poor handwriting provides an occasion for an interesting thought experiment about academia.

Suppose for a moment that the American Medical Association (AMA) becomes worried about the bad handwriting epidemic of the medical profession. Its board of directors hears complaints by pharmacists who struggle to read prescriptions. Or, perhaps a high-profile malpractice case springs up where a patient received the wrong treatments due to illegible blood pressure readings. In response, let's suppose the AMA board directs its staff to arrive at a solution to the handwriting problem. The AMA's board decides to amend its rules for obtaining a medical license. In addition to completing standard classroom instruction, medical residencies, and degree conferrals, all new doctors seeking to practice medicine in the United States must now complete a one-semester course on penmanship.

In response to the rule change, medical schools adapt their curriculum and degree requirements to incorporate the new course. They charge the same price per credit hour as any other course, but because doctors—including doctors who work as college professors—have notoriously bad handwriting, medical schools must also hire *others* to teach the new class.

There's a precedent here, believe it or not. In the nineteenth century, penmanship was a fairly common academic requirement, even at the college level. Undergraduates were often trained and then graded on their proficiency in written script. Several early business schools also offered formal classes in handwriting as a part of their curriculum for bookkeeping and accounting. Accurate record-keeping, after all, was crucial, and a sloppy written figure could throw off a company's entire balance sheet and threaten the business. Technology, of course, made most classes in penmanship obsolete. For the same reason, colleges no longer offer training (as they once did) in the operation of telegraphs. Penmanship in the modern era, accordingly, has a much smaller presence in academic life—most colleges don't even offer it, and in the rare instance that they do, it is usually taught as a niche fine art skill such as calligraphy.

Returning to our scenario, though, suppose that medical schools found a willing group of penmanship instructors among this underutilized group of calligraphy experts and professionals. The AMA's rule breathes new life into the reconstituted penmanship department and suddenly fills its classrooms with tens of thousands of would-be doctors. Medical schools hire many new penmanship faculty, who unexpectedly receive larger salaries and experience more job security than was the case in outside work.

Now suppose a few years pass. A new generation of doctors has been trained in formal penmanship in addition to diagnosing diseases, setting broken bones, performing surgeries, and any number of other specializations. Much to its chagrin, though, the AMA continues to receive complaints from pharmacists about doctors' terrible handwriting. The now-flourishing penmanship department explains the problem: "True mastery of the written arts requires practice—including more practice than can be obtained in a single semester. The obvious solution," they conclude, "is to add a second semester of advanced penmanship to the curriculum." Although the AMA doesn't require a second or third penmanship class, many medical schools decide to adopt such a practice, especially given that the sunk cost of the first semester is already in place. The growing penmanship department is, of course, eager to oblige its school—this means twice as many medical students to teach and thus more money and more jobs for penmanship professors.

A few more years go by, and the handwriting complaints from pharmacists continue to flow into the AMA. Frustrated by the lack of results from the previous several years of curricular changes, they decide to investigate. They conduct a few studies comparing handwriting samples from a group of medical students before and after the two penmanship classes. The studies show that the penmanship classes produce no meaningful improvement in handwriting, although the students are now worse off by six credit hours' worth of tuition and time.

Let's continue one step further in this increasingly absurd scenario. After years of seeing no discernible results from the ever-growing penmanship classes, a few of the regular medical school faculty try to persuade the school to cancel the penmanship requirement. Bad handwriting may still be a problem, they suggest, but the evidence shows the classes simply aren't working, that they are a waste of the students' time and tuition dollars. Furthermore, every now and then a student even shows up in human anatomy class peddling a pseudoscientific claim about homeopathy or alternative medicine he or she may have learned from a calligraphy instructor.

Unfortunately, there's a problem. The once-small penmanship department is now large and entrenched. They've hired multiple new faculty to meet the teaching load, which, in turn, has attracted a new pipeline of calligraphy MFA students of its own—all of them hoping to land a faculty position teaching penmanship. When the medical school faculty raise the issue of the penmanship course's ineffectiveness, they're met with not only vigorous resistance to altering the curriculum but also renewed pressure to add even more penmanship courses—perhaps it's simply the case that medical students are "remedial" in their handwriting and need an additional semester of prerequisite penmanship training before they are ready to take the two regular semesters of classes.

When the penmanship faculty hear rumors of possible cuts to their discipline (on the grounds that their classes have not delivered results), they aggressively organize to protect their turf. They enlist the help of the local American Association of University Professors (AAUP) chapter to ensure the security of their jobs, vigorously dispute the characterization of the classes as wasteful, lobby administrators for more resources to make their classes "effective," and even write opinion pieces to the local newspaper and higher ed presses stressing the innate value of the art of penmanship. They claim the medical school dean is captive of a neoliberal ideology or "corporatist agenda," or they complain that he works for Big Pharma. A few calligraphy faculty circulate articles calling up horror stories about patients who suffered severe harm because of an illegible annotation on a prescription pad to remind the university of the dangers of poor penmanship. The university administration, not wanting to deal with the controversy of laying off faculty let alone the insinuation that they are endangering patients, discourages the medical school from making any curricular changes that would reduce or remove the penmanship requirements.

Even if the AMA could be convinced to relax its penmanship/calligraphy requirements, eliminating this largely useless class is now politically difficult if not impossible. Penmanship classes are a permanent and growing fixture on campus.

Welcome to the world of academic rent-seeking.

The good news is that medical schools don't actually suffer from this problem. The bad news is that undergraduate schools seem to suffer from it in droves. We have good reason to believe that many, perhaps even most, general education requirements for undergraduates are a form of academic rent-seeking. Their purpose is *not* really to give students breadth, make them well rounded, or introduce them to new areas of research. Their real purpose is to line professors' pockets at students' expense.

WHAT IS RENT-SEEKING?

The term "rent-seeking" is a technical term among economists, but it refers to a phenomenon with which we're all well-acquainted.

Briefly summarized, a rent-seeker is anyone who uses a political process—as opposed to supplying a productive service—to obtain, extend, and preserve the flow of income or other benefits to him- or herself at others' expense. Rent-seeking refers to when a person or group tries to rig the rules of the game to get a special advantage at the expense of others.

For a hypothetical example, imagine "craft sodas" become popular and start to cut into Coca-Cola's market share. Now imagine Coca-Cola responds by lobbying Congress to pass a law requiring all soda pop manufacturers to hire a full-time chemist whose job is to test water purity. Suppose that this safety measure isn't necessary—in fact, there is little risk of water poisoning. Nevertheless, Coke knows it can easily absorb this cost (since it's a big corporation), but small-scale craft soda makers cannot afford it. So, as a result, many of the craft soda companies go out of business, and Coke regains its market share. In this situation, Coke has engaged in *rent-seeking*—it manipulated the legal environment to benefit itself at its competitors' and the public's expense. It gained a "rent" for itself by using the political system to secure customers.

Or, recall our "Students for Organized Rock Climbing" example from Chapter 2, another hypothetical example of rent-seeking. We asked you to imagine that a small group of fifty students who value rock climbing at $150,000 lobby the student government to install a $300,000 rock climbing wall, with the costs split among the university's 50,000 undergraduates. The fifty students who actually use the wall get a good deal—they each pay only $6 for the wall, but they get $3,000 in enjoyment. The other 49,950 students get a bad deal—they each pay $6 but get nothing. Still, because the benefits are concentrated among the few and the costs diffused among the many, we'd expect the other 49,950 to not even learn about the wall, to not bother lobbying against it, and to just suck it up and pay the fee. The rock climbers win and the other students lose, and the losers lose more than the winners win.

Or, recall our example of ADM from the last chapter, a *real* case of rent-seeking. ADM lobbies Congress and various bureaucracies for subsidies and tariffs. This hurts us more than it helps them, but they get away with it because the benefits are concentrated and the cost diffused among taxpayers, consumers, and smaller competitors.

We asked you to imagine how penmanship classes could become gen eds in medical schools, and then told a plausible story by which penmanship faculty could entrench themselves even if, or perhaps *especially if*, their courses don't yield good results. If that story sounded familiar, just replace "med school" and "penmanship classes" with "undergrad college" and "freshman composition."

A TALE OF TWO DISCIPLINES . . .

People who get PhDs usually want to work in academia. This means they want universities to hire people in their field. But if students don't want to take their classes, there won't be enough jobs for them. So, one way to solve the problem is to lobby academics to *force* students to take their classes. This leads to the following prediction: The disciplines with the worst job markets, the lowest student demand, and/or the weakest opportunities for outside funding will also be the disciplines that push hardest to require students to take their classes. Now go glance at various universities' gen ed requirements, and you'll see our prediction holds true.

Academics love to complain about the poor job market for new PhDs. Simply put, there are significantly more people seeking to become college professors than there are jobs to employ them.

But not all academic disciplines and departments are beleaguered. Let's take the economics profession as an example. According to US Department of Education statistics, the economics profession has consistently produced about 1,000 new PhDs per year since the mid-2000s. Going back further, we find that the economics profession has grown over time—but at a stable rate. In 1970, there were 794 new economics PhDs. In 2014, there were 1,056—representing a difference of 262 new PhDs per year.[3] Overall, the long-term trend is up, but the growth of new economics PhDs was gradual.

Available job statistics do not go back nearly as far and do not precisely measure how many of those positions are entry-level versus senior jobs. The American Economics Association (AEA) nonetheless tracks the number of annual job listings for economists on its website. In 2016, they reported 3,673 job listings, of which 2,642 were in academia; the rest tended to be government, policy, and private-sector jobs requiring economists.[4] All things considered, the job market for new PhDs in economics is and has been very healthy. Some estimates suggest that well in excess of 90 percent of new economists are able to find full-time work within a year of graduating, with over half of them securing jobs in academia the first year.[5] The unemployment rate among PhD economists is less than 1 percent.[6]

The humanities—especially English and modern languages—have far gloomier prospects. In English, new PhD production has fluctuated dramatically over the past forty years. There were 1,213 new English PhDs issued in 1970, although that number spiked to over 1,800 by 1972. Following a drop to about 900, on average, in the 1980s, it rebounded aggressively to over 1,400 per year in the 1990s. In 2014, new English PhD production was 1,393.[7] Also note that these figures do not include degrees issued in other closely related fields, such as comparative literature and creative writing, both of which have overlapping job markets in English departments. [They are called Modern Language Association (MLA) disciplines.]

See Figure 7.1 for a breakdown of the total number of English and economics PhDs conferred per year from 1967 through 2014.

In contrast with economics, the job market for English PhDs has remained poor for two decades. English appears to be acutely afflicted with "adjunctification" as well. One 2012 survey estimated that

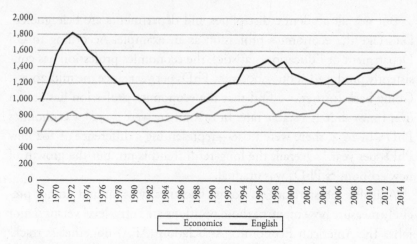

FIGURE 7.1 Total Number of New English and Economics PhDs Conferred per Year, 1967–2014

Source: US Department of Education, IPEDS survey. 2015

16.4 percent of the entire adjunct workforce teaches in an English or literature department, and another 5.3 percent teaches in one of the modern languages other than English. Only 0.7 percent of the adjunct workforce is employed in economics.[8] A 2016 analysis by the Modern Languages Association observed a large drop in annual academic job postings by both English and foreign language departments over the previous decade. English posted 1,680 new jobs and foreign languages 1,826 new jobs in 2008. As of 2016, they sat at 851 and 808 respectively.[9] These figures, it should be noted, include upper-rank positions for midcareer faculty. They also do not account for the backlog of carryover applicants who failed to land a permanent job during a previous cycle and are applying again.

The fundamental problem is that the total number of new PhDs is growing at a much faster rate than the academic job market can absorb, and these numbers have remained stable or even slightly increased over the last decade. As a result, as many as half of all new English PhDs may not receive a full-time academic position in weaker job market years.

Remember, there are important differences between the disciplines of economics and English. For one, economists have more diverse career opportunities in private-sector and government work that English

PhDs lack. Only 13 percent of new English PhDs who secured a job in 2015, for example, worked outside of a university.[10]

But one more point of comparison will come as a surprise in light of the statistics we've just offered. Despite a significantly worse annual job market due to a glut of new and carryover job-seekers, overall academic employment in English is actually expanding—and has been expanding at a much faster rate than economics, even given the economics hiring boom of the past few years.

It may sound paradoxical, but English has consistently outpaced economics in terms of its overall academic employment numbers for as long as these statistics have existed. In fact, English is often one of the largest departments on campus of any discipline and usually the largest of the academic core disciplines after one excludes preprofessional programs. In 2015, the Bureau of Labor Statistics (BLS) estimated that over 75,000 people are employed as English faculty at two- and four-year postsecondary institutions in the United States.[11] These estimates derive from surveys and include so-called full-time adjuncts who string together enough classes to approximate full-time working hours.[12] The total numbers nonetheless dwarf those of most other disciplines. Economics, by contrast, employs only 13,580 professors. The numbers for political science (17,460), sociology (16,160), history (23,680), chemistry (21,460), computer science (33,760), physics (14,310), and psychology (38,380) do not come anywhere close to English. One has to look to faculty in large multidisciplinary, preprofessional programs such as business (84,890) and nursing (57,390) to find comparable numbers.[13] "Business" is not really one field, but rather multiple fields and departments, including accounting, finance, marketing, management, and others.

To add some further perspective to the size of English's existing workforce compared to other disciplines, consider the other traditional humanities where the academic job crunch is especially severe. The field of English alone makes up almost half of the approximately 160,000 faculty currently working in the humanities. When the other MLA disciplines are factored in, English and foreign-language literature together constituted over 64 percent of humanities employment in 2015.[14]

Returning to our comparison with economics, another fascinating pattern emerges. Student demand for certain degrees varies dramatically across disciplines. The popularity of economics as a major has increased over the past twenty years. English, by contrast, remained stagnant for most of the 2000s and has faced a large decline since 2012. Despite this, the number of long-term jobs in English have actually grown at a much *faster* rate than in economics, although not fast enough to accommodate all the new PhDs. These results may be seen in Figures 7.2 and 7.3, which use Department of Education and BLS data to compare the ratio of professors employed in each discipline to the number of bachelor's degrees issued.

In case you're thinking that economics is exceptionally strong at attracting majors, the stats suggest they are fairly typical by social

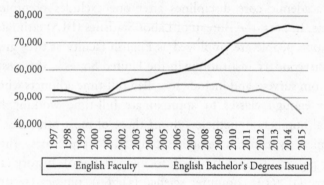

FIGURE 7.2 Number of English Faculty versus Bachelor's Degrees Issued, 1997–2015

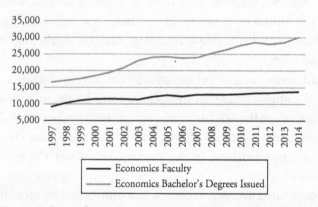

FIGURE 7.3 Number of Economics Faculty versus Bachelor's Degrees Issued, 1997–2014

science standards. Table 7.1 shows the faculty-to-degree ratios for a sample of "core" academic disciplines. English and its MLA cousin, foreign languages, are the clear outliers.

Thus, student demand for economics is up, but economics departments aren't keeping pace; student demand for English is down, but English departments are growing their faculty at a faster rate than economics, even though the number of jobs listed in the MLA is lower than the number of jobs listed at the AEA.[15] Odd. Imagine how bizarre it would be if you saw this happening in the private sector. Imagine Apple and Samsung use the same production methods. Imagine that demand for iPhones has gone up by 40 percent, while demand for Galaxies has only increased 20 percent. Yet you observe Samsung hiring lots of new workers at a much higher rate than Apple. You'd probably

TABLE 7.1 2015 Faculty to Bachelor's Degree Ratio in Selected Disciplines

Department	Faculty	Bachelor's Degrees	Faculty/Degree Ratio
Foreign Languages	30,120	15,579	1.93
English	75,730	44,172	1.71
Chemistry	21,460	14,477	1.48
History	23,680	27,709	0.85
Biology	51,640	74,179	0.70
Education	60,260	87,217	0.69
Sociology	16,160	28,980	0.56
Computer Science	33,760	64,405	0.52
Political Science	17,460	35,440	0.49
Economics	13,580	32,681	0.42
Psychology	38,380	117,440	0.33
Engineering	37,270	124,009	0.30
Agricultural Science	9,680	37,005	0.26
Business	84,890	371,694	0.23

Source: US Department of Labor, Bureau of Labor Statistics, 2015, *Occupational Employment Survey*; US Department of Education, Institute of Education Sciences, National Center for Educational Statistics, 2015, *Digest of Education Statistics*, Section 325.

think the company was being mismanaged. But, as we'll explain next, the key difference is that academic departments are not funded the way for-profit businesses are—they don't have to win customers.

Imagine that deans around the country are reading this chapter and universally conclude that English departments across the nation have too many faculty. Suppose they decide to cut their English departments so they maintain roughly the same faculty-to-degree ratio of 0.5 that the "core" social sciences exhibit. This would put English right around where political science stands now and above economics. This newly reduced workforce of English professors would include just over 22,000 faculty to service 44,000 bachelor's degrees per year. In other words, universities nationwide would have to lay off a total of over 53,000 current English professors simply to reach parity with several other middle-of-the-pack "core" departments on campus.

Of course, we aren't actually advocating mass firings in your English department. Nor are we making any normative claim about the quality of English degrees versus economics degrees, or any other subject for that matter. Students choose to study different areas for a multitude of reasons, many of them deeply subjective. We are suggesting, however, that English has a numerical presence on campus that might be legitimately described as bloated *despite* ample evidence of its declining popularity. And economics has a comparatively spartan presence on campus *despite* its reputation as one of the most widely employable areas of study outside of the STEM fields.

To briefly recap, economics has a healthy academic job market with a stable growth rate in PhD production, nearly full employment for new PhDs, and stable growing demand from undergraduate majors that outpaces faculty hiring. English, by contrast, has a wildly fluctuating rate of new PhD production, an academic job market where as many as half of all new PhDs are unable to find permanent employment, and a declining number of undergraduate majors. Yet, despite this, the number of English faculty grows at a faster rate than many other disciplines on campus.

Accordingly, we see a seemingly paradoxical situation where an extremely healthy and growing department occupies only a small footprint on campus, but a department with a perennially troubled job market and declining student interest has one of the largest faculty presences in the entire university system—and is still continuing to grow in faculty size relative to healthier disciplines. Even more curious, faculty in this discipline have managed to cultivate a popular image of themselves as being constantly beleaguered and subject to a perhaps-warranted contraction in size relative to other departments. This image is often repeated without question, even though the BLS statistics point to unambiguous English faculty employment growth over the last decade that outpaces academia as a whole by over 10 percentage points.[16] English, in short, has all the telltale signs of being a university resource gobbler.

THE GEN ED JOBS PROGRAM

Most college students are bad writers. Many first-year students arrive unable to write at a college level. Many lack an understanding of basic grammar and syntax. Some do not understand how paragraphs work, what constitutes a sentence, or what the structure of an essay should be. Many do not know how to argue for a position coherently, or how to summarize another person's ideas. When Jason was a teaching assistant for introductory classes at the University of Arizona, half of the papers he had to grade did not even qualify as argumentative essays. They lacked identifiable thesis statements, arguments, or conclusions, or evidence, and most sentences had no relation to or relevance with the others. During his first semester as a teaching assistant, Phil assigned a short research paper for an upper-level course. The assignment revealed widespread issues with basic syntax, grammar, and argument construction, even among students who had already been in college for several years. In future semesters, he added an optional one-hour session on writing expectations at the beginning of the course.

This problem also spills over into the postcollege workforce. (That's not surprising; as we discussed in Chapter 3, most students don't learn much in college.) A 2015 survey prepared for the American Association of Colleges and Universities asked a group of graduating students to self-evaluate their level of common workplace skills. Of the student respondents, 65 percent rated themselves as having "excellent" written communication skills. In contrast, only 27 percent of employers shared this assessment.[17] So, students are not only bad writers, but also appear to severely overestimate their own writing skills.

Both faculty and employers began to complain that students couldn't write. Most colleges and universities in the United States responded to this problem by *requiring* an introductory class in writing composition. The overwhelming majority of these classes (roughly 85 percent) are taught, in turn, in English departments.

"Introductory composition," in one form or another, is the most commonly taken class at two- and four-year colleges and universities in the United States. There isn't a great amount of information on college course enrollment patterns; in fact, the last comprehensive study for the United States was conducted in 1992. It nonetheless showed that writing composition was the uncontested leader of the pack, with over 85 percent of college students taking the course. Aside from introduction to psychology (70.6 percent), in each of the next-closest college classes—introductory history, sociology, biology, and economics—enrollment spanned 40 to 45 percent of college students.[18]

Introductory composition's dominance in college curricula has increased since the 1992 study. In fact, its presence in college general ed requirements has continued to grow steadily since at least the early 1970s. One benchmark may be seen by comparing the results of a 1973 survey of composition course requirements with a more recent replication of the same survey in 1998. In 1973, approximately 76 percent of colleges required at least one composition class. By 1998, this number had grown to 97 percent of all colleges. So, at the turn of the twenty-first century, nearly every college required students to take intro composition.

The total number of semesters of required composition classes also increased dramatically. In 1973, 41 percent of colleges required only one semester, while the remaining 59 percent required just two semesters. By 1998, the number of colleges requiring only a single semester of composition dropped to 26 percent. Those requiring two semesters increased to 64 percent, and an additional 10 percent of colleges now require *three or more semesters* of composition.[19]

We don't have data on exactly what percent of students actually take these classes. We know that about 600,000 students a year take Advanced Placement (AP) English classes in high school, and some unknown subset subsequently receive an exemption from intro comp in college.[20] But the majority of colleges now require at least *two* courses

in composition. (Perhaps part of the reason so many colleges now require two courses is that too many students were using AP classes to
exempt themselves from the first.)

Nearly all incoming college students today must take composition
in some form. Because about 85 percent of these courses are also taught
in English departments, and because the demand for English degrees
is down, this ever-growing curricular presence is probably the main
reason why universities keep hiring more English professors.

Similar numbers hold for foreign-language requirements. Recall
that MLA disciplines have the same problem as English—departments
graduate far more PhDs per year than there are jobs for PhDs. Although
they are not in as bad shape as English, the number of foreign-language
majors has plateaued for over a decade.[21] Although the interest of college students in this subject is stagnant, most must nonetheless take
one or more semesters of a foreign language. The last major study of
the foreign-language requirement is unfortunately two decades old,
showing again how the lack of consistent measurement remains an ob-
stacle to understanding the full extent of gen ed growth. As of 1999,
though, 75.4 percent of all four-year college degree programs required
at least one semester of a foreign language. This number shot up from
68 percent only four years earlier, and anecdotal observations suggest
that the percentage of colleges with a language requirement has only
grown in the time since then.[22]

Just as our imagined handwriting class for doctors kept alive the
calligraphy department, composition requirements appear to sustain
English departments. Unfortunately for many English PhD holders,
this means most of their teaching is entry- or even remedial-level classroom instruction. The hiring pattern devolves into something of a vi-
cious cycle—increased instructional needs for required Composition
101 (and 102 and 103) courses drive English faculty hiring to service
these teaching loads. For example, at Arizona State University (ASU),
approximately 400 of the 550 undergrad classes the English department
offered in Fall 2018 were introduction to composition classes.[23] In contrast, only about 10 percent of ASU's econ classes are introductory, split
between intro micro and macroeconomics.

Note that a much smaller number of these new hires are able to
teach more desirable upper-level classes that explore advanced themes

in literature and poetry, which makes the English professor career a highly appealing one at the elite levels of the discipline. Even though most applicants will never reach this level, the allure combined with ever-expanding and composition-driven teaching needs is sufficient to attract a continuous flow of job-seekers to the English discipline. With the teaching opportunities created by composition classes, more job-seekers, fueled by decades of English PhD overproduction, enter the already saturated job market for English faculty and do so at a higher rate than the number of new jobs created by the same growth in composition requirements. As a result, many of these faculty settle into teaching-heavy positions servicing the general education curriculum. Furthermore, the glut of job-seekers ensures that some of these applicants fall short of even a teaching-heavy full-time position. Instead, a number of them settle for adjunct jobs and wages, while the overall English job market continues to worsen due to new PhD creation and carryover applicants from the previous year.

But why are composition classes multiplying in number in the first place? We seem to have a classic "Bootleggers and Baptists" scenario, a case where two or more parties with very different reputations and motives nonetheless come together behind a common political goal.[24] Here, the Baptists are all the professors who want to improve their students' bad writing. The bootleggers, by contrast, are the senior ranks of English faculty as well as university administration. Rather than reducing their hiring and budgeting patterns to reflect declining English majors and lower demand for literature classes on obscure niche subjects, these senior professors instead get administrators to force students to take and pay for additional classes in writing composition. As a result, there are more jobs for English faculty than student demand would warrant on its own, and more tuition dollars are then tied up in a mandatory general education curriculum.

We, of course, don't have a smoking gun transcript of secret English faculty meetings where they admit this is their intention. (Our friends at other universities state as much and we have witnessed professors admitting to this during gen ed meetings, but these are just lots and lots of anecdotes rather than representative data.) And, as the last chapter explained, we might even expect English professors to sincerely believe that they are pursuing students' welfare rather than their own. So, our argument here is essentially an argument over the best explanation: Are composition requirements best explained A) as a means to improve student writing or B) as a form of rent-seeking by the English department?

To help answer that question, we should ask another: Do composition courses *work*? If they don't, then the rent-seeking explanation becomes ever more plausible.

DO REQUIRED COMPOSITION AND FOREIGN-LANGUAGE COURSES "WORK"?

Writing composition course requirements have rapidly expanded in recent decades, but the empirical results on learning outcomes are largely ambiguous. There's almost no evidence that Composition 101 actually improves student writing abilities.

Let's revisit (from Chapter 3) the work of sociologists Richard Arum and Josipa Roksa on student learning. They paint a dismal portrait of the effects of writing instruction at the college level. The authors of this study analyzed results from the Collegiate Learning Assessment (CLA) exam, a standardized test administered to college students at the start of their freshman year and again at the conclusion of their sophomore year. The test, in part, aims to measure improvements in student learning objectives during their first two years of college. This period directly overlaps the semesters where most students encounter their ubiquitous writing composition requirements, giving a "before" and "after" snapshot of any changes in their performance.

Although the standardized testing format is often a point of criticism for analyzing educational outcomes, the CLA exam is specifically tailored to capture the primary claimed objectives of courses such as Composition 101. A core portion of the test gives students ninety minutes to respond to a short writing prompt about a problem-solving scenario. Essays are then scored based on how well they display critical thinking, complex reasoning or problem-solving, and written expression—all widely touted benefits of formal writing instruction at the college level.

Arum and Roksa found no meaningful evidence of student improvement in critical thinking, complex reasoning, or writing in the first two years of college. The average student who took the test in the fall of 2005 showed only a 7 percentage point improvement in these three categories by the end of the Spring 2007 semester. The measured gains, they note, were negligible.[25]

Just as telling, Arum and Roksa's analysis suggested that modern results from the CLA exam compared unfavorably to older studies in the 1980s and 1990s that attempted to measure aspects of critical thinking. Student learning outcomes from these classes might actually be getting worse. These dismal findings from the CLA exam also remain after adjusting for a range of socioeconomic variables and comparing to survey data on student study habits.[26]

The lack of discernible improvement in writing and related analytical skills coincides with the growth of the same mandatory composition curriculum that seeks to address these problems. While *some* students in select writing-intensive degree concentrations did show larger gains on the CLA exam, the average typical college student appears to emerge from almost two years of writing instruction without meaningful improvement. For most students, introductory composition classes are likely a waste of time and money.

Even the results of specifically *remedial* writing classes evince ambiguity at best. A vast pedagogical literature exists on methods and strategies for writing instruction at the college level, yet there are comparatively few attempts to measure outcomes in any detailed or replicable way.[27] One 2008 survey of the academic literature on remedial college education found "very little rigorous research analyzing its effectiveness" and suggested a number of steps that could be taken to improve this situation.[28] These findings were echoed in a 2012 review of thirteen studies on remedial writing instruction. Most of these studies focused on instructional strategies, with little robust information in the way of assessment or measurement. As the literature review's authors concluded, "The body of studies of the effectiveness of reading and writing instruction for underprepared college students is small and undermined by methodological flaws."[29]

Perhaps some specifically remedial writing classes better equip students to navigate more advanced courses. There is also a selection problem: Students who take remedial classes, on average, have weaker study habits.

That said, the empirical literature on remedial writing reveals one reason why university administrators would want to increase composition requirements, even if they don't successfully teach students how to write. Remedial writing instruction appears to increase student enrollment and retention patterns. For example, one recent study of students at public colleges and universities in Ohio found that certain remedial writing (as well as math) classes increased retention and, eventually, graduation rates among underprepared students.[30] Another study found that a specialized remedial curriculum in Baltimore community colleges accelerated the "mainstreaming" of underprepared students into regular freshman and sophomore English classes, thereby increasing their retention and completion rates.[31] Note that such outcomes could be worthwhile goals for other reasons. But they don't validate the pervasiveness of writing composition requirements, or their claimed instructional benefits.

In short, given the ambiguity of evidence for remedial writing classes, and the complete lack of evidence for general writing composition classes, the case for current levels of curricular investment in writing composition classes is exceedingly weak.

How about foreign-language courses? Do they fare any better?

Defenders might assert that foreign-language courses have a host of hard-to-measure benefits. But one thing they rarely do is create fluent speakers of foreign languages. Among American adults, fewer than 2.5 percent claim that they can speak a foreign language "very well" or "well" as a result of instruction at school.[32] As Bryan Caplan notes, these are citizens' self-reports, so the real numbers are probably lower (people tend to have an inflated view of their own skills).[33]

Students vary widely in the value that they could receive from mandatory foreign-language gen eds. A student intending to pursue a career in the foreign service needs to be fluent in other languages. But is the same true for a philosophy major? (No: English is the dominant language of Western academic philosophy.) An economist? (No: English again dominates.) A prospective doctor? A biologist?

Despite the obvious diversity in students' actual needs, faculty in foreign-language departments have favored a one-size-fits-all approach that extends their gen ed curricular presence even further. A recent report from an MLA foreign-language faculty task force called on colleges and universities to "[e]stablish language requirements (or levels of competence) for undergraduate students majoring in fields such as international studies, history, anthropology, music, art history, philosophy, psychology, sociology, and linguistics, as well as for students preparing for careers in law, medicine, and engineering."[34] Although some students in these fields may wish to develop a foreign-language skill, it is far from an essential feature for all students in all cases. Many students in these fields will find mandatory foreign-language classes costly, ineffectual, and of little relevance to their chosen career paths. Others may only make sparing use of language skills and find that their needs are adequately met by translation services or computer technology. The only unambiguous beneficiaries are the faculty, who now have classrooms flush with gen ed students.

OTHER GEN ED REQUIREMENTS

By now, you probably see the general pattern.

First, someone (employers, deans, adminstrators, faculty, students) makes the case that students should have some skill or body of knowledge. For example, "We need to make sure students know how to write before they take other classes" or "Every student should understand basic calculus" or "Our students need to know a foreign language" or "Our students need to be exposed to a wide range of different styles and areas of research."

Second, someone proposes what seems like an obvious solution: "Great, let's *require* students to take two semesters of foreign-language instruction" or "Let's require students to take ten classes from ten different disciplines."

All this could be well-intentioned. But it invites abuse. Once you start requiring students to take classes *for their own good*, you thereby create a system where professors can lobby to make students take classes *for the good of the professors*. Insofar as money, prestige, power, or hiring lines are tied to student enrollment, professors have an incentive to manipulate the gen ed system to ensure that students fill the seats in their classrooms. And so, Step 3 is that professors now engage in rent-seeking through the gen ed system.

And, as a delicious final touch, the best part is that if the mandatory courses don't work, you can then lobby for *more* classes! If money comes attached to students, then your department should be careful to ensure that students need two helpings of your courses rather than one. All the while, you can wring your hands and say, "Well, it's too bad we have to force students to do this. But I guess we need to."

In principle, the rent-seeking hypothesis is open to some empirical testing. For instance, first, you'd want to obtain some measure showing to what degree, at different colleges and universities, money and other resources are allocated on the basis of enrollments. Second, you'll want some measurement of the gen ed requirements at these different schools. Third, you would then expect to find that schools allocating money according to enrollment tend to have more gen ed classes, and departments that are the most enrollment-dependent tend to be overrepresented within gen ed requirements.

We focused on English because first-year composition is a such a beautiful example. Almost everyone has to take it, there's no evidence it works, comp is clearly in English departments' self-interest to expand, and English has clearly increased its footprint on campus relative to other disciplines with lesser stakes in the gen ed curriculum. But it's easy to imagine these same patterns afflict other academic disciplines, or that they similarly exert an outsized influence on curricular decisions.

For example, one increasingly common curricular practice over the last thirty years has been the growth of "First-Year Experience" (FYE) courses that are intended to introduce incoming freshmen to university life. Unlike writing composition, there are no multidecade statistics that track the rise of FYE classes. Based on descriptive discussions in the higher education literature, though, they appear to have become increasingly trendy in the early 1980s and have grown such that most colleges and universities today create some version of a first-year class or course sequence for all incoming students. There are reasons to suspect that these courses provide faculty in certain fields of study with more students than they would otherwise draw on their own, much as English faculty gain students from writing composition requirements.

FYE courses are usually taught by faculty from across multiple disciplines, but their content is, by nature, more conducive to the humanities, arts, and softer social sciences. "Understanding College with Physics and Engineering" would likely make a poor first-year experience class for all students except future physics and engineering majors. By contrast, a FYE course featuring a general introductory survey of art, history, and cultural studies has fewer entry barriers and, at least ostensibly, a broader ecumenical appeal across an incoming class, even if comparatively few of those students ever major in art, history, or cultural studies. We might accordingly expect to find a greater percentage of art, history, and cultural studies faculty teaching FYE classes than STEM discipline faculty, at least on average. This may also be the case, even if majors in those disciplines are stagnant or declining. Just as writing composition provides an enrollment lifeblood to the English department, FYE classes and other similar general education requirements ensure enrollment and thus budget resources and employment for the faculty who teach them.

Note that these observations are true regardless of what one might think about the intellectual value of FYE courses, or the overall effectiveness of writing composition. By requiring a course as part of a general education curriculum, the college itself determines specific enrollment patterns for that course and ties them to the conferral of a degree itself. Even if most students in FYE classes never intend to major in a humanities subject, and most students in writing composition never intend to major in English, all students must still take FYE and writing classes in order to graduate. Note that this pattern could also be true of any number of other classes. For example, most colleges have a foreign-language requirement. And a math requirement. And a physical sciences requirement. Some have less common requirements, such as fine art or physical education.

The important takeaway is that, in each case, enrollment is guaranteed by the college's curricular requirements. And this guarantee, we contend, is highly susceptible to academic rent-seeking by faculty who exercise influence over the very same curricular requirements. It's also amenable to administrators who measure academic "success" by bodies in seats and by retained enrollment. But such classes are difficult to get rid of once established, even if it could be conclusively shown that they do not serve their original purposes. After all, to return to our original analogy, if the calligraphy department's funding or very existence depends on enrollment, but it's an unpopular or declining major, what better way to guarantee growth than to make it *required* for all medical students?

THE ETHICS OF GENERAL EDUCATION REQUIREMENTS

Let's consider some putative justifications for making specific courses mandatory for a degree. The most obvious justification is that universities aspire to provide a well-rounded education. While students are expected to specialize in a relatively narrow area of study, universities historically arose from a tradition of liberal education that sought to instill core knowledge through an introductory survey of the hard sciences, social sciences, arts, and humanities. This function is retained today through general education requirements.

Yet as we have seen in the writing composition example as well as the rise of FYE classes, general education requirements have changed over time at most colleges. It's an empirical fact, for example, that college students today have to take more semesters of writing composition, on average, than college students in 1973. In the case of FYE classes, many colleges did not even offer this more recent curricular creation in 1973.

So, even if we accept the basic thesis that universities should provide a well-rounded liberal education, this does not explain why, over the past forty years, universities have ramped up the number of English composition classes they require, or any other type of class for that matter.

But if we accept that some academic rent-seeking is occurring— that is to say, we accept that some faculty support and even pressure for curricular changes that fill their own classrooms and justify their department's budgetary intentions—it follows that not all curricular requirements are in the best interest of the students. Rather, students end up being forced to take classes that add little value to either their degrees or their general skills sets.

Let's put our cards on the table. We the authors agree that college graduates should be well rounded. We think English majors should also know science, economics, and mathematics. We think mathematics majors should be able to read Shakespeare. We think college graduates should be able to order dinner in at least one foreign language. We find the ideal of liberal education attractive.

But—and this is a big but—none of this suffices to justify gen ed or other class requirements. The problem is that the following line of reasoning is fallacious:

1. Graduates should know X.
2. Therefore, we should require students to take at least one course in X.

Statement 2 doesn't follow from statement 1. The reason it's a fallacious inference is that this argument tacitly assumes *taking courses in X* works. But we can't just assume that. We need to *check*.

Consider as an analogy: It's one thing for the government to mandate that every child receive a measles vaccine. Measles vaccines at least work. But it would be absurd for the government, in an effort to eliminate measles, to mandate that every child receive psychic healing treatments. Psychic healing treatments don't work. If you're going to force someone to do something for his or her own good or for the public good, it had better actually *be* in that person's interest or the public good. But the most popular gen eds—composition and foreign languages—don't appear to pass this basic test.

Another putative justification for gen eds goes as follows:

Distribution for Discovery's Sake
In high school, most students only take mathematics, chemistry, physics, biology, English literature, foreign language, and history. They have almost no exposure to the vast majority of academic disciplines, including economics, philosophy, art history, sociology, anthropology, geography, and so on. Many of them would major in these fields if only they were exposed to them, but arriving at college, they have no knowledge that these fields even exist. So, we need to require them to take classes in a wide range of fields so they can make an informed choice about their majors.

There's something to this kind of argument. Of course, it wouldn't justify forcing students to take three semesters of composition or two semesters of Italian. But this new argument prompts two questions. First, do these requirements succeed at expanding the breadth of student knowledge and exposure to new ideas? We'd want data showing that gen eds often help students discover new fields and choose their majors. (Unfortunately, we couldn't find any studies showing this to be the case.) Second, is there an *easier* or *cheaper* way to solve this problem? For instance, most universities have some sort of first-year orientation week. Instead of filling that week with ice cream socials or ideologically loaded reading groups led by administrators, we could have students attend ten or so one-hour introductions to different fields of study.

We should also ask, when we examine arguments on behalf of gen ed requirements, who bears the burden of proof? Now, we agree that deans and curriculum committees need to have some freedom to experiment. They often don't or can't know if a new curriculum design "works" unless they first mandate it and then measure the results. But, in general, they bear the burden of proving their ideas work. Just as the government would not force everyone to get a vaccine without first establishing that it worked, so deans should not force everyone to take classes (after perhaps a short experimental period) unless they know the classes "work," that is, they actually succeed in imparting the skills and knowledge the classes are supposed to impart.

The problem is that gen eds have both a high monetary cost and a high opportunity cost for students. If students must take—and pay for—a largely superfluous and ineffectual class, that burden comes out of their time and their bank accounts. And if that student's education is subsidized by the government, the costs of the superfluous course requirement may extend onto the taxpaying public, who, in turn, receive an ineffective and overly expensive outcome from these public investments.

Suppose Juanita is required to take two semesters of composition and two semesters of a foreign language. This costs her 180 hours in class plus whatever time she spends outside of class studying. She also pays tuition for these classes, which could be as low as $4,000 for the four classes at a relatively inexpensive state university or as high as $26,000 if she's paying the full sticker price at an expensive private school. Her opportunity cost is whatever her next best options were. If we hadn't forced Juanita to take these four classes, which classes would she have taken instead? Forcing Juanita to spend a year in (as far as we know) ineffective writing and language classes comes at the expense of her picking up a minor in something she actually cares about.

Universities have a fiduciary obligation to not waste students' time or money. By extension, universities that receive public funding are also obliged for the same reasons to be good stewards of public resources. They owe students a class with intellectual value in return for their tuition dollars, particularly if participation in that course is a mandatory general education requirement.

Let's illustrate this proposition by way of an extreme example. If a university threatened to withhold degrees from all students unless they paid for and completed a single-semester class in magic crystal healing, the university will have wronged the students in at least two ways: first, by providing false instruction in a pseudo-scientific medical topic, and second by using the threat of blocked graduation to extort participation and payment for a largely useless and potentially harmful class. And if that university receives public funding, it will have wronged the taxpaying public by misallocating the resources placed in its trust in similarly destructive ways.

But what if the class is something more mundane, such as a third semester of composition or an additional FYE seminar? The pseudo-scientific element of the crystal healing class diminishes in this scenario. The extortive element in terms of possibly blocking graduation remains, though, especially if the classes fail to instill the advertised skills.

Now recall that a fair amount of evidence suggests writing composition classes accomplish very little for most students. If these classes are also mandatory despite delivering almost no discernible improvement in their promised outcomes for most students, they are a waste of time and tuition. They are courses students only take and only pay for because they have to jump through those hoops in order to qualify for graduation.

We may also identify a couple of secondary effects from a class of this type. By wasting time and tuition, every hour spent in an ineffective writing class is an hour missed in another class in one's major, or even in a more interesting subject taken strictly for personal consumption and interest. As we will discuss in Chapter 9, students are also more likely to cheat in classes that they dislike or do not care about. The wasteful but mandatory class may therefore encourage other forms of bad behavior.

Let's take the cynical approach a step further and assume that the mandatory class in question was adopted mainly out of bootlegger motives in order to justify the employment of more faculty. For example, let's suppose a college adopted a fourth semester of required writing on top of its longstanding three-class writing track. And let's suppose this happened after a curricular review committee chaired by an English professor pushed for the additional requirement. In our example, assume this English professor is acting out of self-interest. He knows that the added course will redirect thousands of students to his department, justifying both a stronger claim to a bigger share of the university budget and several new faculty lines for teaching-heavy positions. Since he's a senior member of the department, those new faculty lines will also allow him to shift one of his own current Composition 101 sections onto the new hire in exchange for being able to teach a small upper-level seminar class on seventeenth-century Dutch religious poetry, the topic of his own scholarly research. The faculty member in this scenario, as described, is engaging in a play for more budgetary resources for his department. He is an academic rent-seeker. More importantly, though, his rent-seeking is not merely wasteful—it actually imposes a new and largely unwanted expense directly onto students in order that he may enjoy greater comfort in his job.

It's difficult to avoid the conclusion that the responsible professor is inappropriately exploiting the student's needs to meet the university's graduation requirements.

There are at least two other hidden costs to academic rent-seeking. First, gen ed requirements reduce the incentive to teach courses well. Imagine if the government mandated that you eat breakfast at Burger King. Burger King wouldn't have to compete for breakfast customers anymore, so you'd expect the quality of their breakfasts to decline. Something similar could happen with other academic departments. If English knows it's guaranteed 1,000 students a year, it doesn't have to compete with other departments to win those students. The English department could then afford to assign these classes to its worst faculty, or perhaps staff them with low-paid and underskilled adjuncts rather than its star professors. (To be fair, though, the department has some incentive to teach the classes well, as they might get a few extra majors by doing so—unless attracting majors has no bearing on their funding, as could be the case in a department that has completely turned itself over to mandatory gen eds.)

Second, rent-seeking diverts faculty attention away from scholarly activities and into academic politics. Any professor who has served on a curricular review committee can attest that faculty become aggressively territorial when new courses are added and old courses are removed from the catalog. They bicker over prerequisites and cross-listings, debate enrollment potential, parse minute details of course content, and indulge in endless comparisons of their own respective teaching commitments to determine where the proposed addition places their own workload in relation to their colleagues. Even small curricular changes may be dragged through months of tedious meetings and committee work. Major changes, such as the creation of a new degree track, the establishment of a new major, or the revision of a core course requirement, sometimes take years to complete. This diversion of time and energy into jockeying for desired curricular outcomes has its own associated costs of less time spent in the classroom and less time devoted to research.

We don't have the data to support our claim because they have never been measured, but we've seen this behavior firsthand. For instance, Jason was once part of a committee that tried to create a new major *at the request of students*. Another department killed the major for blatantly selfish reasons that they didn't even try to conceal. The department head just said, "If we create that major, our department will lose enrollment, because students would rather major in that. So, no, we're going to veto it." Phil has witnessed cases where professors in other departments, and even in other branch locations of the university system, have used their positions on curricular review committees to ensure that their own courses are cross-listed as degree fulfillment options in a completely different department. And we've both seen too many cases to count where professors lobby to protect their turf in an underperforming course that has been "threatened" with changes in the catalog.

SUMMARY AND CONCLUSION

Sitting in an armchair, it seems easy to justify gen ed requirements. Surely, one says, students should know X, Y, and Z, and master skills A, B, and C. So, let's make them take classes in all these subjects.

Yet, if those classes don't actually work, all we've done is waste students' (and donors', taxpayers', and other funders') time and money. We've made our students take classes they don't want instead of the classes they do.

But the situation is even worse than that. The problem is that at most colleges and universities, individual departments receive funds and jobs in proportion to how many students they enroll. So, professors have a stake in *gaming* gen eds for their own benefit. They have a selfish incentive to manipulate gen ed requirements to force students to take their classes. Furthermore, they may even have a perverse incentive to ensure that skill classes *don't work*, in order to justify forcing students to take additional classes.

We're not saying gen eds are a complete disaster. And there are some schools, such as the University of Chicago, that have well-designed curricula that really do so seem (anecdotally) to create well-rounded, liberally educated students. But what most universities do is require students to take a smattering of unconnected classes from here and there, plus a stream of classes in the most enrollment-dependent department(s). This is best explained as academic rent-seeking, as a means for professors to exploit students for their own benefit. And regardless of the professors' background motives, it sure looks like a waste.

8

Why Universities Produce Too Many PhDs

ASK A HUMANITIES PROFESSOR, or read the *Chronicle of Higher Education*, about the academic job market, and you'll probably get a story like this:

> This country just doesn't value the humanities anymore. Funding for humanities research is drying up. Faculty positions are being cut across the board, and entire programs are being eliminated. The main reason there are so many humanities PhDs seeking long-term academic employment—and settling for low-pay adjuncting gigs—is that there are no longer enough tenure track jobs to support them. Students also suffer because they are losing access to important but unmeasurable skills that teach them valuable lessons in critical thinking and cultural literacy. And highly skilled faculty are being denied the ability to share their knowledge due to a near-constant state of underemployment and devaluation in their fields. If only we got our priorities straight, and learned once again to value liberal education, we'd fix the problem.

There is a glut of underemployed PhDs, especially in fields like English or modern languages. By definition, a glut means the quantity of job-seekers supplied exceeds the quantity of positions demanded. The standard story blames this on a *drop* in demand—society no longer cares about these subjects and so purchases too few academic workers. Many blame the Republicans especially for alleged budget cuts to higher ed at the state and local levels.

If the standard story were true, we'd still have to ask an important business ethics question: Given that the humanities PhD primarily trains people to work in academia, and given that there are not and (pending radical change) will not be enough academic jobs to absorb all new humanities PhDs into the academic workforce, do graduate programs have a duty to stop producing so many new PhDs? And more fundamentally, why do so many programs continue to pump out new PhDs despite such bad job prospects?

When we started writing this book, we presumed the standard story would turn out to be true, and we planned to ask those questions. However, to our surprise, the standard story doesn't hold up. In fact, even as student demand for instruction in the humanities declines, the number of new jobs for humanities professors either keeps pace with the general growth of the academic population, or, more surprisingly, grows *faster* than many other academic disciplines. We noted one such example in the previous chapter. Although the demand for economics degrees appears to be rising while demand for English degrees contracts, English still hires more full-time faculty per year than economics (in 2015, there were 479 new PhDs hired in English and literature departments compared to 270 economists).[1]

The reason a humanities PhD glut exists is *not* that the jobs are going away. Rather, the jobs are mostly staying stable or growing relative to the overall college population, but humanities departments over the past few decades started overproducing PhDs at even faster rates, rates that far exceeded the ability of academia to employ them. The humanities are not victims; they are responsible for their own plight.

Even though the empirical evidence contradicts the standard narrative, we must still ask the same questions: Given that the humanities PhD primarily trains people to work in academia, and given that there are not and (pending radical change) will not be enough academic jobs to absorb all these new PhDs, do graduate programs have a duty to stop producing so many advanced degrees? And why do so many programs continue to pump out so many PhDs despite such bad job prospects?

Our answer to the first question is a qualified yes. Our answer to the second is self-interest—faculty and administrators have selfish incentives that lead them to overproduce new PhDs.

ORIGINS OF THE HUMANITIES PHD GLUT

In 2015, just over 55,000 students received a doctorate of some form from one of the 432 institutions in the United States that issue advanced terminal degrees. Students have a wide range of career aspirations and trajectories; many of them will never return to a university. Nonetheless, roughly 7,400 of these students reported having postgraduation commitments in academia in the United States, and another 9,800 indicated intentions to pursue postdoctoral study of some form.[2] These figures derive from a self-reported survey of newly minted doctorates and only include people who have already accepted full-time academic positions at the time of graduation. But they still give us a snapshot of new entrants into academic employment. Furthermore, most new PhD students in the humanities indicate that they intend to seek academic employment after graduation if they do not have a position lined up already; for them, a professorship is the first-choice gig.

As we discussed in the last chapter, academic disciplines often differ widely in job opportunities. We contrasted economics, which has a healthy job market approaching full employment, with English, where as many as half of all job-seekers may fail to find their desired level of employment for some years. Both of these patterns extend to other fields as well.

The humanities, in particular, have a reputation of being perpetually beleaguered. Although English, history, philosophy, foreign languages, and a few other fields indeed count too many job-seekers, these circumstances cannot be blamed on a simple shortage of humanities jobs. When we look at other metrics, a more complicated picture emerges. Although you probably wouldn't know it from reading the standard account we noted in the introduction, typical of outlets such as the *Chronicle of Higher Education*, the humanities have actually been expanding their footprint on campus relative to other disciplines in recent decades.

Figure 8.1 shows faculty employment growth by field between 1999 and 2015, as estimated by the Bureau of Labor Statistics' (BLS) Occupational Employment Survey (OES). Note that the OES is a survey and therefore only approximates employment totals. It also uses statistical smoothing tied to prior years' totals, so it's better at gauging

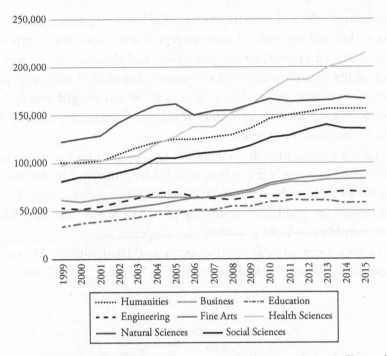

FIGURE 8.1 Number of Faculty in Two- and Four-Year Colleges by Academic Discipline, 1999–2015

Source: American Academy of Arts and Sciences, Humanities Indicators.

long-term patterns than shorter year-to-year fluctuations. But the twenty-year trends depicted are unambiguous: Despite their notoriously saturated job markets, the humanities have grown at substantially faster rates than STEM disciplines, social sciences, or almost any other category of faculty. The lone exception is healthcare, which benefits from a booming array of preprofessional programs in medicine and nursing.

The OES estimates are not the only sign of humanities growth. The aforementioned survey of new PhDs with "academic commitments" (defined as having signed an employment contract for the next year at the time of graduation) suggests that the humanities actually claimed the lion's share of academic hiring in 2015, relative to other areas of the university system. In total, the humanities reported 1,383 hires among newly minted PhDs. The social sciences showed 1,215 hires (excluding psychology, which is sometimes categorized as a preprofessional discipline); life and agricultural sciences posted 920; math and computer science posted 441; engineering posted 399; and physical sciences posted 246 faculty commitments from the newest class of PhD students.[3] The picture that emerges is clear (Figure 8.2). When gauged strictly on trends in total number of faculty hired, the humanities, in fact, do *better* than most other fields.

There's a twist, though. Humanities employment on the whole has been increasing, yet it is nowhere near the level that will be needed to absorb all the new humanities PhDs who desire academic jobs. Thus, the famous job glut materialized. The growth of new humanities PhDs consistently exceeds the growth of new academic jobs.

In 2015, some 5,891 doctoral students graduated with an American humanities PhD—the highest number in history.[4] Not all students

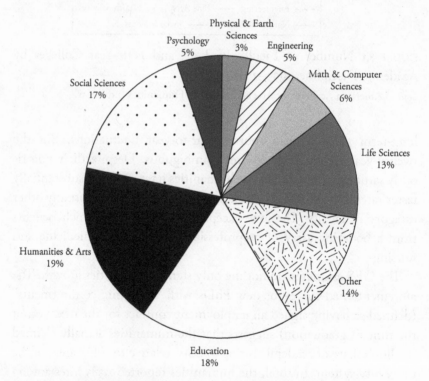

FIGURE 8.2 Academic Job Commitments at Graduation
Source: Survey of Earned Doctorates, 2016.

desire faculty positions, but the humanities have far less employment sector diversity than almost any other area of academia. In recent years, just shy of 80 percent of humanities PhDs with job commitments went into academia, and in English and foreign languages that number grew to 87 percent. This figure contrasts with 60 percent in the social sciences, 46 percent in life sciences, 32 percent in math and computer science, 24 percent in the physical sciences, and 14 percent in engineering. All these other areas of study have substantial PhD employment markets in the private sector, non-profits, and government. But for a few recent initiatives by academic professional associations to expand "alternative" career paths for their graduates, the humanities, by and large, do not.[5]

To compound the problem further, recent growth rates in humanities PhD production show no sign of dissipating. As Figure 8.3 shows, new PhD creation has been on the rise most years since the mid-1980s. Although this recent growth pattern is smaller than the short-lived historical surge in PhDs that (not coincidentally) accompanied the Vietnam War, it is unmistakably positive—even after the 2007–2008 financial crisis. English leads the pack by a long shot with almost 1,398 new PhDs in 2015 (a figure that does not include creative writing PhDs

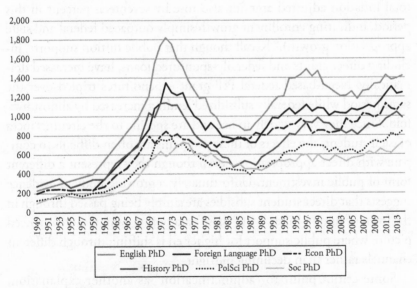

FIGURE 8.3 Number of New PhDs Issued by Year, 1949–2013
Source: Digest of Education Statistics, 2016.

and MFAs, who also compete for some English faculty jobs). History follows at just over 1,005, and foreign-language literature comes in third at 751, plus another 165 graduates in comparative literature studying two or more languages.[6] The English and history totals also exceeded the number of faculty jobs listed with their respective professional associations (including jobs for senior candidates and midcareer moves). This pattern has persisted for the past five hiring cycles.[7]

Many humanities scholars blame job market woes on budget cuts or an alleged devaluing of their subjects, but again the numbers are more complicated than the standard narrative suggests. Spending on higher ed has fluctuated in recent years and especially in the wake of the 2007–2008 financial crisis, but a decade later overall state appropriations are on the clear rebound. According to one recent estimate, state-level spending on higher education increased by 20 percent between 2013 and 2018 alone.[8] Direct public appropriations for higher education have also given way to a tuition-dependent model that relies more heavily on student enrollment.

One popular narrative cites this shift as evidence of a declining investment in higher ed. When measured by direct appropriations per pupil, public investments are down by eight percent since 1992 (although the total inflation-adjusted amount also rose by seventeen percent in this period, indicating enrollment growth simply outpaced federal and state appropriation growth).[9] Recall though that public tuition supports, including direct grants and federally-sponsored loans, have increased dramatically. Need-based federal Pell grant expenditures tripled over the same period while federally subsidized lending increased by almost fivefold. Since they vary widely in use and are specific to the circumstances of each student, the effects of these programs are often difficult to compare with direct appropriations, even though they represent a different form of public investment. Unfortunately, a growing body of evidence suggests that direct student subsidies are simply being passed through in the form of tuition hikes.[10] But these data points paint a more nuanced picture where public support for higher ed is shifting through different channels rather than declining outright.

Some critics point to "adjunctification" as another explanation, noting that the number of adjunct faculty in the humanities and especially English are higher than in most other disciplines within the university system. But adjuncts, at most, explain only a small portion of the humanities workforce. As we discussed in Chapter 6, the student-to-full-time-faculty ratio for US academia has been remarkably stable for the past four decades, hovering around 25 to 1. Adjunct hiring *supplements* full-time hiring, especially when you take away the adjunct-heavy, for-profit higher ed sector and only concentrate on traditional colleges and universities.[11] The OES statistics we use here do include some "full-time adjuncts" who work multiple low-paying teaching jobs at different universities, although salary percentiles suggest that people in this category make up only a small segment at the tail of the distribution.[12] More so, other surveys that only measure full-time faculty respondents have also hinted at the growth of the humanities relative to the STEM fields in recent years.[13]

On occasion, we hear stories about how various departments and degree programs are being targeted for elimination. Usually, this leads to hyperbolic reactions from faculty in other departments and plenty of media coverage and discussion. But this might be an example of how "man bites dog" is news, while "dog bites man" is not. While undergraduate *majors* are occasionally eliminated due to declining enrollments (although the departments that teach them are usually just shifted over to the gen ed curriculum, minus a major of their own), the elimination of a graduate programs appears to be a relatively rare event. We know of just one recent example of this pattern. In 2018 the University of Akron announced the phasing out of ten of its existing PhD existing as part of a university-wide restructure. All but two were in professional career programs in highly specialized areas of engineering, nursing, and counseling, and all ten faced severe enrollment declines. In total, these programs graduated, on average, only 20 students per year between them during previous three year period.[14] The decision, although it was denounced in some quarters as proof of a declining investment in education, likely reflected the much simpler reality that very few students wanted these degrees.

Anecdotes aside though, cases such as Akron appear to be exceptions to the norm. On the contrary, most universities are *adding* doctoral programs at a faster rate than they are eliminating them. The total number of doctorate-issuing universities in the US has grown almost every single year since these figures were first tracked in the early 1970s, as seen in Figure 8.4.

"Aha!," the watchful humanities professor might exclaim here. "Those figures are for universities with doctoral programs of any type, and the recent surge in STEM emphasis and professional degrees hides the fact that our history, philosophy, and foreign language departments are losing their traditional PhD programs." But that's not what the available evidence says either.

Stats on the number of operational PhD programs by discipline are admittedly harder to come by than the total number of universities with active doctoral programs. Some professional associations as well as independent ranking publications and websites maintain lists, but these are almost always oriented around the top 20, 50, or 100 ranked institutions. Operational PhD programs vary greatly in size as well. A few of the largest departments grant as many as twenty degrees in a single field each year. The smallest departments only issue a single degree, and a few even have gap years where no PhDs are issued. To get a discipline-specific glimpse at the number of operational PhD programs in the US, we have to turn to a close proxy measure in the

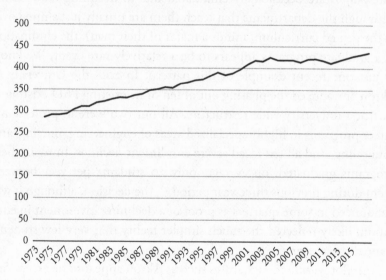

FIGURE 8.4 Doctoral-Granting Institutions in the United States, 1973–2015

Source: Digest of Education Statistics, 2016.

form of degree-issuing departments by year. These figures are obtainable from the Survey of Earned Doctorates going back to 2006 or 2007, depending on the subject area. Since the closely related narrative of higher ed budget cuts coincides with the financial crisis of 2007–2008, we may accordingly use these numbers to get an approximation of the number of PhD programs operating in specific disciplines across the subsequent decade. The results for three humanities and three social sciences are given in Figure 8.5.

Other than a slight drop in political science programs between 2007 and 2009, the number of operational PhD programs in all these fields is either stable or rising. In fact, English and history—two of the most beleaguered disciplines in the humanities—showed the clearest upward trajectories. The stats suggest there are roughly fifteen to twenty-five more operational PhD programs in these fields today than was the case a decade ago, just before the financial crisis. Note that some programs were perhaps eliminated during these years. Even if true, whatever cuts have occurred are outpaced by growth, leading to a net increase. In short, the conventional narrative—that budget-conscious administrators duke it out with humanities faculty trying to save liberal education—is the exception rather than the rule.

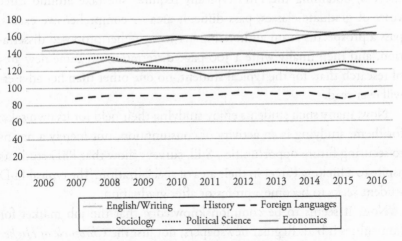

FIGURE 8.5 Departments Issuing a PhD by Type, 2006–2016

Source: Authors' calculations, Survey of Earned Doctorates, 2016.

The humanities expand their faculty at a rapid pace, but expand their PhD production at an even faster pace. The result: unhappy, unemployed PhDs. With PhDs still expanding at a faster rate than new jobs, the existing glut appears as if it will only get worse for the foreseeable future. So this leads us to ask: Why do humanities departments produce too many PhDs?

THE BAD INCENTIVES OF GRADUATE PROGRAMS

From the outset, we've stressed how incentives explain bad behaviors among academics. PhD programs are no different. Let's consider for a moment who the players are and what they want from a PhD program.

Students

The most obvious stakeholder—but the one hardest to explain—is the PhD student herself. This person is usually a highly intelligent individual with strong analytic, writing, and/or mathematical skills. She already holds at least a bachelor's degree but decides to forgo possibly lucrative private or public-sector employment to pursue advanced study in a highly specialized subject. She devotes anywhere from three to ten years, and sometimes more, to obtaining a doctoral degree. In the US, obtaining the PhD typically requires she take around three years of graduate classes, pass difficult area or comprehensive exams, pass a prospectus exam authorizing her to write her proposed dissertation, and then finally write a 300-page dissertation on some new area of research that, for the typical student, no one other than her advisers will ever read.

Now, many such students enjoy studying their field for its own sake; for them, studying is an activity of consumption, not merely a means to securing future opportunities. Still, surveys show that PhD students aspire to a lifelong career in their area of specialization. The typical PhD student seeks to become a professor after graduation.

Now, it seems to be common knowledge that the job market for humanities is bad. Regular newspapers, not just the *Chronicle of Higher Education* or *Inside Higher Ed*, often run news stories about the job market woes of academia. We couldn't find any surveys indicating what entering graduate students know about their prospects, however, so we're forced to speculate. Do students realize how bad the market is? Do they know it's bad, but generally believe they will beat the odds? Are PhD students—presumably highly intelligent people with a far-above-average ability to search for and analyze data, and to detect bullshit—somehow bamboozled by slick marketing materials encouraging them to pursue a PhD? We don't really know.

However, some research indicates that, in general, PhDs who fail to obtain long-term faculty jobs land on their feet and instead find good jobs elsewhere. According to the BLS, in 2015, the unemployment rate in the United States for PhD holders was 1.7 percent.[15] Empirical work shows that most PhD holders, after they stop trying to secure permanent college faculty positions, find employment elsewhere, for instance, as academic administrators, as high school teachers, in non-governmental organizations (NGOs), in government, or in private business.[16] Most people who obtain a PhD do not end up securing a long-term academic position, yet the majority do find full-time employment elsewhere.[17] So, perhaps PhD-seekers are more rational and better informed than they seem at first glance—they might hope to become full-time professors, but they know they aren't doomed to homelessness or permanent adjuncting if that falls through.

Money is another consideration for the student. Students forgo wages by becoming PhD students, but not as much as you might think, if you are unfamiliar with how PhD programs work. While undergraduate and even master's students (or their parents, guardians, or governments) pay to go to college, PhD students—at least at any halfway decent program—instead get *paid* to obtain their PhD.

The typical PhD student receives a stipend, usually between $15,000 to $30,000 a year. That won't make her wealthy, but it's not insubstantial either. The stipend does not just keep her alive; it also reduces the opportunity cost of completing the PhD program. (Would you rather get paid to handle insurance claims for $60,000 per year or get paid $30,000 per year to study microbiology? If microbiology truly interests you in ways that insurance claims do not, this trade-off in salary might appear worthwhile.)

Sometimes the stipend is an unconditional fellowship grant. Sometimes, in exchange, grad students must work 15 to 20 hours a week as a teaching or research assistant, although in many cases the actual workload is lighter than that. For instance, when Jason was a teaching assistant, he really "worked" only 6 hours during the typical week and maybe 10 hours during exam weeks. Phil worked as a teaching assistant in grad school. In a typical week, he averaged about 3 hours in the classroom plus another 3 hours tutoring students, grading papers, and preparing for class. Of the graduate programs in which Jason has participated, grad students who actually spend 15 to 20 hours a week teaching were, in general, bad time managers and didn't flourish.

In addition, most PhD students don't pay tuition. They receive tuition waivers that are nominally worth as much as $30,000 to $60,000 a year at top-ranked private institutions and frequently tens of thousands at state schools. Of course, there is no real market to determine tuition for these degrees, so we cannot take the sticker tuition price for PhD programs at face value. But a tuition waiver is clearly worth something substantial to the student who obtains it.

At the same time, some graduate students pay out of pocket or take on debt to pursue their degrees. They do so at different rates, however, and unfortunately it's the students in the *weakest* academic job markets who are the most likely to pay out of pocket or assume debt. In most STEM fields, fewer than 5 percent of PhD graduates are paying out of pocket for their degrees. In the humanities, this number jumps to 20.5 percent; in the social sciences, almost 25 percent.[18] PhD graduates in STEM fields consistently report substantially lower amounts of graduate school–related debt than the humanities and social sciences. In 2015, the average math or engineering PhD graduated with about $6,300 in grad school–related debt. For the physical sciences, that number was approximately $6,000; for the life sciences, $11,500, on average. By comparison, the typical humanities debt was $21,700 and the average social sciences debt $26,700.[19] In general, highly ranked graduate programs fully fund all their students, whereas lower-ranked programs are more likely to actually charge tuition. Thus, the common dictum: For most fields, if you have to take on substantial debt to pursue a PhD, you should not get a PhD.

The chances of landing a job, and what kind of job one gets, depend on the prestige of one's school. Once again, we see clear evidence of this in English, which also made up 35 percent of humanities job commitments in the 2015 survey of earned doctorates and consistently ranks as the largest humanities department on most campuses. A 2015 study by economists David Colander and Daisy Zhuo tracked English PhD job placements from 2008 to 2011 in an attempt to better understand this saturated market. They found that having graduated from a top 6 English program dramatically improves both the type of position a candidate is able to secure and the ranking of the hiring institution. About 55 percent of graduates from top 6 programs who go into academia net tenure-track jobs at a university or four-year college. By comparison, they estimate that 44 percent of graduates from "tier 4" programs (or those ranked 63rd or higher) obtain tenure-track jobs. Similarly, the lion's share of tenure-track jobs at upper-tier research universities and elite liberal arts colleges go to students from top 6 programs. Students from tier 4 schools basically have no chance of placement at anything higher than another tier 4 university or a low-ranked liberal arts college, and even PhD graduates from the two middle tiers (with overall ranks of 7 to 62) very rarely land jobs above tier 4.[20]

Colander and Zhou offer tough medicine for English as a discipline, concluding that "at most, the United States needs only about half the graduate English programs (as currently constructed) that it currently has."[21] Given the elite bias in academic hiring, any cuts would almost certainly have to come from lower-ranked programs. These authors also offer mitigating advice to lower-ranked programs, such as improving their self-reporting of job placement rates and offering greater specialization in skills and training for non-academic roles with an English PhD. But the numbers are nonetheless bleak for the foreseeable future.[22] Nor are these findings simply a case of nosy economists intruding on English's turf. They parallel similar statistics from within the humanities that note almost identical elite hiring biases, differing only in the solutions they offer to address this situation. Whereas economists suggest the possibility of cutting low-ranked programs, other scholars who study elite biases in academia tend to call for proactively rectifying the "injustices" and "inequities" of a hiring system that disproportionately draws from Harvard, Princeton, and Yale by expanding interviewing opportunities downward as an ethical obligation for the hiring department.[23] Although this call often sparks widespread concurrence in the academy, there's little evidence that anyone actually takes the associated actions.

Some humanities and social science students pursue doctorates *despite* a known weak job market and having to take on debt. These students are the most puzzling. Perhaps as many as a fifth of the students graduating from certain humanities fields are essentially pursuing their degrees as personal consumption goods. They typically lack stipends and fellowships, obtain admission to lower-ranked programs, and willingly assume debt to finish their degrees. They're often paying large amounts of money to continue their studies in a subject that they find personally enjoyable though academic employment opportunities are slim. These education consumers, by and large, would probably welcome a job in their selected areas of study if provided the opportunity. But for many, no such opportunity materializes.

So far, we've focused almost entirely on the incentives for graduate students. But note that undergrads also have a stake in their universities offering strong graduate programs. Faculty at R1s have incentives to research rather than teach, and to teach graduate students rather than undergrads. (We'll discuss why in just a moment.) So you might think undergrads would be better served at small liberal arts colleges where professors' main job is teaching undergrads. However, most students prefer to attend more elite and prestigious schools when they can, and in general, the most prestigious places are research-intensive R1 universities, such as Harvard, Princeton, Yale, MIT, Caltech, Chicago, Stanford, and so on.

Faculty

Faculty are far easier to explain. They face perverse incentives to graduate too many PhDs and to create and maintain even marginal PhD programs where students have little hope of securing long-term faculty jobs.

We presume most faculty members want their graduate students to find an academic job. Faculty often view their PhD advisees as a point of pride. PhD graduates are their own long-term legacies in the academy, a way to influence future generations of college students long after the advising faculty member has retired. The more students you place, the more leverage you have, and the important you are. Indeed, Thomas Kuhn, the great theoretician of scientific change, goes so far as to suggest that intellectual change comes about as much from getting your students jobs as it does from winning arguments in journals.[24]

But with persistent PhD overproduction in some fields, it's not possible to place every single student advisee in a full-time academic job—particularly when the student comes from a lower-ranked program. In general, the best academic jobs still go to graduates of elite programs, although what counts as "elite" varies from field to field. (For instance, in philosophy, Rutgers is more elite than any of the Ivies.)

We suppose—horror stories aside—that most faculty genuinely care about their PhD students and want them to succeed. Nevertheless, faculty have selfish incentives to inflate the number of PhD students.

For starters, teaching PhD students is often more fun and less laborious than teaching undergrads or professional students. A professor teaching Biology 101 to a crowd of 200 undergrads might be lucky to have 5 students who genuinely find the material interesting; most take the class because they want the credential. The undergrads may have no idea that the professor is a big shot in her field; they often do not even know their professors create new knowledge and cannot distinguish endowed research chairs from adjuncts or teaching faculty. In contrast, PhD programs draw students who self-select into their disciplines and, by and large, enjoy studying the same topics as their professor. They know about and admire the professors' accomplishments and want to be like him or her. So, consider: Would you rather teach 200 unskilled, bored undergrads, or 10 highly skilled "fans" who hang on your every word?

For the professor, graduate teaching usually means fewer papers to grade, better-quality work from students, and better in-class experiences. Lessons and reading materials approach the level of a discussion among peers as opposed to a traditional lecture format.

Graduate-level classes also explore more niche topics that align more closely with a professor's own interests and expertise. An undergrad history class might entail something like "Survey of American History to 1877," while a typical PhD class might focus narrowly on "Military Strategy in the American Revolution" or "Gender Roles in the Plantation South." An undergrad class might use a survey textbook, but a PhD class means the professor can assign readings from her own books and focus on her own current research. By the way, don't assume that's irresponsible—if you're a professor at a top-ranked grad program, your current research *is* the cutting edge, so teaching your grad students what you're doing is teaching them what's important for them to know.

But wait, there's more. Faculty also benefit when full-time graduate students receive funding and tuition stipends for their degrees in exchange for working as a teaching or research assistant. To the professor teaching in a PhD program, this puts skilled labor at his disposal. For instance, when Jason was at Brown, he taught a 200-person survey class, but PhD students did all his grading. (To be nice, Jason chose to grade ten papers per assignment, to get a sense of how students were doing. He didn't have to do that.) Grad students can relieve professors of the drudgery of grading tests. They can lead small discussion sections for an undergraduate survey class and hold extra office hours, thereby freeing up the supervising professor's preparation time and allowing her to focus more on research. (Recall from Chapter 2: Research, not teaching, is where the money is.) Having PhD students means having someone to do data entry work, chase down references for a research project in the library, conduct experiments you design, run a lab, or assemble the literature review for a paper. If the PhD student is advanced enough in his or her program, it may even mean a coauthor to assist in the writing of an article, thereby increasing the supervising professor's own research output in time for tenure and promotion decisions.

But wait, there's even more. Doctoral programs also bring greater prestige, higher salaries, and more job security for the professors who teach in them. A 2011 survey by the *Chronicle of Higher Education* placed the average salary for an assistant professor at a doctoral-granting university at almost $73,000. The same position at a baccalaureate-only institution averaged $56,500. These gaps only widen as faculty advance in rank.[25] Full professors at R1 universities average $148,984.[26] At the more elite bachelor's only colleges with an arts-and-science focus, they average a mere $103,245.[27] At the less elite, "diverse fields" bachelor's only colleges, full professors average a paltry $71,690.[28] So, brand new 35-year-old assistant professors at doctoral universities make more money on average than full professors at non-elite four-year colleges.

In general, faculty at PhD-granting universities, even low-ranked ones, make significantly more money than faculty elsewhere.

Part of the reason for this wage gap is selection: You need to hire better researchers for PhD programs, but only a minority of faculty can consistently publish in top outlets and so command a higher wage. But part of the reason is probably treatment. If your department can convince a dean to add a graduate program, you can justify increasing your salary because you have more responsibility. You can then argue more easily that you need a stronger, more diverse, better faculty to serve those grad students. You can justify reducing your own teaching load so that you can spend time on research. This research focus, in turn, facilitates mentoring opportunities for your grad students so they too can focus on publishing. You can access greater amounts of outside funding (there's more money for research grants than for pedagogical developments). And you can enjoy the perks and comforts that come with each.

Doctoral programs also carry other nonmonetary perks, such as higher social status. They generally come with lighter course loads, more departmental resources for faculty to utilize, more in-house intellectual opportunities such as guest speakers and visiting faculty, more appeal for hiring top job candidates to fill junior faculty roles, and greater mobility for professors seeking to climb up the ladder into a higher-ranked institution. Again, some of this is selection—some schools have more money, and that's why they can both afford all these perks and afford a PhD program—but some of it is causal. A dean allocating scarce resources will probably give more money to a PhD-granting department than a merely BS-granting department on her campus; after all, she'll think, a proper PhD program needs to have research funds, a speaker series, a larger faculty, and the like.

Administrators

In Chapter 2, we noted that administrators and faculty to some degree are adversaries, as a dollar spent on faculty salaries could have been spent on administration. But they are to some degree complements, and sometimes their selfish interests align.

Administrators also have a stake in PhD programs. For higher-level administrators especially, PhD programs increase the prestige of their university and thus their own personal prestige. Furthermore, housing PhD programs means having a more sophisticated university to administer. This translates into perceptions of greater responsibility, which makes it easier to argue for more personal pay, a larger budget, and more external funding from private or public sources. PhD programs expand access to other administrative priorities. Large universities with graduate programs generally charge higher tuition, have access to more grant opportunities, and, if public, receive larger shares of state appropriations than their four-year undergraduate-only counterparts.

The administrative stake in graduate programs is not exclusively positive, and indeed we hear from time to time about university administrators targeting underperforming programs for elimination. The disputes that emerge around program cuts are notoriously fraught with academic politics. One influential study on program elimination, in general, depicted a pattern of recurring divides between administrators, who often approach the issue in the language of costs and benefits, and the targeted faculty, who argue their cause in the language of "justice" to their programs.[29] Program elimination is often cited as an example of the alleged "corporatization" of higher education, with one education scholar even referring to it as a form of "academic terrorism" to control and extort faculty into compliance with administrators.[30]

However, as we previously saw, this threat is overblown. While some schools cut underperforming programs from time to time (usually on account of their inability to attract students over several successive years), overall the number of schools with PhD programs has been increasing. The number of individual PhD-granting institutions in supposedly beleaguered fields such as English or history has either remained stable or is increasing.

If anything, a closer look at the incentive structures of administration shows why the real scenario, new program growth, is more common. Although they may differ on the specific priorities in determining how money is used, administrators as a rule of thumb like spending money—and especially spending money that leads to other revenue sources and building a case for more appropriations in the future. In optimal circumstances, a PhD program, including a low-ranked one, fits this bill on several counts. Remember: It's useful to model bureaucracies as budget-maximizers.

High-level administrators especially have a strong incentive to increase spending. Imagine you're a dean at Mid State U hoping to make the jump to president at another university. One of the most valuable accomplishments you can list on your résumé is that you managed to raise an additional $X in private or state funding for programs at your university. But to raise money, you have to spend it. Furthermore, showing you *need* the money makes it easier to raise it, but you don't need money if you already have a big pile of cash. (We don't want to overstate that. Harvard has a $38 billion endowment but also little trouble raising more money.)

Still, let's take a closer look at incentives. First, PhD programs mean another intake pipeline for students. Granted, adding five or ten new PhD students per year is seldom a game changer in the world of university finances. It can still become a revenue stream—particularly if those students enter a low-ranked program with fewer funding opportunities and therefore pay for their graduate education out of pocket or by taking on student loans. But let's assume that a PhD program is still bleeding money relative to its operational costs due to generous tuition waivers and other student outlays. One popular option to reverse this course is to add or expand an accompanying master's degree program in the same subject using the same faculty or even a condensed and overlapping version of the same curriculum. Unlike PhD students with stipends, master's students are almost always paying the actual sticker price for their degrees. They're often professionals, teachers, government employees, or even intellectual consumers who are willing to pay for advanced study for reasons entirely outside of an academic career. Thus, a PhD program in literature that admits four fully funded doctoral students a year might be paired with a master's program that admits thirty paying students, most of them teachers in local public schools seeking to advance up the promotion ladder.

There are many effective strategies for running even a small PhD program in cost-effective ways from an administrator's perspective. Cross-listed and shared classes on advanced subjects can be used to make the entire graduate program economical by allowing them to satisfy both master's and doctoral coursework requirements. Many doctoral programs utilize cross-listed master's classes as their prerequisites or first-year "core" classes for PhD students. Others offer advanced seminars on highly specialized subjects as electives that can be taken by both master's and doctoral level students. Many programs even offer students who fail to complete the post-coursework phase of their doctoral degree (comprehensive exams, field work, and dissertation-writing) an option to graduate with a master's degree, provided they completed the equivalent level of coursework in their first two years.

Several studies have found that university administrators exhibit the classic characteristics of utility-maximizing bureaucrats. In other words, they utilize the tools under their control to essentially "over-supply" the functions and services of their own offices. The motives for doing so are multifaceted. Some administrators seek new streams of money to maximize their own budgets and the various perks that come with each. These streams may include both public appropriations and student-derived payments such as tuition and fees. Others want job security, particularly the type that comes from entrenching oneself as a gatekeeper of university resources.

To this end, university administration appears to be a prime incubator for "bureaucratic accretion," or the explosive growth of administrative personnel relative to a more modest expansion of the tasks and services they perform. Several studies have similarly found evidence that university administrators exercise varying degrees of control over the means and numbers of student admission as a strategy for servicing their own objectives.[31] In some cases, this may mean expanding enrollment beyond an optimal level to maintain curricular quality at an institution, simply because doing so brings in additional revenue. Think about a large third- or fourth-tier state college with open admissions regardless of SAT/ACT score, or even a graduate program that offers advanced degrees to almost anyone willing to pay the tuition. In more selective institutions, an administrator might seek to maintain a tuition premium by artificially restricting admissions to an "elite" group of students exhibiting the highest test scores, although this scenario is less applicable to the case of low-ranked graduate programs.

In any case, what we see from most bureaucracy models of academic administration is a tendency to make programmatic, hiring, and spending decisions on criteria linked to the administrator's own tenure, comforts, and job security. Even though administrators do not typically aim to saddle students with debt or low-value degrees, the incentives of administrative budgeting often operate in ways that lead to precisely that outcome. And when an administrator's budgetary objectives align with faculty perks and the prestige of offering a graduate program, the student is often left to bear the brunt of the costs.

THE ETHICS OF PHD OVERPRODUCTION: LET THE STUDENTS BEWARE?

A PhD is more like a JD or MBA than a BA. What this means is that it is a degree to train people for a particular kind of job: a researcher, and in particular, a researcher in the academy. Now, some PhD holders, especially those in STEM or economics, can obtain research jobs outside the academy. Nevertheless, faculty jobs are the nail for which the PhD is the hammer.

Surveys indicate most PhD students want an academic job, even if their chances of securing one are low. So this leads us to ask, who should be held responsible when they don't get a job due to PhD overproduction? Is it even a moral problem?

Let's outline two broad answers to that question:

1. *Blame the Students*: PhD programs offer a course of study but make no promises. It's not the professors' responsibilty to ensure their students get the jobs they want, or even have a decent shot at getting such jobs. Potential students have a duty of due diligence: they should learn the risks, research their chances, and make an informed decision about whether the PhD is worth their time. If they fail to do so, that's on them.

2. *Blame the Faculty and Administrators*: PhD programs advertise themselves as preparing students to become professors. They know most of their students want professorial jobs. They also know that while their students may worry about poor job prospects, students rarely know just how good or bad their chances would be if they got a PhD from a particular school. Faculty are supposed to mentor and professionalize their students, not merely teach them how to do research. PhD students are apprentices, and it is wrong to take on an apprentice who has little to no chance of getting the job she wants.

We can see the attraction of response 1. (To our surprise, many of our most left-wing colleagues—those who complain the most about job market exploitation—advocate 1.) Grad students are adults, not kids. We the authors generally want to treat adults as adults, and that means expecting them to take responsibility for their choices. The kinds of people who become grad students tend to be smart, excellent at analyzing data, and conscientious. Thus, it makes sense to hold them responsible for deciding whether to incur the risks of attending graduate school.

But we can also see the attraction of response 2. The problem is that while most people know the market is bad, it is hard to find data explaining just *how* bad it is, and furthermore, just how bad it is for *students at a particular school*. Many graduate departments do not keep, let alone publicize, data about how their students perform on the academic job market. They often list recent graduates who found a job, but fail to mention the students who did not. They often mention students' current positions, but fail to mention how long it took them to get those full-time jobs. They often list where students got jobs, but neglect to mention whether such jobs are tenure-track, full-time but not tenure-track, short-term visiting, or mere adjuncting. The school job placement websites are often inaccurate or hopelessly out of date.

A priori, maybe there is no obvious reason to prefer response 1 to 2 or vice versa. Perhaps both are acceptable.

But an ethical problem arises when some departments operate on principle 1 and others on principle 2. Goods and services—including education—are bought and sold in light of certain background conventions and expectations. For instance, when you order food at a restaurant, you agree to pay for it, even though you never explicitly say, "I agree to pay." When a taxi picks you up, the driver implicitly agrees to take you on a short, efficient route to your destination, though he never explicitly promises to do so. The problem we face is the following: Many departments express or signal that they regard themselves as the trustees and fiduciaries of their students, so graduate students reasonably fail to recognize that many of the "buyer beware" departments are, in fact, buyer beware departments.

Perhaps, then, the best solution is for departments to make it clear, on their webpages and in their promotional material, what their philosophy is toward their graduate programs. They should post detailed data about what happens to all their students, not just the ones with jobs. They should indicate to what degree they will work to get their students jobs and to what degree they will take a hands-off approach. If they do not fully fund all their students, they could make it clear why taking on debt to obtain a PhD is usually a bad idea. When a department says, "We're offering our program as is," then the responsibility clearly shifts to the students. But many departments get away with selling their product as is because they benefit from the spillover effects of reputation from more conscientious departments selling their product with higher standards.

DON'T HOLD YOUR BREATH WAITING FOR REFORM

It's worth re-emphasizing why professors and administrators lack strong incentives to reform their practices, reduce their PhD output, or even follow the rather modest advice we offered in the last section.

Suppose Fourth Tier State University, or FTS for short, is a regional branch campus of a large state university system. It's publicly operated and funded, and it has famously lax admission standards that make it a "safety school" for high school students living nearby.

FTS also offers many advanced degree options, although they are not prestigious. The history graduate program, which issues several dozen master's degrees and a few doctorates every couple of years, is ranked 148th out of 162 departments. FTS runs a graduate program in business that technically issues several finance PhDs as well as several dozen MBAs each year, although almost none of these students are academia bound—rather, they are midcareer professionals in local businesses finishing a degree at night and the program itself is something of a cash cow for the university. FTS also offers an unranked graduate program in creative writing that came into existence three decades ago during a wave of public investment in the state university system by a governor who ran on an education platform. The MFA has gone through ebbs and flows, but in a good year it, too, functions as an income stream from students paying the full sticker price.

FTS's graduate admissions process is uncompetitive. They give a limited number of stipends to their top three or four PhD applicants, but regularly admit classes of fifteen or twenty to each program provided that certain (very) minimum admissions test scores are met and, importantly, tuition is paid—usually out of pocket and backed by heavy loans. It helps that many students qualify for a heavily subsidized in-state rate.

Even the best FTS PhD graduates also have trouble on the academic job market and most seek employment outside of higher education. FTS MBAs do fine, securing jobs in local companies and industries. But the creative writing program housed in the English department has only resulted in three academic job placements over the last decade despite graduating three dozen new PhDs and a hundred MFAs. Numerous other students are also slowly working through this program on a "ten-year plan" to finish their dissertation.

Suppose a well-meaning external auditor proposes eliminating FTS's unranked creative writing graduate program to the state higher education curriculum board. The program's continued operation seems to only clutter the job applicant field with low returns and dozens of disappointed students. Perhaps its budget could be reallocated to tuition breaks for low-income students, or used to shore up a different department with better—albeit undergraduate—job placement rates.

Enter the current creative writing department chair, Professor Pamela Statusclimber, who immediately recognizes the threat that the auditor poses to her own comforts on the job. Pam is an accomplished scholar compared to many of her colleagues at FTS, and holds a PhD in comparative literature from a top program. The faculty hiring market being what it is though, she settled into her current role at a low-ranked school a decade ago and has tried to make the best of the situation by working her way up the department ranks. Being able to run a PhD program, even if it is a poorly performing one, is a major perk of her job. It gives her status in the profession, even compared to several of her former classmates from the Ivy League who now teach at liberal arts colleges with no graduate programs.

Cutting the program will cost Pam the ability to hire two PhD students as teaching assistants, who grade her undergraduate class essays for her. The proposed cuts will also likely mean fewer resources for her department's budget after phase-out, as the university will want to recoup expenses associated with the program's operations and reallocate them elsewhere. Pam may accordingly lose her department's administrative assistant, who dedicates one-third of his time as graduate student coordinator. Pam also had long-term plans to expand her department by requesting two new faculty lines over the next five years, in part to service the graduate program's operations. Those will now be off the table. Shuttering the graduate program will additionally amount to a loss of prestige that comes from teaching even lower-quality doctoral students.

Pam vigorously protests the proposed cuts, denounces them as a pattern of "devaluing higher education" and subjecting it to "corporatization," writes an article for the *Chronicle of Higher Education* or a similar outlet about the humanities' vital role in ensuring an educated populace, and quickly succeeds in mobilizing the FTS faculty senate to her cause. Pam's behavior is entirely rational.

Across campus, the proposed elimination of the creative writing graduate program causes a different kind of angst for Thaddeus Spendangrow, the Associate Vice President for the Office of Strategic Marketing Compliance at FTS. Unlike Pam, Thad is not an academic by training. A career administrator with decades of experience in the ranks of the public university system, he came to FTS with a specialized master's degree in something called "Higher Education Administration" with concentrations in communication and enrollment management (yes, this is a real degree offered at dozens of universities). Most FTS faculty regard Thad as a bureaucrat who overinvests university resources in projects they consider nonessential, such as a new lighted scoreboard at the baseball stadium or perhaps a YouTube marketing campaign about how the "FTS lifestyle" caters to the entertainment interests and hobbies of the current generation of students.

Whereas Pam associates her job with higher appeals to cultural enrichment, Thad speaks primarily in buzzwords from management books, marketing seminars, and motivational speakers. He constantly talks about improving "metrics" such as student evaluations, even though everyone knows they are persistently inaccurate (just as we demonstrated in Chapter 4), and he views "success" synonymously with the number of students in classroom seats, regardless of their skill level and intellectual drive. He's deeply interested in "expanding the reach" of all current FTS programs, as well as every classroom technology fad that promises to do so. On any normal day, Thad is the university's in-house face of "corporatization," administrative bloat, and diminishing faculty governance. But something is different when it comes to the audit threatening the creative writing graduate program. The interests of Thad and Pam actually align more than either realizes.

Thad knows that FTS's annual budget allocation from the state is closely tied to the numbers he cares about—to student enrollments, retention levels, graduation rates, and the sort. He also knows that FTS's rankings, although admittedly poor, improve on the margins by maintaining a low ratio of professors to students in the classroom. He's even made classroom attention per pupil a central selling point in a newly launched ad campaign to recruit students by promising them "Personalized Excellence for Your Future Now" (recall what we discussed in Chapter 3 about advertising). It was the result of six months of focus groups and committee meetings with other administrators, all of which will be for naught if the program goes away. There are other incentives as well. Importantly, the state's funding allocation formula automatically classifies graduate degree–granting institutions in a larger appropriations tier than four-year colleges, which, in turn, operate on a higher tier than community colleges and so forth.

Thad knows that student numbers and associated funding formulas are what matter at the end of the day. Like Pam, he ultimately buckles in to fight for the entire program despite its poor record at securing desirable jobs for its graduates. It turns out that he wants the numbers and funding, just as she wants graduate assistants and departmental prestige. In the process, both Pam and Thad act in their own interests while largely neglecting that of the students being served by their program. Note that neither actually wants FTS graduates to fail when they enter a saturated job market with a low-ranked PhD, weak research background, no publications record, and possibly tens of thousands of dollars in student loan debt. Those concerns simply aren't strong priorities relative to other factors.

Although our scenario is hypothetical—or, rather, based on composites of actual scenarios we've witnessed—note the patterns of incentive it highlights. Pam and Thad have different conceptions of what a university should be and what their respective roles mean to the institution. They may even despise each other personally. But the advantages of continuing the creative writing graduate program benefit them both in ways that extend well beyond the needs of students— for Pam, it's all the perks associated with teaching in a department with a graduate program, and for Thad, it's numbers, seats in chairs, and sources of operating money. Good luck getting either of them to change course.

9

Cheaters, Cheaters Everywhere

MOST UNDERGRADUATES CHEAT IN some small way at least once in college. The extant research indicates that around half commit at least one serious act of academic dishonesty. Somewhere between 20 to 40 percent cheat over and over again.[1]

Why?

Here, popular bloggers, pundits, and even a few researchers in the less rigorous academic fields are quick to blame poltergeists. Supposedly, awful things such the "consumer mentality"[2] or "neoliberalism" have possessed academia and students, causing them to engage in systematic bad behavior. For example, activist and adjunct professor Warren Blumenfield says there is a "culture of cheating at our universities" and blames it on competitiveness brought on by our "neoliberal age."[3] Education theorist Elizabeth Buckner and anthropologist Rebecca Hodges have started studying cheating behavior at colleges in the Arab world; they, too, blame the problem on the "outcomes-oriented 'neoliberal student.'"[4]

But these ghost stories don't make much sense. The problem is that the consumer mentality or neoliberal attitudes supposedly started infecting universities in the late 1970s or early 1980s, with the rise of Ronald Reagan and Margaret Thatcher. However, students have been cheating at high rates for as far back as the research on cheating goes. In the early 1960s, William Bowers did the first major, systematic study of undergraduate cheating and found that 75 percent of students admitted to engaging in at least one form of academic dishonesty, and about

50 percent admitted to engaging in at least one of the more serious forms of dishonesty.[5] More recent replications of that study, by Douglas McCabe and Linda Treviño, find that students admit to cheating at roughly the same rates, or in fact, slightly lower rates.

Back in the early 1960s, before neoliberalism and the consumer mentality supposedly infected the university, everyone cheated. Then, after neoliberalism and the consumer mentality supposedly took over the university, students *continued* to cheat . . . at more or less the same rates, or perhaps slightly lower rates.

We don't have to posit mystical poltergeists to explain why students cheat. Instead, students cheat because it's easy, because they're bad at time management, because they expect it to work, because they reasonably expect not to get caught, and because they believe their peers also cheat. If they believe their peers cheat, then they have strong incentives to cheat. If we want to reduce cheating, we have to change the students' environment.

EVERYBODY CHEATS A LITTLE; SOME CHEAT A LOT

It's hard to know exactly how many students cheat. We don't catch 'em all. The best we can do is survey students anonymously and hope they'll be forthcoming.

However, we know that, in general, on anonymous surveys, respondents will exhibit "social desirability" bias: They will tend to answer questions in ways that make them look good. Even on anonymous surveys, people will lie and overestimate, say, how much they give to charity, and underestimate, say, how much they lie and cheat.[6] Accordingly, we should treat these surveys as giving us a lower bound. If 50 percent of students say they plagiarize, we should assume the true number is higher.

The most comprehensive and controlled surveys on cheating come from William Bowers's 1962–1963 work, along with Donald McCabe and his coauthors' subsequent replications. Here, we'll present the summary McCabe, Butterfield, and Treviño offer in their most recent book.[7]

Table 9.1 displays the percent of students at universities that lack a strong honor code system who admit to having engaged in various forms of academic dishonesty at least once in their undergraduate careers.

TABLE 9.1 Percent of Undergraduate Students at Schools without an Honor Code Who Admitted to Various Forms of Dishonesty at Least Once

Type of Cheating	Bowers 1964	McCabe 1991	McCabe 1994	McCabe 2000	McCabe 2010
Copying a few sentences without attribution	53	41	54	45	36
Padding a bibliography	35	25	29	26	13
Plagiarizing from public material on papers	36	19	26	19	6
Receiving exam questions from students who already took the exam	43	19	29	56	30
Copying from another student during a test	31	31	52	34	14
Did collaborative homework although professor forbids it	14	40	49	51	42
Turn in papers partially or entirely written by other students	20	13	14	8	6
Giving answers to other students during an exam	27	27	37	27	11
Using crib notes during an exam	21	21	27	19	8
Any of the above behaviors	83	74	87	83	63

Overall, the rates of academic dishonesty seem to have slightly declined over the years, although McCabe and his coauthors caution that students might simply be less forthcoming in online surveys that, in principle, could be hacked and traced. Most students admit to having engaged in at least one form of dishonesty, and about 50 percent in each survey year engaged in at least one of the more severe forms of dishonesty.[8]

So, most students cheat, and at least half cheat in a severe way, at least once in their undergraduate careers. Surveys and studies find somewhere between 20 to 40 percent are chronic cheaters: students who have cheated three or more times.[9] However, these are probably lower bounds—people generally underreport bad behavior in anonymous surveys, in part because, in order to avoid cognitive dissonance, we often fail to remember our misdeeds.

In terms of *who* cheats, the results may not surprise you. Male and female students cheat at about the same rate. Most studies find that students with lower GPAs cheat more than students with higher GPAs, although some studies examining more detailed data claim that students with very high GPAs cheat more than students with merely good GPAs.[10] Students in professional schools or with preprofessional majors generally cheat more than students in liberal arts, social science, or science majors.[11] (Perhaps professional students regard schooling as merely an instrument to getting a job, and so are more inclined to cheat.)

THE PSYCHOLOGY OF CHEATING

From an economist's point of view, the belief that cheating is wrong operates as a kind of distaste for cheating. If a person genuinely believes cheating is bad, this means cheating has disutility for her, and she'll cheat only if the expected benefits of cheating overcome the inherent disutility of cheating and its other expected costs (such as the risk of getting caught).

But economics on its own cannot tell us how much people disapprove of cheating. So, let's turn to psychology.

Moral psychologist Dan Ariely is perhaps the leading researcher in the world on the question of what causes people to be honest or dishonest. In many of his experiments, he asks subjects to complete the "matrix task": They receive a worksheet with many different grids; in each grid, they must identify the two numbers (e.g., 3.44 and 6.66) that sum to 10. To motivate his subjects to do the math, Ariely pays them for each correct answer. In most of his experiments, he uses a control group whose responses he or one of his assistants scores, and an experimental group in which the subjects or respondents get to grade themselves and then inform the researcher how many questions they got right. The experimental group thus has the power to cheat. It turns out most who can cheat do. (Ariely has devised a way of anonymously checking how much they cheat after the experiment is over.)

Ariely finds that the amount of money at stake affects cheating in surprising ways. A sociopath's calculus is simple: The bigger the expected payoff, the more he cheats. But regular people act differently. Ariely finds that normal people cheat more when he pays them $2 per correct answer than when he pays them $10.

Ariely explains this by positing what he calls the "fudge factor" effect. Everybody lies and cheats a little bit on little things; only some people lie and cheat a great deal on big things. Think of it this way: Most of us are fairly decent people, and we want to maintain a self-image as such. We don't aim to be angels, but we aren't devils. If moral character were graded on an A through F scale, we aim to be a good solid B or B–. So, Ariely claims, we lie, cheat, and steal only as much as is compatible with having a pretty good character overall.[12]

This theory helps explain a few things. First, it explains a phenomenon known as *moral accounting*: Many experiments show that we keep a kind of moral tally sheet for ourselves. Right after a person does something unusually good, she'll act worse than normal for a short time. After a person does something bad, she'll act better than normal for a short time. The idea here is that you're aiming for a B–, so if you just got a good grade on the last pop quiz, you can slack off a bit. If you just got a bad grade, you have to work a bit harder. Second, it explains why most students do not continuously cheat, but only cheat on occasion and generally in smaller amounts. Many students copy and paste a few unattributed sentences in a paper, but fewer hand in an entirely plagiarized piece.

Ariely's research explains, in part, why students cheat: Because most of us aim only to be "pretty good" rather than morally perfect, dishonesty is normal and widespread. Students cheat in college not because something bizarre and bad happens in college, or because colleges have a corrupting influence, but because cheating and lying are normal behaviors. People lie and cheat a little bit all over the place, and college is just another place.

With all that in mind, we'll want to see if certain environmental or contextual factors tend to induce higher or lower rates of cheating.

Ariely himself has modified the matrix task experiment to examine how different factors affect people's cheating behavior. For instance, it turns out that people behave more nicely when they smell cleaning fluids.[13] They cheat more when they believe a peer (someone like themselves) is also cheating, but cheat less when they believe a hated rival is cheating.[14] People are more likely to cheat when they suffer from conflicts of interest, when they are skilled at rationalizing their behavior, when they believe others will benefit from their dishonesty. They cheat less when they are asked to pledge their honesty ahead of time, when they are surrounded by "moral reminders" (such as crucifixes), or when they feel like they are being watched.[15]

In a book on cheating, James Lang summarizes a wide range of research and concludes that four basic background factors tend to increase cheating:

1. *A heavy emphasis on performance*: The more students are pressured to excel, the more they cheat.
2. *High stakes*: When individual projects, papers, and tests are worth a high percentage of a grade, students cheat more. Students cheat more when given one large assignment rather than many small assignments.
3. *Extrinsic motivation*: If students don't care about the skill or knowledge being tested for its own sake, but instead just need the grade to pass the class, they cheat more. The more they care about grades for their own sake, the more they cheat.
4. *Low expectation of success*: Students who think they need to cheat to do well cheat more.[16]

As an example, Lang discusses the research of George Diekhoff, who examined differences in cheating rates between American and Japanese college students. One might expect that because American students are more individualistic and less concerned with honor, they would cheat more. But Diekhoff found that Japanese students, in fact, cheat at higher rates. The reason, it seems, is that American college students usually have multiple small assignments over a semester, mandatory class attendance, and multiple pop quizzes. In contrast, Japanese students usually have one major exam at the end of a semester worth

100 percent of their grade. As Lang summarizes: "The higher the stakes you load onto any specific exam or performance of any kind, the more you are tempting students to engage in any means necessary to succeed."[17]

Part of the problem also has to do with what students regard as cheating. Students might think cheating is wrong, but then cheat because they do not realize they are cheating. Or, they might cheat because they regard cheating as less serious a violation than others do. As McCabe, Butterfield, and Treviño document, students and faculty have very different attitudes toward different forms of academic dishonesty. For instance, 14 percent of high school students think using crib notes during a test is not cheating *at all*, as do the 23 percent who think having their parents do half their work isn't. In contrast, all faculty regard these forms of dishonesty as cheating, and nearly all think it's *serious* cheating.[18] Only 26 percent of high school students think having their parents do more than half their schoolwork for them represents *serious cheating*.[19]

CHEATING FROM A GAME THEORY PERSPECTIVE

Contextual factors influence how much students cheat. Not surprisingly, the research tends to show that students cheat more when they believe their fellow students cheat more.

Student cheating is socially destructive. To the extent that students cheat and the public knows, it lessens the value of the university degree. It reduces the value of the signal that the degree provides.

It's tempting to wag our fingers at students and demand they do better. But there's a problem: If almost everyone else is cheating, then doing it starts to become the rational and maybe even reasonable choice for you, too. That depends, in part, on how grades are determined and what kind of value grades have.

Let's take a step back: There may be cases where a person engages in socially destructive behavior, but the behavior is excusable or even justifiable. To illustrate one such case, consider a hypothetical game called modified dollar auction, a variation of an economics game developed by Martin Shubik.[20] Suppose we force fifty strangers to play an auction game with the following rules:

Modified Dollar Auction[21]

1. The opening bid must be $1.
2. Each new bid must increase by an increment of $1.
3. The highest overall bidder pays her bid and wins $50.
4. All losing bidders pay their highest bids, but win $0.
5. All losing players must also pay a fee of one-tenth of the winning bid.
6. All players must pay a minimum fee of $5 regardless of whether or not they bid.

This game is designed to escalate quickly. Jason sometimes plays this game on the first day of a new class. His students will bid into the hundreds. The rules of the game make it rational—as a matter of self-defense—for losing players to always increase their bids. So, for example, suppose the highest bidder right now has just offered $50. The second highest bidder will have offered $49. This player should then bid $51 rather than stay at $49. She will lose less money that way.

Modified dollar auction causes players to engage in socially destructive behavior. However, it is not clear that any of the bidders are blameworthy or doing anything wrong. They are victims of the rules. The rules pit them against each other. They do not wish to exploit or harm their classmates, but just want to reduce the extent to which they are themselves harmed and exploited. The game generates plenty of socially destructive behavior, but the players are not obviously blameworthy for their actions. The problem lies with the rules of the game, not the players' actions. The game forces players to choose between exploiting or being exploited, harming or being harmed. The rules are designed to turn players into mutual enemies.

By bidding, they harm others, but they are plausibly seen as excused for doing so. They are not trying to victimize others, but instead attempt to protect themselves from victimization. They face a choice: Exploit or be exploited.

Or, more simply, consider the classic prisoner's dilemma game. The prisoner's dilemma game gets its name from a hypothetical story in which two suspects are given the opportunity to rat on one another or stay silent. In the abstract, the game works as follows. There are two

TABLE 9.2 The Prisoner's Dilemma

	Player 1 Cooperates	Player 1 Defects
Player 2 Cooperates	1 wins. 2 wins.	1 wins big. 2 loses big.
Player 2 Defects	1 loses big. 2 wins big.	1 loses. 2 loses.

players, each of whom has two moves, *cooperate* or *defect*. They move at the same time. The payoffs are as outlined in Table 9.2.

In the prisoner's dilemma, mutual cooperation is a win-win scenario. Mutual defection is a lose-lose scenario. Both parties are better off if they cooperate. Nevertheless, the game gives both players an incentive to cheat—regardless of what the other player does, they do better if they defect.

The smart way to play prisoner's dilemma depends on whom you play with and how many times you play. If you play it once with a random person, never to be seen again, you serve your self-interest by defecting. But suppose you play it with the same person over and over again. In that case, the player will *react* to your previous moves. If you cooperate repeatedly, she might learn she can trust you and so will play cooperatively. If you cheat or defect repeatedly, she might learn you are untrustworthy and so punish you in the next round by defecting herself. In the end, a strategy of "tit for tat"—start by cooperating, then do whatever the other player did in the last round—works best.[22] When the other player plays nice, you play nice; when the other player tries to take advantage of you, you fight back.

Student cheating is in many respects a variation of modified dollar auction or the prisoner's dilemma game. When students cheat, they do not simply break a covenant with their school or play cat and mouse with the professor. Rather, they are reacting to their fellow classmates. They cheat, in part, because cheating is a rational response to *other students cheating*.

To illustrate with the most dramatic example, imagine a course graded on a curve rather than an absolute scale. The curve turns grades into zero-sum competition among the students. One student's grade can rise only if another student's grade falls. Suppose Kevin has no choice but to take this course. (Perhaps the course is a general education requirement, or perhaps it is now too late for him to drop it.) Imagine that cheating is widespread in this particular class. In fact, every other student, except Kevin, cheats. The professor and the administration are unable or unwilling to stop the cheating. Suppose also that cheaters routinely do better gradewise than noncheaters.

Suppose Kevin knows that if he tries to keep his hands clean and just does his best without cheating, his grade will suffer. The cheaters—the kids with the crib sheets—have an advantage over the noncheaters, just as defectors in the prisoner's dilemma get an advantage over the cooperators. Since the course is curved, the better others do, the worse Kevin does. The curve means their cheating does not simply improve their grades, it also lowers Kevin's grade. Suppose in a classroom devoid of cheating, Kevin would earn a B, but in this cheater-inundated class, he will earn at most a C unless he also cheats.

In this case, it's not clear if we should blame or condemn Kevin should he choose to cheat. Through no fault of his own, he is stuck inside a corrupt academic system. He faces a prisoner's dilemma where he knows ahead of time the other players are going to cheat (Table 9.3).

In this class, if Kevin cheats, he does not thereby disadvantage or take advantage of competing students. He does not impose harm on innocent people. Instead, he levels the playing field. Kevin cheats in self-defense. Kevin does not take unfair advantage of others. Rather, when he cheats, his cheating brings the world closer to the outcome that would have resulted if others had acted rightly. The other students threaten him with their cheating behavior, and by cheating, Kevin prevents them from harming him.

When others are playing by the rules, we have good moral reasons to play by the rules as well. However, if others are committed to not

TABLE 9.3 Kevin's Cheating Dilemma

	Others Cheat
Kevin Refuses to Cheat	Kevin gets a bad grade. Cheaters get an advantage.
Kevin Cheats	Kevin gets a better grade. Others lose their advantage.

playing by the rules, and if playing by the rules then just makes us suckers who will be exploited, then we sometimes lose our obligation to play by the rules. We could not demand that Kevin remain honest when, through no fault of his own, he is stuck in a situation where honesty will just make him a victim of dishonest people. Kevin has a moral duty to be honest to those who deserve his honesty, not an absolute moral duty to be honest no matter what.

We would not go further and argue that Kevin has a *duty* to cheat, or that it would be wrong for him not to cheat. In fact, it may be admirable and praiseworthy for Kevin to take the high ground and refuse to cheat, despite the costs, simply because he is not the kind of person who cheats on a test. If Kevin takes a stand against cheating, bearing all the costs, he might deserve our admiration. Our point here is just that if he decides to cheat like the others, he does not deserve blame.

This is an extreme case, and the less the classroom looks like this extreme case, the less excusable Kevin is. To the extent a professor grades on an absolute scale rather than a relative scale, Kevin's blameworthiness goes up. As fewer and fewer students cheat, his blameworthiness rises, as he's no longer simply playing self-defense, but starting to hurt other innocent people. Kevin's blameworthiness also depends on how much cheating "works": Does it actually succeed in raising a student's grade?

Now, Kevin's case is extreme and unrealistic. In fact, not all courses are strictly curved, although many instructors do maintain a kind of rough, informal curve. In general, professors will give the best papers As and grade other papers relative to those. Thus, even in uncurved classes, when other students cheat, the noncheaters might reasonably worry that this cheating comes at their expense.

In Kevin's class, we stipulated all other students cheat and Kevin knows this. But in reality, only some students cheat. Given that McCabe and others' survey evidence suggests that at most only 40 percent of students are chronic cheaters, then a properly informed student should expect that in any given class, most of her classmates will *not* cheat. However, it seems students are not well informed; in fact, they overestimate how many other students cheat and how frequently they do so. For instance, in one study, Reva Fish and Gerri

Hura asked students how often they might have used another author's ideas, phrases, sentences, paragraphs, or an entire document without attribution. Many claimed they never did so, and only a small minority admitted to doing so regularly. However, when asked how often they believed *other* students did so, they tended to overestimate the amount of cheating their classmates engaged in by a factor of 2 to 10. Their perception was that they themselves have cheated rarely and in small ways, but their classmates frequently cheated in big ways.[23] Other studies find similar results.[24] Because they overestimate how much others cheat, students may feel less guilty about cheating and so cheat more than they otherwise would.

Does cheating actually work? To our surprise, there are few studies directly testing this. Many studies examine the relationship between GPA and cheating; in general, they find that people with lower GPAs cheat more, although some studies find instead that people with especially high GPAs also cheat more than others.[25] One experiment with online tests did not quite find evidence that cheating worked, in the sense that the students who chose to cheat during the experiment did not perform better.[26] However, the problem with many such studies is that we'd ahead of time expect a strong selection effect: The students who expect to do worse will probably cheat more. Accordingly, it may be that the cheaters do worse overall than the noncheaters, but nevertheless, cheating improves their scores somewhat. Furthermore, even if cheating turns out not to work—it doesn't objectively improve grades much—students might still *believe* it works and thus cheat more than they otherwise would.

SOLUTIONS

Student cheating is widespread—most cheat a little, and some cheat a lot. Thanks to social desirability bias, surveys give us a lower bound on how many and how often students cheat, so the truth is that more students cheat and more often than the surveys indicate. So, what should we do about it?

Here, moralizers might be inclined to gnash their teeth and talk about society's moral decay. Conservatives will blame the decline of traditional values and the sense of honor. Leftists will blame corporatist,

consumerist, or neoliberal ideology. But, in reality, we have no empirical evidence that any such factors are causing the problem. On the
contrary, as far back as we've measured student cheating, students have
been cheating at about the same rates. Furthermore, as Lang documents,
cheating appears to have been widespread thousands of years ago in the
Olympics and in the Chinese imperial examinations.[27]

When cheating is this widespread, it's pointless to blame character.
We have to change the environment in which students find themselves.
We have to reduce their incentive to cheat and structure the classroom
in such a way as to make cheating more difficult or less likely to pay off.

Douglas McCabe and his coauthors have documented at length
the fact that honor codes, when internalized by a student body and
controlled by student honor councils, seem to work. Students, like everybody else, are conformists who want to fit in and be esteemed by their
peers. When they are studying at a school where everybody cheats and
no one cares, they, too, start to cheat and feel little remorse. But when
they enter a university where students themselves take pride in their
academic honesty, and where fitting in means being honest, students
cheat far less.[28]

The good news is that once a university has a reputation for academic honesty among students, this behavior tends to become self-
reinforcing. The bad news is that dishonesty is also self-reinforcing. The
other bit of bad news is that changing from the bad equilibrium (lots of
cheating) to the good one (little cheating) is difficult.

Professors can reduce cheating in their own classes fairly easily,
simply by changing the kind of assignments they give. It's harder to
cheat on in-class assignments than out-of-class assignments. Students
will cheat more if the professor uses the same essay prompts or exam
questions year after year; they will cheat less if the professor varies
essays and questions. Students will cheat less if they are given many
small assignments worth a small percent of their grade; they will cheat
more if given one or two big assignments worth a large portion of
their grade.

Many studies show that students cheat more when they don't care
about the content of the class and cheat less when they do care. So, one
way universities could foster increased "intrinsic motivation" would
be to give students more freedom to choose their classes, rather than

saddling them with a large number of gen eds that students don't want to take.

But notice that—given what we've argued in the previous chapters—reducing student cheating probably comes at professors' expense. As we made clear in Chapter 2, professors generally have financial incentives to reduce the time spent teaching and to increase the hours spent on research. Having to grade many small assignments takes much more time than having to grade one or two large assignments. Having to produce new exams or new essay prompts every year is time-consuming, especially if it requires professors to assign new readings and thus prepare new lectures. It's easier for professors to just recycle the same lectures, exams, and learning material year after year. Finally, as we argued in Chapter 7, gen eds are largely a form of academic rent-seeking: The point of forcing students to take two English composition classes isn't to make them better writers, but instead to increase the English department's budget. At most universities—where butts in seats equal money in department pockets—professors have little incentive to reduce gen ed requirements. Administrators also have little such incentive; for them, it's easier if departmental budgets and student enrollments are stable and predictable, rather than rising and falling year after year as students' tastes change or as faculty compete for student enrollments.

In the end, it's not all that hard to reduce student cheating significantly. Any given professor could choose to make her class cheating-proof. However, professors have little incentive to do so and many incentives not to.

We'll end with one easy-to-implement suggestion from some of Jason's students at Georgetown: Faculty know that cheating happens at their university, but they don't know how much cheating occurs in their own classes. But professors usually have the option of adding custom questions to their anonymous course evaluations. They could add a question or two about academic dishonesty, for example, "Did you engage in any form of academic dishonesty in this class?" Some students will undoubtedly underreport their level of cheating, but many will fess up. (We know—given that they're willing to insult their professors on such surveys—that students believe they won't be punished for what they write.) Suppose a professor follows this recommendation and learns that 25 percent of the students cheated in her class. That information alone may well induce her to change her assignments and class structure in order to reduce cheating. Why not make such questions standard? As we showed in Chapter 4, course evaluations are largely a waste of time, but we could easily make them truly useful.

IO

Three Big Myths about What's Plaguing Higher Ed

Blame Canada! Blame Canada!
It seems that everything's gone wrong
Since Canada came along
. . . We must blame them and cause a fuss
Before somebody thinks of blaming us!

— "Blame Canada," *South Park*

OVER THE PAST NINE chapters, we've examined all sorts of bad behavior from faculty, administrators, and students. To explain *why* they engage in this bad behavior, we haven't had to talk about gremlins or poltergeists. We've been able to explain most of it just by looking at the perverse incentives individuals face because of the way universities are structured.

Nevertheless, many commentators seem to believe that three powerful forces haunt academia. They are, supposedly:

1. the *corporatization* of higher ed.
2. *neoliberal* ideology.
3. the threat of impending *technological disruption*.

In Chapter 1, we warned readers not to blame the failings of higher education on gremlins and poltergeists when a more *natural* explanation will do. In the rest of the book, we looked for and examined those natural explanations. But in this chapter, we pause to show that these three supposed threats are greatly exaggerated.

MYTH #1: THE CORPORATIZATION OF HIGHER ED

The most nefarious and hated poltergeist in the higher education press is "corporatization." The term refers to a philistine cost–benefit, profit- and results-driven mindset imported from the business world.

As one recent article in the American Association of University Professors' magazine asserted, universities are facing an onslaught of "corporate values, corporate management practices, corporate labor-relations policies, and corporate money."[1] The corporatization poltergeist has spawned a vast and growing academic literature that usually pits students and faculty in a struggle with administrators who allegedly devalue education in the service of vaguely referenced yet all-encompassing concepts such as "the market." The theory of the corporate poltergeist purports to explain university spending priorities, hiring practices, student recruitment, curricular decisions, campus amenities, and above all administrative growth.[2]

Certain parts of the "corporatization" narrative ring true and explain its appeal. The total number of university administrators has more than quadrupled in size since the mid-1970s, and the use of slick branding and advertising campaigns to "sell" higher ed to prospective students and their parents certainly has a slimy business feel to it.

Blaming corporatization for these and other observed ills often works at the surface level, but the approach begins to fall apart with only minimal probing. The "corporatization" poltergeist is belied by the lack of a discernible profit mechanism and the persistence of sustained budgetary bloat throughout the American university system.

The "corporatization" story is misdiagnosis built upon superficial understandings of two key concepts we have stressed throughout this book: incentives and institutions. While administrators certainly re-spond to incentives of their own and the institutional constraints in which they operate, there's nothing uniquely "corporate" about how they do so. From an economic standpoint, nearly all colleges and universities, whether public or private, behave and function far more like government agencies than for-profit corporations.

The reason comes from the nature of their product, education. Universities sell education in the form of a credential—a degree or certification that a student has demonstrated proficiency in a specific subject or set of subjects. Outside of the small and low-quality "for-profit higher ed" sector and a few exec-ed business programs, this product is not conventionally sold for profit in any traditional "corporate" sense.

If anything, universities are distinguished by unusual institutional features that reduce or eliminate the profit mechanism's effect on how higher education is structured. As economists James M. Buchanan and Nicos E. Devletoglou pointed out, the breakdown occurs in three specific areas of university operations.[3]

First, the consumers of education—the students—are usually not the direct buyers of the product. Their tuition payments usually come from one or more indirect funding sources that, cumulatively, dampen their price responsiveness to the degree they are seeking: scholarships, public aid and subsidies, student loans, and even their parents. Students have little incentive to shop around for the best deal in an opaque pricing structure, and universities are similarly insulated from the feedback signals that a price provides to them about the degrees and services they are offering.

Second, the main producers of education—the faculty—are not the actual sellers of its degrees. They depend on the university administration to recruit and house students, to establish curriculum standards, to maintain accreditation and good scholarly standing, to comply with government regulations, to manage university finances, and to operate the facilities where instruction occurs. Sometimes the productive incentives of faculty do not align with what students want. Faculty often prefer to teach upper-level specialty courses that service their personal intellectual interests over core classes in their disciplines, and similarly tend to place a high value on niche programs and departments that have trouble attracting majors. Faculty prioritize their own research and rationally do so given the incentives of academic hiring and promotion. But this also dampens the incentives to service student demands in the classroom and reprioritizes budget expenditures away from the university's core educational products.

Third, the actual ownership of almost any given university is usually several layers removed from both its administration and faculty.

Public universities are technically owned by the state and managed by an appointed board of governors. Private institutions are usually set up as non-profit entities under the direction of a board of trustees. These roles tend to attract philanthropic and political appointees who have other careers and obligations besides running a university. They therefore devolve most tasks of actually running the university onto a full-time administration, checking in only periodically or in the event of a problem that rises to the level of their attention—including outside political pressures. In both private and public institutions, a gap exists between the legally empowered ownership of the institution and the people who are tasked with its daily operation.

The effect of these three characteristics—consumers who do not directly pay for education, producers who do not directly sell education, and owners who do not directly administer their institutions—is to reduce the responsiveness of all three to the costs, demand, and operational efficiency within the university system. In other words, the allegedly "corporatized" university lacks all the basic signals that would otherwise be necessary for a university to operate as a profit-maximizing firm, even if its administration *wanted* to do so.

So how do universities actually operate? The most common complaints about the modern university can be diagnosed through the extensive body of scholarly literature on the study and operation of bureaucracy. In fact, the most common problems in university administration are the same as those in government agencies: budgetary misallocation and waste, growing or bloated administrative staffs, redundant functions, inefficiency, and poor customer service.

The reason is simple. Rather than operating as profit-maximizers, bureaucracies tend to maximize their own budgetary expenditures and do so with few meaningful checks against wastefulness or feedback mechanisms to ensure accountability. (Note that we are *not* suggesting here that universities should simply become profit-maximizers, and indeed the for-profit higher ed sector is currently plagued by a host of its own problems. Rather we are using the term profit-maximizer descriptively to illustrate that traditional universities do not exhibit these characteristics). As we saw in Chapter 8, accountability failures might entail expanding enrollment at the expense of educational quality, or extending the operation of a graduate program well beyond its ability to place students in their desired jobs. It could also mean enjoying the perks of office, including a large staff, control of funding, and access to campus amenities.

When academics complain about the "corporatization" of the university, they are usually noticing real and tangible problems but then misdiagnosing them as features of a "corporatized" management strategy, as if corporatization were something people pursued for its own sake. Now, we admit that corporations also suffer many of the problems built into large bureaucracies. But universities have more in common with the Department of Motor Vehicles than they do with Disney or McDonald's, and the reasons have to do with both the way they receive money and allocate scarce resources between their components.

Universities turn to bureaucratic administrative models because of internal budgetary competition over scarce resources between two or more of its components. The witnessed problems are thus a feature of that competition, and various strategies used by both administrators and faculty to secure resources for themselves and their functions within the university system.

The bureaucratization of higher ed may seen in Figure 10.1, which documents administrative growth since the mid-1970s. Whereas faculty and executive-level administrators (presidents, vice presidents, deans) have both grown at fairly stable rates in conjunction with the expansion of the university system, a clear outlier exists in another type of staff growth. Lower-level professional staffers have skyrocketed in number, far exceeding the growth rate of both the executive-level administrators and the faculty. They have also grown faster than student enrollment at most institutions. These positions include personnel in student affairs and student services, admissions offices, financial offices, accrediting and regulatory compliance roles, residency and dining, university life, and dozens of other smaller administrative functions in the noneducational ranks of the university system. Some of these functions are necessary and even essential to university operations, but their growth rate and the ever-expanding amount of university resources they consume are relatively recent developments.

Although most of the aforementioned administrative functions have expanded in recent decades, the most pronounced growth appears to be in noninstructional student services—a broad assortment of functions

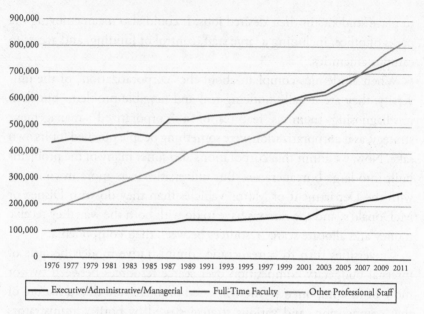

FIGURE 10.1 Administrative Growth in US Higher Education, 1976–2011
Source: Author's calculations, Digest of Education Statistics, 2015

that include campus life activities, counseling services, admissions, student organizations, intramurals, noncredit workshops, and an ever-growing assortment of extracurricular miscellany that takes place outside of the classroom. A 2016 study by the Delta Cost Project, a think tank initiative that tracks university spending patterns, showed a pronounced increase in student services spending between 2003 and 2013 across almost all types of universities. Spending on student services, measured per equivalent full-time student, increased 22.3 percent at public research universities and 29.9 percent at private research universities during this period. Instructional spending in the same period grew by 10 percent or less, depending on the university type.[4] With each passing year, administrators tasked with noninstructional roles appear to be consuming an ever-larger portion of the typical student's tuition payments.

Take an example from one of Phil's former universities to see how administrative functions come into being and then rapidly expand into permanent bureaucratic fixtures. A few years ago, somebody in the administration decided to create a new "green sustainability" office. The campus had managed to get along just fine without this office for prior decades, but it proved to be a popular idea with a narrow but active constituency on campus. As one of the new office's main jobs, it doled out a total of $100,000 per year in small grants to students and faculty for environmentally themed projects on campus. Among the projects funded in its first five years of operation: a campus bikeshare program,[5] multiple organic gardens on empty land around campus, a $6,000 environmental ad campaign targeting the dining hall, the establishment of an on-campus beehive station, the installation of picnic tables with solar-powered phone charger outlets (at a price tag of over $12,000 each), and an unsuccessful attempt to attach kinetic energy converters to stationary exercise bikes in the fitness center.

Note that like our rock climbing wall from the first chapter, a small number of students may benefit from these environmental projects and services. The majority probably ignore them entirely, and a few may even find their ideological and political connotations overbearing. The one certainty, though, is that the money and personnel they use must come from somewhere in the university's funding model. Usually, that means money taken from student tuition and fees, or if not them the taxpayers. Soon enough, the sustainability office (or expanded intramural sports program, or art and cultural outreach center, or media affairs office, or diversity training center) becomes a permanent fixture with a sizable and growing staff bureaucracy that also happens to actively lobby for the expansion of its own budget. Hiring ensues, leading to a swelling of administrative personnel involved in increasingly peripheral tasks around campus that are far removed from the provision of education and its associated credentials.

In fact, this same pattern often plays out in common and longstanding areas of student life. Another example that Phil witnessed involved a more traditional office that supported campus recreational activities. Over the course of barely a decade, this office transformed from a single person who shared his time with other athletics offices into a team of three dedicated full-time staffers. The basic services they provided did not change, but the larger version became more bureaucratized over time. It created its own internal governance "council" of students and staff to allocate once-simple budget requests that previously went through a single channel. It adopted complex layers of forms and paperwork to perform previously routine tasks. And toward the end of this period, it imposed a new "dues" structure aimed at collecting supplemental participation fees from students. In all probability, the new hires to this office sincerely believed they were providing "better" services than a decade ago. But the costs of this expanded set of functions—in time, in paperwork, and eventually in direct fees—fell mostly on the students.

Faculty ire against "corporatization" is misplaced. The corporatization narrative does correctly identify many ills in the university system. But it misdiagnoses the causes. The problem isn't that leaders are importing private-sector concepts and nonexistent "profit" motives. The culprit is instead institutional designs that foster internal bureaucratic growth and accompanying inefficiency.

MYTH #2: THE NEOLIBERAL TAKEOVER OF THE UNIVERSITIES

What's wrong with universities? Many faculty will say "corporatization." Many others will instead blame the problem on a different, less easily identifiable poltergeist called "neoliberalism."

"Neoliberalism" is an odd term. Its deep origins may be traced back to the first half of the twentieth century. One of its earliest modern uses was as a term of disparagement. In 1920s Germany, both left-wing and right-wing anti-capitalist intellectuals adopted the moniker to attack their shared adversary, the proponents of a "laissez-faire" free-market liberal philosophy.[6] The term came up again in the late 1930s among the mostly European intellectual followers of American journalist Walter Lippmann, though Lippmann himself never used the term. Lippmann's larger project sought to revitalize political liberalism as an alternative to socialism and fascism in the wake of the Depression, while also shedding some of the perception and blame that its reputation had acquired. At a 1938 conference in Paris, these intellectuals batted around the name "neoliberalism" as a potential designation for their effort, likely seeking to claim it from the earlier pejorative uses of the 1920s.

The name never really stuck outside of a small number of adherents, even though some modern writers have attempted to extend its history back to Lippmann's time.[7] The word appears only a handful of times in academic publications between 1930 and 1950, with no clear pattern of association to Lippmann or any other group or cause.[8] Few persons, it seemed, ever claimed the phrase as their own in its supposed years of origin beyond the aforementioned examples. The loose assemblage of ideas around Lippmann's interwar philosophy eventually morphed into the distinctively termed "Ordoliberal" school of postwar Germany— essentially an attempt to blend classical concepts of free-market economics such as deregulation and free trade with a robust social welfare state, modest progressive taxation, and conservative but active central banking. Based around a group of economists at the University of Freiburg, Ordoliberalism's influence peaked at midcentury as a guiding influence behind the West German Wirtschaftswunder of the 1950s, an ideology suited to the geography and politics of the peak of the Cold War. Scholarly literature at the time associated the term "neoliberal" almost entirely with this narrow postwar German school of economic thought.[9]

The modern concept of "neoliberalism" is divorced from even these obscure roots. The concept's fashionability as an academic catchphrase dates only to the mid-1980s at the earliest, and likely follows from its popularization in a set of 1978–1979 lectures by the French philosopher Michel Foucault.[10] The supposed tenets of today's neoliberalism remain notoriously ill-defined. They have been said to encompass both a non-interventionist "laissez-faire" government and a robust welfare state, the latter presented as something of a "third way" between capitalism and socialism; to merge the economic nationalism of stimulus packages and state-sponsored growth programs with the globalist internationalism of free trade and non-intervention in the economy; and to manifest in everything from market-oriented Western democracies to autocratic military regimes in the developing world. Purported adherents of modern neoliberalism include an array of figures from competing and often inconsistent political backgrounds. Alleged neoliberals extend from economists Milton Friedman, Ludwig von Mises, and Alan Greenspan to political figures Ronald Reagan, Margaret Thatcher, Al Gore, and Tony Blair, to novelist Ayn Rand, and frequently to Chilean military dictator Augusto Pinochet, and even to rival candidates such as Donald Trump and Hillary Clinton. "Neoliberalism" is an amorphous, ill-defined word referring to who knows what. But whatever it is, it's bad, and many academics think it's also running and ruining our universities.

It's not even clear if any of the persons or institutions associated with the term actually is a neoliberal; hardly anyone describes him- or herself as such. Part of the problem derives from the term's use to describe an excessively broad and sometimes self-contradictory array of beliefs, concepts, figures, and institutions. On an even more fundamental level, though, the term "neoliberal" is still applied pejoratively to discredit a targeted person, policy, or belief system. A study by political scientists Taylor Boas and Jordan Gans-Morse tracked the term's rise as an "academic catchphrase" by surveying its use in scholarly journals between 1990 and 2004. After sampling 148 articles that used the term "neoliberalism" and its variants, they found that only 31 percent even offered a working definition of the concept. And 45 percent depicted neoliberalism in a negative way, while only 3 percent presented it favorably. The remainder of articles were either mixed or neutral in their portrayal, but the overwhelming ideological assessment of the term's alleged effects skewed in a hostile direction.[11] While the authors of this study expressed hope of salvaging the term in a more constructive direction with better definitions and fewer normative biases in its use, the patterns they describe have only intensified in the intervening decade. Between the entire period from 1930 to 1980, the word "neoliberalism" appeared in only a few hundred academic works, but it received over 23,000 books and article references in 2015 alone. Meanwhile, certain Critical Theory journals have even published bizarre, profanity-laced tirades against the concept—they're engaging in exorcism rituals against the "neoliberal" poltergeist.[12]

So, what bearing does this term have on the university system? Quite simply, "neoliberalism" is now a favorite poltergeist of higher education. Like the mayhem-causing spirit, it is an ill-defined concept with largely imaginary professed adherents, yet it is blamed for all manner of ills, problems, and malicious acts in the university system.

A widely cited 2003 article by film and media professor Marc Bosquet illustrates this pattern. Bosquet's initial objective in his essay was to explain why a famous prediction about a coming era of abundance in the academic job market had fallen flat. In 1989, William G. Bowen, then president of Princeton University, and graduate student Julie Ann Sosa anticipated a coming "substantial excess demand for faculty in the arts and sciences" starting around 1997—in short, an academic job surplus in many of the most beleaguered fields today.[13] Bowen and Sosa's prediction never came true. They had nevertheless made certain assumptions about the growth of student enrollment and related faculty hiring patterns.

The faulty prediction was particularly pronounced in the humanities, as Bosquet's updated statistics illustrate. Now, if we wanted to figure out what had actually transpired, we might gather data to answer the following questions: How did the student demand for degrees in these fields change over time? Did new faculty hiring reflect the shifting popularity of certain majors over others? What was the relationship between academic job growth and the production of new PhDs in English, history, philosophy, and similar fields? Did the number of new PhDs issued change or accelerate over time? If so, what does this portend given the growth rate in faculty hiring for the same fields?

Although Bosquet briefly waves his hands at these issues, he avoids doing the necessary empirical analysis that could shed light on the problems he presents. Instead, he blames a poltergeist. Bowen and Sosa's predictions, he asserts, did not fall flat because of what turned out to be faulty modeling assumptions in their empirical work. Nope. Instead, it's because their work was "informed by a neoliberal ideology idealizing market epistemology and naturalizing market relationships." They "erred by imposing market ideology on data about the structure and relations of academic labor."[14] Um, okay.

Scholars like Bosquet contend, and appear to genuinely believe, that academia's job market problems are almost entirely ideological in nature. In this argument, a cadre of largely faceless university administrators and academic organizations have adopted something called "neoliberal ideology" as if it were a core mission of the university system. In doing so, they shove aside an ill-defined "labor consciousness" of faculty. "Labor consciousness" is a blanket term invoked to explain academic hiring as a form of class-based political struggle against the same neoliberal ideology. From these unfalsifiable and untestable principles, all other problems of higher ed arise. Any further attempt at empirical investigation becomes both a contradiction of this stylized "fact" and a symptom of further subservience to the methods of neoliberal ideology.

Critical Theory writer Henry Giroux also blames the neoliberal poltergeist in what has become one of the more popular tracts about the problems facing academia. Declaring that "neoliberalism" is waging a "war on higher education," Giroux proceeds to describe the purported attributes of the threat:

> Unapologetic in its implementation of austerity measures that cause massive amounts of human hardship and suffering, neoliberal capitalism consolidates class power on the backs of young people, workers, and others marginalized by class, race, and ethnicity. . . . [N]eoliberalism has wrested itself free of any regulatory controls while at the same time removing economics from any consideration of social costs, ethics, or social responsibility. Since the economic collapse of 2008–2009, it has become increasingly evident that neoliberalism's only imperatives are profits and growing investments in global power structures unmoored from any form of accountable, democratic governance.[15]

The neoliberal poltergeist currently haunts our universities, according to this worldview. Its claimed purpose in higher ed is to promote "a form of economic Darwinism" that "attempts to undermine all forms of solidarity capable of challenging market-driven values and social relations." Neoliberalism supposedly inculcates students with a belief in "unbridled individualism" that is "almost pathological in its disdain for community, social responsibility, public values, and the public good."[16]

To Giroux, neoliberalism's claimed tangible effects are supposedly seen in declining budgets for higher education, in pedagogies that emphasize "test-taking, memorizing facts, and learning how not to question knowledge or authority," and in a curriculum that pushes "shallow consumerism" on students.[17] On the faculty side, the "neoliberal view of higher education" supposedly acts as a "market-driven paradigm that wants to eliminate tenure, turn the humanities into a job preparation service, and reduce most faculty to the status of part-time and temporary workers" akin to "indentured" servants, if not worse.[18] Administrative bloat, the expanded use of adjunct and part-time faculty, the prioritization of workforce-relevant STEM disciplines over knowledge-centered humanities, and the diminishment of faculty governance are all claimed symptoms of the neoliberal poltergeist's destructive rampage on the university system.

Like many works from the Critical Theory genre, Giroux's portrayal of the "neoliberal" university is heavy on jargon and sweeping generalizations but also backed with little data. But this kind of writing is unfortunately typical of a large segment of the academic literature on higher education. Giroux's assessment garnered almost 300 citations in academic journals and books within the first three years of its publication. Similar arguments have appeared in education journals for over a decade, linking universities to a government-driven quest for a "global neoliberal environment" premised upon the notion of an industry-connected "knowledge economy."[19]

As with any poltergeist, though, the "neoliberal university" is an almost imaginary creature. Like the "corporatization" spirits, it receives blame for all manner of observed and speculated ills in higher education. But at least corporations are defined and tangible entities, even if it turns out to not be very useful to compare the bureaucratized modern university to Google or Apple. Neoliberalism, in contrast, is little more than a vague and typically derogatory concept, asserted to be everywhere, and yet never really defined in any useful way except to point fingers of blame.

The "neoliberalism" narrative creates an odd contradiction in its own numbers. There are more scholars and activists decrying neoliberalism's supposed stranglehold over the world than there are actual self-described adherents of neoliberal ideology. Instead, neoliberalism seems to operate as a pejorative stand-in for free-market economics, for the economic sciences in general, for conservatism, for libertarians and anarchists, for authoritarianism and militarism, for advocates or the practice of commodification, for center-left or market-oriented progressivism, for globalism and welfare state social democracies, for being in favor of or against increased immigration, for favoring trade and globalization or opposing the same, or for really any set of political beliefs that happen to be disliked by the person(s) using the term. "Neoliberal" is a term of abuse among certain people on the hard Left, sort of like the word "fascist." Self-identified neoliberals are almost nowhere to be found, however.

Despite being told almost incessantly about the "neoliberal takeover" of higher education, most of this literature offers surprisingly little evidence for the specific claim. Instead, they just complain about budget cuts, administrative bloat, unfair hiring practices, and other general ills of academia.

If neoliberal ideology has infested and is ruining academia, then we should be able to do the following:

1. Identify who the neoliberals are.
2. Determine exactly when neoliberals first appeared and track their growth, especially in positions of power.
3. Show that bad events started to happen at higher rates when the neoliberals appeared or when neoliberal ideology took over.
4. Find some causal mechanism that explains how the neoliberals brought about those bad events.

The people who complain about neoliberalism, of course, don't pursue this approach. But if we take Step 1 and go looking for neoliberals, we find that their story breaks down.

College faculty on the whole are a famously left-leaning group (Figure 10.2). (We're not saying there's anything wrong with that, by the way.) According to a national 2014 survey of faculty political preferences, a full 60 percent of college professors self-identify as either "liberal" or "far-left." Just over 10 percent identify as "conservative" or "far-right," and the remainder state they are "moderates." The survey also showed that faculty opinions have shifted dramatically leftward over the past twenty years. Starting around 2000, both conservative and moderate faculty dropped in number, while self-described left-leaning liberals increased by almost 20 percentage points during the same period.[20]

The shift is even more pronounced if we go back further in time, when university faculty beliefs reflected a more balanced slice of perspectives. Left-liberals have always been a majority, but before 2000, they maintained a stable ratio along with conservatives and moderates. For example, a national faculty survey in 1984 suggested that about 34 percent of faculty identified as politically conservative—only a little shy of the conservative percentage in the general population.[21] Again as Figure 10.2 reveals, those numbers barely sit over 10 percent today. Meanwhile, the American population at large has retained a more stable distribution across the ideological spectrum.

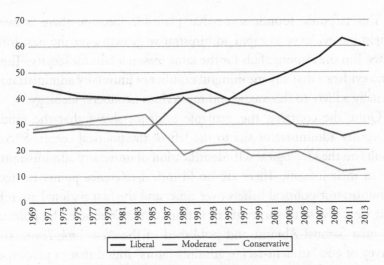

FIGURE 10.2 Political Self-Identification of University Faculty, 1969–2013

Sources: Carnegie Foundation, *National Survey of Higher Education*, 1969–1984, and Higher Education Research Institute, *Faculty Surveys*, 1989–2013.

In noting this leftward shift among faculty, we simply call attention to its implications for the "neoliberal" poltergeist. While neoliberalism remains ill-defined, the term's broad application usually extends to political issues that range from the political center to the political right on a single-dimension spectrum. In other words, if neoliberalization truly afflicted the university system, an independent observer might reasonably expect to see its fruits in the hiring of a greater number of new faculty who adhere to purported neoliberal values from the political right, or at least the center. Instead, we see the opposite phenomenon—the very same types of faculty whom critics of neoliberalism are most likely to describe as neoliberals have shrunk in number as the professoriate shifted leftward. Neoliberalism must be disappearing from, not taking over, the faculty.

"Aha!," a Critical Theorist or other proponent of this poltergeist theory might respond. "Neoliberalism hasn't infected the faculty yet! It's an outside phenomenon, coming from university administrators and the politicians and corporate leaders who hire them while cutting our own department funding! The faculty aren't the evil neoliberals; the neoliberals are the other institutions of power in the academy!"

This response sounds somewhat plausible, because there is overwhelming evidence of rapid administrative growth over the past forty years. But the response fails for the same reason it fails for faculty: There is no evidence that any meaningful number of university administrators actually adhere to this vague and mysterious neoliberal ideology.

Quite the contrary, the available evidence shows that the modal university administrator sits to the left of the political center. Survey results on the ideological self-identification of university administrators are in their infancy. There are no historical reference points to track administrator political beliefs over time, and the first national attempt that we know of to survey them is from 2018. Conducted by political scientist Samuel Abrams and published in the *New York Times,* this survey of 900 "student-facing administrators" found that 71 percent of respondents described themselves as "liberal" or "very liberal," while only 6 percent claimed to be conservatives of any degree.[22] In short, the ranks of university administration appear to exhibit an even *stronger* leftward political tilt than the well-documented leanings of the faculty.

While we cannot track this pattern over time due to lack of survey data, it is directly inconsistent with the claim that administrative bloat is also responsible for pushing a market-oriented "neoliberal" paradigm onto an unwilling faculty. We also have reason to expect that the opposite pattern is true, and that administrative bloat has paralleled the leftward ideological shift among faculty. Note from Figure 10.1 where the largest source of administrative growth in recent decades occurred. Executive-level administrators such as provosts, vice presidents, and deans expanded at a modest pace over the past forty years, but the overwhelming majority of growth actually took place in the lower ranks of the university bureaucracy. In 1976, there were fewer than 200,000 lower-level administrators. In four decades, that number expanded to over 800,000, growing at a faster pace than new faculty hiring.

Strong evidence exists that these lower-level administrative ranks are anything but "neoliberals." Figure 10.3 offers a snapshot of the 2017 Convention of the American College Personnel Association (ACPA), the largest professional gathering of student affairs administrators in the United States. We sorted the roughly 500 presentations and poster sessions on the conference program by topic to search for any content

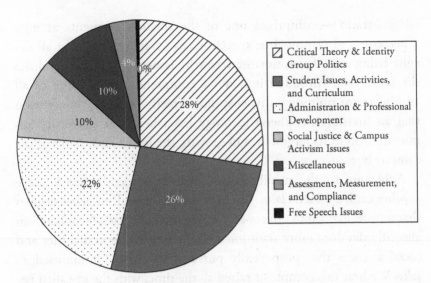

FIGURE 10.3 1969, 1975, and 1984 Carnegie Commission Faculty Surveys of Higher Education in the United States; 1989–present
Source: Faculty Survey, Higher Education Research Institute, UCLA.

that might be broadly described as serving "neoliberal" values within the administrative ranks of American universities.

The topic descriptions contained virtually no evidence of a "neoliberal takeover" of university administration, but it did mirror the progressive-left political skew that may be similarly observed in faculty ranks. Identity group politics (defined as presentations about racial, ethnic, gender, or class identities on campus) comprised the largest component of the schedule at 28 percent. Another 10 percent of sessions pertained to "social justice" causes and engaging in explicitly progressive political activism on campus.

At a combined 38 percent of the sessions, these two overtly political topic areas outpaced other more traditional presentations that would seem more pertinent to the daily job functions of student affairs administrators. Sessions on professional development made up 22 percent of the program. Sessions on the job functions of student affairs administrators (student issues, activities, and curriculum) accounted for just over a quarter. Measurement and assessment—sometimes labeled a distinctive feature of "neoliberal" administration—comprised one of the smallest segments at only 4 percent, and campus free speech issues barely registered at all despite being one of the most newsworthy issues in university politics the same year. Although it is not a comprehensive measure of all administrator opinions, this snapshot directly belies the contention that an invisible neoliberal ideology has taken over university administration in its largest area of growth, the lower-level ranks of the campus bureaucracy.

Adherents to the neoliberalism-is-ruining-academia-theory make another easily falsified claim. They say that neoliberalism prizes degrees that transfer easily into private-sector jobs and industries. Neoliberalism allegedly devalues more traditional disciplines in the humanities and social sciences that purportedly pursue knowledge for knowledge's sake. We hear this complaint raised all the time, with the so-called neoliberal university supposedly prioritizing science, technology, engineering, and mathematical (STEM) disciplines that translate easily into the "knowledge economy" of the private sector. Traditional subjects like philosophy, history, and English are supposedly left on the vine to wither, thereby shifting the curriculum away from a well-rounded instructional basis.

Yet as we showed in Chapter 8, faculty employment in both the humanities and social sciences has grown at faster and more continuous rates than either the natural sciences or engineering, both of which flattened out in the mid-2000s. What's more astounding, the humanities and social sciences teaching workforce continued to grow through the Great Recession of 2008, even as faculty hiring in the STEM fields cooled down. Only health sciences expanded at a faster pace during this period.

Even more significant, expansion in one of the largest humanities—English—took place *in spite of* a stagnant demand for majors in that subject. Between 1997 and 2014, the English faculty workforce grew by almost 50 percent. At the same time, the number of bachelor's degrees in English issued each year still sits at its 1997 level. It would appear that the allegedly "neoliberal" university system is actually ignoring many of the signals of its own growing and contracting majors, aside from shifting the latter into mandatory gen eds as we documented in Chapter 7.

In sum, the theory that neoliberalism has taken over the university system is completely unattested in empirical evidence. There's no indicator that an invisible cadre of "neoliberals" have seized control of faculty or administrative ranks, and evidence of one of the most frequently attributed harms of neoliberalism—the displacement of the humanities and social sciences by job-centric STEM disciplines—isn't anywhere to be found outside of anecdotes that ignore national empirical trends to the contrary. Instead, universities are increasingly full of left-wing faculty and administrators, and they're not giving preference to STEM hires.

Now, perhaps a more plausible version of the "neoliberals are destroying academia" story might go as follows:

> Sure, the faculty, administrators, staff, deans, students, and so on, aren't neoliberals. But neoliberalism has taken over state and federal legislatures, which explains why they're constantly cutting funding to the state universities. Neoliberalism is not some poltergeist haunting the university; rather, neoliberalism attacks from *outside*!

The good thing about this tale is that it's compatible with the almost complete absence of identifiable neoliberals within the university. But is it a good story?

A serious social scientist who asserted such an explanation would try to find some way to operationalize and measure neoliberalism and how much of a hold it has over state legislatures. They would try to show that as state legislatures become infected with neoliberalism, certain measurably bad events occur at the state universities. Furthermore, if the social scientist is being careful and honest, she would examine and debunk competing explanations for why those bad things happened. (For instance, are costs rising because of Baumol's Cost Disease? Are education funds being cut because states have mandatory but unfunded Medicare liabilities, or simply because states had less money after the Recession?[23] Are state legislatures cutting funding because the legislatures are Republican and the professors are all Democrats? Rather than being cut outright, are public funding strategies simply being shifted away from the direct appropriations model and into federal tuition grants and student loan subsidies?) Moreover, she would be careful not to *lie*. For instance, suppose that state legislatures *increase* the amount they spend on universities, but universities' operating costs, tuition, and so on, increase at an even higher rate. In that case, the *percent* of funding the state universities receive from the state would go down, even though the *absolute amount of money* the state universities receive from the state is going up. In this case, it would be either a careless mistake or downright mendacious to say that the state has *cut* funding to the universities.

We haven't found any careful social scientific papers making any such argument. But perhaps someone in the future will manage to do so. For now, the "neoliberalism is destroying academia" theory is, like the Bigfoot theory, an unsubstantiated but widely believed myth.

MYTH #3: THE COMING TECHNOLOGICAL DISRUPTION

A third common myth blames academia's woes not on imagined ghosts, but rather uncertainty over events that have yet to happen. This myth's prediction is straightforward and draws on a grain of truth rooted in recent technological innovations.

The Internet delivers unprecedented expansion in access to human knowledge. Information has never been easier or more affordable to obtain. Information that once required access to libraries or highly specialized levels of knowledge is now available on your cell phone. Millions of pages of academic journals are now online and searchable. Entire university library collections have been scanned and entered into online services such as Google Books and the Internet Archive. Experts from all over the world are even available for real-time advice using a variety of online message boards, video chats, and other specialty services. The same is true of classroom content, which can now be taught online and delivered live to laptops and tablets all over the world. For instance, MIT puts much of its class content online, free of charge. Even traditional forms of communication such as letters have been revolutionized by the near-instantaneous features of email.

But these technological advances leave many faculty and administrators worried. Some claim universities are not prepared to handle the unfolding tech revolution. Others issue apocalyptic warnings that technology may threaten the very existence of higher education itself. As the argument goes, technology-driven expansion of access to knowledge has reduced its cost to little more than time and bandwidth. Whereas universities used to be the cultivators and disseminators of advanced knowledge, that role is in the process of shifting online. When coupled with the rising costs of degrees, this massive expansion of access to knowledge forms something of an existential threat to the very purpose of the university itself. Instead of seeking degrees, prospective students can obtain specialized knowledge for "free" (well, really for the amount of time they choose to invest) on the Internet. Supplanted by this better and more efficient delivery system, the university's purpose withers away. Or, so it goes in the most extreme versions of this myth.

Bolstering the fear of a tech disruption, numerous higher ed commentators point to the emergence of new trends as warning signs of a potential apocalypse: the growth of online courses since the early 2000s; the rise of educational videos on YouTube and similar outlets, containing short specialized lessons in materials that traditionally appeared in the classroom; and since the early 2010s, the emergence of Massive Open Online Courses, or MOOCs, in which an entire university-level class curriculum is offered at little-to-no cost using online lectures, videos, and course readings that the user may access at his or her own pace. These patterns not only display the tangible signs of the mass dissemination of knowledge, they also will allegedly render the classroom-based degree program obsolete.

Versions of this myth fluctuate between the embrace of the potentials of mass access to knowledge and alarm over its claimed disruptive potential. As Kevin Carey contends in his widely discussed book on the MOOC phenomenon, "The great gift of higher education has been locked away from the vast majority of people" for most of recorded history. While he notes the relationship between knowledge and the power to control as a political component of this separation, the most important factor was that "the structures of higher education were limited by available technology"—the written word in books and volumes held by university libraries and interpreted by trained academics. With mixed optimism, Carey predicts a democratization of that knowledge through new technologies that "break" the logic of the traditional university model with easily accessible and widely disseminated information.[24]

To others within the existing university system, the theorized disruption has become a source of both hope and anxiety. When the MOOC phenomenon burst onto the higher ed scene around 2012, *TIME Magazine* speculated that they would put downward pressure on rising tuition rates as well as strip away some of the frivolous excesses of university spending.[25] The president of one large R1 university predicted a nationwide shakeup that would lead to the "end of higher education as we know it." He predicted a coming "shift" toward online platforms that would only accelerate as it caught hold, leading to a complete restructuring of the model and "value propositions" of traditional university education.[26] Other education commentators fretted that MOOCs portended the stratification of the college experience into a small elite sphere for the wealthy and a commoditized content-delivery system, stripped of personal learning interactions, for the rest.[27]

For the first couple of years of the MOOC explosion in the early 2010s, some academics even treated the theorized disruption as an existential crisis. Phil distinctly remembers one conversation from around this time with an academic peer who was exceptionally prone to latching onto new and trendy technological gimmicks. When Phil attempted to show this individual some statistical forecasts about faculty hiring patterns over the next decade, the colleague earnestly interrupted to declare: "We don't even know if universities are going to exist in 5 or 10 years!" Phil jokingly offered to wager a modest amount of money that the overwhelming majority of currently-operational traditional universities would both still exist at the end of the decade, and overall employment patterns would show clear faculty growth, as measured by the total number of full-time faculty employed in the sector. His colleague, who was certain of an impending contraction in traditional faculty hiring, probably would have been a willing taker of the bet. To this day, Phil regrets not actually putting money on the table.

Kevin Carey has since revised some of his predictions on the MOOC trend, writing in 2015 that the coming disruption was dampened by the lack of online platforms offering recognized college degrees. "Free online courses won't revolutionize education until there is a parallel system of free or low-fee credentials, not controlled by traditional colleges, that leads to jobs," he explains.[28] In one sense, he's right. But as we shall see shortly, credentialing is still controlled by traditional colleges and it's a substantial barrier to a competitor product.

There's a grain of truth to the role of technology as a force for change in the way colleges do business. But, to paraphrase Mark Twain, reports of the university system's demise have been greatly exaggerated.

Here's why the tech disruption theory is largely overblown. Tech disruption posits the mass dissemination of access to knowledge, which is true. But as we have seen in previous chapters, universities are *not* primarily in the business of imparting knowledge to students. They are in the business of issuing credentials.

A credential may indeed signify that its holder possesses a type of specialized knowledge in a subject area. Higher degrees also usually signify higher levels of mastery of a subject. It is also true that universities curate knowledge in the form of research output, structured curricula, and instructional methods. But let's think through the purpose of possessing a degree itself, as distinct from simply taking classes and reading books to consume the subjects they curate.

Let's take a hypothetical case of two individuals, Matthew and Melissa, who are intellectually fascinated with the history of the French Revolution. Both became intrigued by the subject in high school upon reading Charles Dickens' classic novel *A Tale of Two Cities*. From this spark of interest, both began consuming everything they could find about the Girondins and Jacobins, about Louis XVI and Robespierre, and about the storming of the Bastille, the Thermidorian Reaction, and the rise of Napoleon. When they get to college, they both take classes on the subject and sign up for a study abroad program in Paris to see the sites they've imagined so much about through books, websites, and documentaries.

From this point, though, their paths diverge. Matthew decides he wants to pursue a career in studying the French Revolution. He majors in history and decides to get a master's degree in museum studies, hoping to work as a curator. He is hired by a museum that holds one of the largest collections of French Revolutionary–era artifacts outside of Europe. He regularly travels to conferences at historical sites in France to meet other curators and archivists, and sets out on a career that involves daily interaction with the subject that sparked his historical imagination back in high school.

Melissa becomes intrigued by another class she takes during her soph-omore year—economics—and decides to switch majors. She graduates with an economics degree and accepts an offer to extend her studies to a master's in business administration. She's hired as a management con-sultant in a private firm and becomes very well off financially. Through all the years of study and work in other fields, she never loses interest in her old hobby of historical reading about the French Revolution. She still buys and reads every new book she can find on the subject, and she returns to France regularly on vacation as an adult to tour museums and historical sites.

Both Matthew and Melissa possess extremely high levels of special-ized knowledge on the French Revolution. Both have read the same books and can recount facts, dates, and major interpretive arguments about the French Revolution in conversation. Both are up to date on their knowledge as well—Matthew by the necessity of his job, and Melissa simply as a hobby. All else equal, both could probably teach an introductory college course on the French Revolution with little difficulty.

Yet Matthew and Melissa still differ in one substantial way: their credentials. And credentials matter for reasons beyond the simple con-sumption of knowledge. Though we might legitimately critique some of the entry barriers that credentialing entails, it effectively means our two individuals have very different career options despite a very similar level of knowledge. Matthew's advanced degree in museum studies is treated as a prerequisite for most jobs in archival work and curation. Melissa is not eligible for the same positions, even though she possesses a very high level of knowledge on the same subject area. (She would, by contrast, be considered for a number of jobs requiring MBAs, where Matthew would stand no chance.) Both Matthew and Melissa likely knew this when they chose their respective degree programs. Their dif-ferent paths of study reflected the credentials they each needed to ob-tain in order to pursue certain specific careers, even as both possess comparable levels of knowledge in the same subject area.

This example serves to illustrate a key feature of the signaling model of higher education: A degree is not a measurement of knowledge it-self, but rather a signifier that a person has completed certain steps and tasks that are—for a wide variety of reasons—expected prerequisites in particular careers. As Melissa's example illustrates, it is entirely possible to acquire high levels of knowledge about a specialized subject without parallel university training. But pathways to prerequisite credentials are more limited to specific tasks, and without them Melissa's high level of knowledge would be of little use in landing a museum job like the one that Matthew holds.

So, what does credentialing mean for the hypothesized technological disruption? As it turns out, everything. Tech disruption theorists such as Carey focus almost entirely on how access to knowledge has never been easier to come by. But credentials are not easier to come by; indeed, they cannot become easier and still function as credentials.

Consider an example. Imagine it becomes possible to download skills and knowledge directly and instantly into people's brains, as in *The Matrix*. (You may recall Neo pressed a button and suddenly he knew kung fu.) Now imagine two people, John and Kate. John has downloaded everything people learn when they get a biology degree at Columbia. Kate actually obtained a biology degree at Columbia. Whom would you rather hire? You might as well pick Kate. One thing you know about her, but not John, is that she is conscientious and perseverant enough to spend four years jumping through hoops to complete a degree. She is more likely, as far as you know, to be a great worker and colleague.

With that simple example in mind, let's now consider the case of the much-discussed MOOCs. In the last few years, hundreds of colleges and a number of private entities have begun offering these online platforms for college-level instruction in a variety of subject areas. According to the tech disruption argument, courses of this type threaten to become inexpensive competitors to instruction using the same content in a traditional classroom. Instead of twenty or thirty students in classroom requiring physical space, the MOOC may reach thousands of people all over the world. The professor need not attend the class in person—she gives her lectures online, or may even be able to record them once and use the video for several semesters in a row. University administrators find this model appealing because it saves them from needing to hire faculty and find classroom space. Non-university entities similarly begin to offer their own competitor products by taking advantage of the low cost to enter the "knowledge" market. Soon enough, the university system itself discovers that its traditional model is being outcompeted and undermined by a low-cost MOOC alternative.

MOOCs induce anxiety about impending obsolescence. But before we throw in the towel for the professoriate, though, let's consider how credentialing alters this narrative. As told in the tech disruption argument, MOOCs threaten to fundamentally change the instructional model of higher education by making knowledge—once a feature of the classroom, and only then at high costs and time investment—available to the masses for pennies on the dollar. That may be entirely true, but it does not fundamentally alter the credential, which, as we've argued, is the real product of the university system.

To this end, MOOCs have proven much less suited for the issuing of credentials than the mass dissemination of knowledge. The reason derives from a matter of reputation.

Suppose you surf the Internet one day and come across a website offering an online degree in philosophy for one-tenth the cost of the same degree at a traditional university. As a casual reader of philosophy, you're intrigued and decide to click on the site. You read about the program and find that its courses are essentially MOOCs, which you can take at your own pace. A few of them even feature guest lectures by "star" philosophy faculty, although they are all recordings that were prepared in advance. To obtain your degree, you must submit nominal assignments to achieve certain "milestones." They are graded by an instructor affiliated with the school who may possess an advanced degree, but otherwise has no major academic distinction—but that's sold as a plus since you get the recorded content of "star" faculty without having to pay the associated price tag. You can complete the courses at your own pace, though, and advertisements on the site even point to other program participants who finished their degrees in only two years, as opposed to four at a traditional college.

There's a hitch, however: The website offering this online degree through MOOC-style classes is not recognized by any educational accreditor. Upon a little further research, you find out that the online university has poor Yelp reviews and appears on a couple of watch lists of institutions that issue "substandard" degrees. It doesn't have a physical campus either in any normal sense and instead rents a storefront office at a strip mall in Oregon, or perhaps a more exotic locale at a former condominium complex in the Swiss Alps. It hosts occasional in-person events at its physical building, but they resemble short weeklong speaker seminars rather than classroom education and they all come with a much heftier price tag than the online product. All these signs strongly portend that few prospective employers will view a degree from this institution as reputable. Is the program's convenience and low cost still worth it to you as a consumer? If your interest is only acquiring knowledge of philosophy as a consumption good, perhaps. If your interest is getting a credential for improved employment prospects in the field of philosophy, almost certainly not.

And herein lies a fundamental trade-off of the MOOC phenomenon—to the extent that MOOC providers seek to enter the traditional credentialing market of universities, their product is necessarily dependent on reputation and accreditation. For this reason, MIT and Cornell might be able to offer an online version of some of their classes at lower cost, and with attached certification credentials or even credits toward an eventual degree upon the completion of certain tasks. In doing so, they are banking on the reputation of their own institutions, which, in turn, is dependent on the quality of their faculty and the accreditation status of their traditional educational functions. An unaccredited storefront university in Oregon has no comparable reputation to attract any sizable number of credential-seeking students to its programs, and those who do complete them will likely be spending money on a degree of little recognized worth.

Note that in this model, MOOCs still serve an intriguing purpose for higher education. It is simply a different purpose than the competitive replacement posited by the tech disruption argument. Rather, they are better understood as ancillary product offerings to expand the consumer base of higher education. Consider people like Melissa in our earlier example, who may sign up for an online course on the French Revolution out of a simple interest and passion for the subject. Melissa does not expect to be handed a master's degree in history upon completing the course or even an extended online course sequence. In fact, she may not want a certification at all—she simply expects to deepen her knowledge of the subject, just as one might do by reading a book or attending a public lecture at a museum.

All else considered, Melissa probably would not be willing to spend $6,000 for course credits in a class on the French Revolution at her local university. She has a career of her own, and the expense and time of taking that course would be hard to justify for pure consumption reasons, especially if she never intended to get a degree in that specialization. But she may sign up for a nondegree version of the same course offered online if she's simply interested in the subject. She may be willing to pay $50 to register for the MOOC simply so she can listen to a series of lectures by an expert on a subject that she finds interesting.

In this sense, the MOOC is filling a role very similar to many other long-standing features of the education economy: It is similar to auditing a course in person for nondegree purposes, or listening to a "Great Books" recorded lecture series during your daily commute to work. The MOOC boom of the 2010s is better understood as a high-tech expansion of these common and long-established university practices to reach an even broader audience of students who desire a structured form of accessible knowledge without the need to complete a full degree program. Far from a disruptive and revolutionary concept that seeks to supplant higher education, the MOOC actually has more in common with such well-known predecessors as the correspondence course, the recorded lecture on cassette tape, and the in-person continuing education class offered to nondegree seekers at a discount.

Colleges are also inclined to offer online courses of this type at low costs for similar reasons: These courses expand the university's student base to a wider pool of consumers, including those who do not wish to commit to or pay for a full degree program. They might provide an entry point to university study for potential students who only wish to test the waters before committing to a degree. They also provide public educational services in the form of low-cost content, thereby building up a university's brand and goodwill in its community. And they might allow a university to price-discriminate on its existing course offerings by extending their content to non-degree seekers at a discount.

Unless there's a complete disruption of the functional role that credentialing plays in the larger employment market, the functions of MOOCs and similar tech-savvy educational products will remain complements rather than competitors.

THE BIGGER PICTURE

The problem with blaming all these poltergeists and gremlins is that we don't have any real evidence they exist or cause difficulties. Throughout this book, we've been able to account for systematic bad behavior just by looking at incentives built into jobs and roles. Complaining about "neoliberalism" or "corporatism" adds next to nothing. Predicting technological apocalypse when a more careful study of a phenomenon reveals stable commonalities with the older way of doing business amounts to alarmism. Instead of pointing fingers at distant objects of blame, we should be looking to the bigger picture of human behavior in the presence of everyday incentives. In the same way that you don't need to posit "God did it" once you understand evolutionary biology, you don't need to posit "neoliberalism did it" once you recognize the incentives built into the structure.

II

Answering Taxpayers

AMERICAN COLLEGES AND UNIVERSITIES spend about half a trillion dollars a year on direct operations.[1] The National Center for Education Statistics reports:

> In academic year 2014–15, postsecondary institutions in the United States spent $536 billion (in current dollars). Total expenses were $336 billion at public institutions, $182 billion at private nonprofit institutions, and $18 billion at private for-profit institutions.[2]

Federal, state, and local governments cover a large portion of these expenses. The Pew Charitable Trusts report:

> In 2013, federal spending on major higher education programs totaled $75.6 billion, state spending amounted to $72.7 billion, and local spending was considerably lower at $9.2 billion. These figures exclude student loans and higher education–related tax expenditures.[3]

The numbers cited include over $30 billion in Pell Grants (to pay students' tuition), about $10 billion in state-funded tuition assistance, about $25 billion in federal research grants, and $53 billion in state general allocations to higher ed. So, excluding government-sponsored loans, in 2013, the federal, state, and local governments spent about $158 billion on higher ed. If we include government-sponsored student loans, this jumps up another $104 billion to $262 billion total.[4]

Overall, colleges obtain about 37 percent of their revenue from the government.

This number still does not include indirect spending, such as the public goods that colleges consume without having to pay taxes. Colleges don't pay for roads, police, fire departments, military defense, or whatnot in the communities where they operate. They also enjoy substantial tax benefits on everything from the property they own to the purchases they make to the way they invest money under their endowments. So, colleges receive other hidden subsidies and perks not reflected in those numbers.

A dollar spent on higher ed is a dollar not spent on medicine, art, music, aid to women with dependent children, police protection, housing the homeless, or some other cause. To justify government spending and subsidies to higher ed, one has to explain why it's a better use of the money than any of the available alternatives. Think of all the possibly good and wonderful things governments could do with $262 billion and then ask, why not do those things instead?

For instance, left-wing economist Jeffrey Sachs argues in *The End of Poverty* that rich first world countries could rid the world of extreme poverty with an additional $60 billion to $130 billion in aid funding per year for the next decade or so.[5] Maybe he's wrong and it's not that easy. But, if Sachs were right, we'd have to ask: Why not cut US spending on higher ed by $60 billion and instead use that money to end world poverty?

Or, we often hear people complain that US infrastructure is crumbling. The American Society of Civil Engineers (ASCE) claim the government needs to spend $1 trillion just to bring the highway and road system "up to date," and that doesn't include other needed repairs for dams or railways.[6] (Of course, we don't take ASCE's claims at face value—after all, ASCE's job is to advocate for civil engineers, the very people who would make lots of money if the government rebuilt the roads, railways, and dams.)

Students do repay some, if not all, of their federal and state loans, so you might balk at us including government-subsidized loans in our numbers. However, federal and state student loans still need to be justified as public expenditures. For one, they give preferential economic benefits to people who spend money on higher education.

After all, you probably don't think the government should offer low-interest-rate loans for people to buy sports cars, high-gain tube amplifiers, singing lessons, or Caribbean cruises. If the government offers people loans, those loans better serve some legitimate *public* purpose. The government isn't Citibank; it's not and should not be in the personal loan business. Second, there's a growing body of evidence that suggests publicly subsidized loans are at least partially driving the rise in college tuition levels. One recent study estimated that as much as 60 cents of every dollar spent on subsidized federal loans gets passed on as tuition hikes. Another analysis suggested the rise in tuition attributable to subsidized loans may actually crowd out some of the new enrollment it is intended to stimulate.[7] Thus, public subsidies of loans also have substantial spillovers on the price tag of college, whether you use a loan or not. But if for some reason you disagree about tabulating student loans along with other public expenditures on colleges, that's fine: Just read the rest of this chapter as talking about the other $158 billion American governments spend each year.

Now ask: What would it take to show that this money was well spent?

ACADEMIA AS A PUBLIC GOOD?

A very common argument for why the government should pay for higher ed goes as follows:

The Public Goods Argument
1. Higher education is a public good.
2. Public goods must be financed by the government, since the market will underprovide them.
3. Therefore, the government should finance higher ed.

Even if, for the sake of argument, we grant premise 2, this argument has two big problems. First, it doesn't tell us *how much* government should pay for—it doesn't tell us what the optimal level of public goods provision is. This argument might show that government should finance higher ed, but it doesn't tell us whether we should increase spending, keep it the same, or decrease it. In the same way, if you demonstrate that a public park is a public good, that doesn't tell you by itself how many parks to build or how nice the parks ought to be.

But second, and more importantly, premise 1 is overstated. Higher ed is not really a public good.

Hold on. Don't get angry.

"Public good" is a technical term in economics. The term does not mean "a good the government ought to pay for." We might believe that the government should provide aid to poor families, but that doesn't make such aid a *public good* per se. Rather, the word "public good" refers to a good that is *non-excludable* and *non-rivalrous*. To say a good is non-excludable means that when you provide it for some, you provide it for all, and you can't keep others from using it. To say it's non-rivalrous means that when one person consumes the good, it doesn't come at the expense of or prevent others from consuming it. So, an example of a genuine public good would be an asteroid defense system—if you protect one person from asteroid strikes, you protect them all.

Universities are both excludable and rivalrous. Harvard's admission rate is under 5 percent; they're leading experts at excluding would-be consumers and brag about just how much excluding they do. Furthermore, access to education is rivalrous—as you increase class size, you decrease access to professors and other resources. A 1,000-student class has a different dynamic from a 5-person class. As for the research portion, research may not be entirely rivalrous, but thanks to subscription requirements and the like, it is excludable.

A more sophisticated version of the public goods argument says instead that while higher ed is predominantly not a public good, it nevertheless has certain positive spillovers or externalities. Paying people to do research and educating students creates certain costs for society as a whole, but—according to the argument—left to its own devices, the market would underinvest in this research or education.

This kind of argument might well be sound. But whoever asserts it bears a burden of proof. That person would need to identify what the positive spillovers are, demonstrate that there really are such spillovers, identify how valuable those spillovers are, and then determine how much governments should spend to create those spillovers. "Universities are good for society, so let's pay *more*" isn't even the beginning of a serious argument. Maybe universities are good for society, but right now we're spending $10 in subsidies for every additional $1 of social value. Maybe it's the other way around. We'd need to check. There is an optimal level of public investment in higher education, and we don't know a priori whether we're below or above that level.

Moreover, universities do many different things, research and teach many different subjects, and conduct many different activities. Perhaps some of these have greater public returns than others. Biology and medical research that leads to better cancer treatments are easier to justify than research on obscurantist art and poetry. (And we say that even though one of us loves obscurantist art and poetry.)

We're not philistines who lack appreciation for fine art. We're happy to accept the mantra that medicine keeps you alive but Shakespeare gives you a reason to live.

But do universities actually help teach people to appreciate the humanities? As Bryan Caplan argues in *The Case Against Education*, there is scant evidence that college education induces appreciation for highbrow culture or is particularly useful for keeping such culture alive.[8] It tries to induce appreciation for the humanities, but it usually fails. That's too bad, but when you discover a medicine doesn't work, you don't keep prescribing that same medicine.

WHAT DO UNIVERSITIES DO, AND WHY SHOULD THE PUBLIC PAY FOR IT?

Let's just make a list of the possible functions of the university. We can then ask what it would take to show that the public should pay for any of these functions:

1. *Universities as museums of ideas.* According to this model, a university is like an art museum, but it houses ideas rather than paintings. It preserves and protects big ideas, displays these ideas to the public, and tries to induce appreciation for these ideas.

For this justification to succeed, you'd need to show that however much you're spending on this purpose, the ideas are worth protecting and preserving at such a price, that displaying the ideas to the public "works," and that your spending actually succeeds in inducing appreciation for those ideas.

Furthermore, you'd always need to show that the price is worth it. We the authors might believe it would be wonderful if the average person came to appreciate the French philosopher Michel Foucault, but we wouldn't say it's worth $10 million to get 10 people to read and understand Foucault. Note that it could still be true that Foucault inspires brilliance in students. It could also be the case that Foucault is difficult to understand even among specialists. Or, maybe he's just not all that insightful or useful outside of a small number of Foucault specialists. Those and other questions about the return to the public are pertinent when asking about using tax dollars to fund an intellectual museum to Foucault studies.

In addition, academia doesn't seem to function as if were a museum or if it even wants to be a museum. Museums are usually run with some active concern for the public interest. They specialize in styles of art, branches of science, periods of history, or specific types of artifacts that have both specialist and generalist followings. They often try to tailor their displays and subject matters to the visitors they expect to attract, and they run special exhibits to generate interest in their collections. In contrast, universities research whatever the professors feel like researching. They hire whichever professors the other professors feel like hiring. To a significant extent, they offer whatever classes the professors feel like teaching, and even game the gen ed system to force students to take classes in unpopular subjects with declining enrollment. Now perhaps this model unintentionally leads to a good museum environment, but the public good sure isn't on professors' minds.

2. *Enlightening and ennobling students.* According to this model, the purpose of the university is to make students smarter and better. Universities are supposed to cultivate certain virtuous habits of mind, including curiosity, open-mindedness, critical thinking skills, the ability to integrate disparate ideas, the ability to apply principles to novel but analogous cases, tolerance, and so on.

Again, even if you could show that universities succeed in doing these things, you still have to ask, "Is the amount of enlightenment and ennoblement we get worth the price we pay?" Some may balk at the idea of putting a price on virtue. But, au contraire, we all do so every day. Instead of watching *Game of Thrones*, you could train your brain with logic games. Instead of spending $5,000 on trip to Fiji, you could take art appreciation classes or undergo anti-racism training. Every time we chose one thing over another, we implicitly put a price on everything else, including virtue. So, however much virtue universities induce in their students, we have to then question, "Is that increase in virtue worth the price society paid for it?"

But this may all be moot. As we saw in Chapter 3, it's far from clear universities do much to enlighten and ennoble students. In the *short term*, it looks as if half of students learn nothing, 40 percent learn almost nothing, and only 10 percent learn a great deal. In the long term, much of that learning probably fades away. There is little to no evidence higher education does much to foster students' moral virtue.

3. *Training for future employment.* Here, the idea is that colleges train students to become better employees. Colleges impart the skills students need to succeed in their future jobs.

But this argument faces a few major problems. First, it's unclear why it would then be the government's job to provide such training. They'd have to show they're generating a public rather than purely private benefit. After all, the government doesn't subsidize Chick-fil-A by paying to train its nugget fryers. Why should it subsidize Goldman Sachs by paying to teach people how to calculate net present value?

Second, as Chapter 3 illustrated, it's not clear that most students get any real training. Most of what students learn is irrelevant to their future jobs. They forget most of what they learn. Their soft skills do not develop much. And there is little evidence that students transfer the few skills they learn in college to their future jobs.

Third, employers seem quite willing to train employees at their own expense. Private employers provided roughly $410 billion in informal training and $180 billion in formal training per year in recent years.[9] Private employers spend far more training their employees than the US federal and state governments spend in total on postsecondary education. Now, perhaps this amount turns out not to be enough, but if you believe that, you need to provide real evidence to that effect.

4. *A sorting mechanism for future employers.* In this model, the purpose of education isn't to make employees better, but to help potential future employers separate the wheat from the chaff. Completing a four-year college degree at a good school demonstrates to employers that you are probably smart and perseverant, and will likely interact well with others.

Even higher ed's biggest critics agree education plays this sorting function.[10] But the problem is that it's unclear why governments should pay hundreds of billions a year just to reduce employers' search costs. Why not have employers pay those costs instead?

Furthermore, this model predicts that people will seek ever better credentials to distinguish themselves, leading to a credentials' arms race that is individually rational but socially destructive.[11] Subsidizing employer search costs *increases* the total amount spent on search costs.

To illustrate what we mean, imagine the manager at Chotchkies Restaurant wishes to assess which of his waiters are the most enthusiastic and perseverant. Suppose he can't easily measure this directly, so he uses a proxy: the amount of "flair" his waiters wear. If the average waiter has three pieces of flair, then he can distinguish himself by wearing four pieces. But, because this is true for everyone, four pieces of flair will become the new normal, so waiters looking to demonstrate their superiority will wear five. And so on. Three years later, you find all the waiters wearing at least twenty pieces. The manager's ability to distinguish the best from the rest hasn't changed—it doesn't matter to him whether the average number of pieces is three or twenty—but the waiters are engaging in progressively more expensive behavior to achieve the same distinction. Search costs have increased dramatically, but the system is no more efficient at separating the wheat from the chaff.

The same thing happens with educational credentials: If everyone has only a high school diploma, then everyone develops an incentive to acquire a BA. If everyone has a BA, then you distinguish yourself with an MA. Insofar as governments are paying for people to obtain better credentials, they are also inducing everyone to acquire ever better credentials.

The downside of this model is that you fill classrooms with people who don't care about learning; they just want the credential. This is a simple anecdote, but illustrative: One of our German colleagues complains that half his *PhD students* are seeking the PhD not because they love generating new knowledge or doing research, but because it helps them get choice jobs with the most prestigious corporations.

We also know several faculty colleagues who teach extra evening courses in various master's programs on public administration or political science. These degrees are hot commodities in the Washington, DC, region, because several companies that contract with the federal government also base their promotions on the number of credentials attained. Very few students in these programs take them because they are interested in the academic study of American government, but almost all are interested in the pay increase that frequently comes with an advanced degree. In some public-sector jobs, this credentialing arms race is even formalized. To move up in level on the state or federal pay scale, you sometimes have to reach a certain level of certification or obtain a more advanced degree. Although the added credential may not actually improve your performance on the job, you can now check a box that places you in a higher salary bracket.

5. *Knowledge creation.* According to this model, the purpose of the university is to create new knowledge. Universities are not simply museums of ideas; they are idea-generators.

This model faces some familiar problems. Even if we believe research or new knowledge is good, we have to ask how much good it is, and how much we should spend on it. Perhaps we already overspend, or perhaps we underspend. To take a stance either way, one needs to provide plausible evidence of the public benefit of certain forms of research and knowledge, find a way to attach a monetary value to that benefit, and then finally show that society *profits* by paying for this research, because the public value of the research is higher than the price the public pays.

In addition, not at all research is the same. It's relatively easy to demonstrate a public benefit from medical or engineering advancements.

It's harder to justify public expenditures on history or political philosophy. It's even harder to justify public expenditures on twelfth-century, avant-garde Romanian poetry. Not all knowledge is the same. Some new knowledge—such as how to cure cancer, or perhaps how to reduce wasteful spending in higher ed—might be worth the price the government pays. Other bits of knowledge, such as assessing whether Plato and Aristotle had the same tastes in food, might intrigue a few people, but don't seem like a wise public investment.

Furthermore, this kind of justification—that universities are knowledge-generators—at best applies to a minority of professors and a small number of universities and colleges. The Carnegie Classification of Institutions of Higher Education categorizes American institutions of higher ed according to various categories, including what kinds of degrees they offer, what kinds of students they serve, how large they are, and how much research they produce. Out of the 4,660 institutions they list,[12] only about 300 are research-oriented universities producing significant amounts of research. Now, some liberal arts colleges (e.g., Amherst or Williams) have faculty that produce significant research, while some "R3" universities have faculty that publish very little. Some professors with 4-4 teaching loads manage to publish books and articles, while some professors with cushy 2-2 loads at R1s publish nothing. Still, the majority of professors in the US are teachers first, researchers second. Only a minority consistently publish year after year.

The Higher Education Research Institute at UCLA conducts a biennial survey of professors' behavior and attitudes at four-year or more colleges and universities. Their results are self-reported, so thanks to desirability bias, professors probably exaggerate their number of publications. Still, the survey indicates that a minority of faculty produce the majority of research. Twenty-eight percent of faculty say they have published nothing in the past two years, while another 31 percent admit they've published only 1 or 2 papers. So, about 60 percent percent of faculty average less than 1 publication a year. Another 20 percent published 3–4 pieces over the last two years, 14.7 percent published between 5–10 pieces, 3.9 percent between 11–20 pieces, and 1.8 percent published 21 or more.[13]

Their data are not fine-grained enough for us to say something as precise as "X percent of the faculty publish Y percent of the research."

But we can make a low estimate. Let's charitably assume that all the professors at the low end of the survey always hit the maximum of their publication range. (For example, assume everyone in the "3–4 publications over the past two years" category each published only 4 articles.) Let's also assume that highly productive faculty all hit the minimum of their range. (For example, assume that all the professors in the "5–10 articles" category each published only 5, all the professors in the "11–20 articles" category each published only 11, and all the professors in the "21 or more articles" category each published only 21.) Even based on this heroic assumption, the 20 percent of faculty in the high range of publication published more than the 80 percent in the low range. So, at a bare minimum, 20 percent of faculty publish at least 52 percent of all research.

Suppose we instead assume that the faculty, on average, publish in the middle of their survey range. For the 1.8 percent who published 21 or more pieces in the last year, let's assume they, on average, published 25 pieces. Based on these assumptions, the top 20 percent of faculty published 2 pieces for every 1 piece the bottom 80 percent published.[14]

In fact, these numbers seem to inflate how much publishing professors end up doing. The HERI survey also contains data about how many *total* pieces faculty have published over their careers. In fact, 63.2 percent have never published a book, 44.9 percent have never published a chapter in an edited volume, and 17.2 percent have never published a peer-reviewed article. Only about 21 percent have published 21 or more articles in their careers, while about 70 percent have published 10 or fewer articles in their careers.[15] Basic arithmetic tells us that the 20 percent of faculty who have published at least 21 articles have, *at bare minimum*, published as a group (over their careers) almost twice what the remaining 80 percent of faculty have collectively published over their entire careers.[16]

Maybe part of the point of higher ed is to produce original research, but this justification for government spending can only account for a small percentage of faculty. Most faculty produce only a small amount of research. That said, *perhaps* if governments spent more on knowledge generation, a higher percent of faculty would become consistent knowledge-generators. After all, as of now, professors at research-intensive universities (RIs) produce research at a higher rate than others. But these professors also have the lightest teaching loads and the most research funding. It is no surprise that professors who teach two to three classes a year and who get automatic research sabbaticals every seven years publish more than professors who teach eight to ten classes a year and rarely receive research leave. So perhaps increasing the full-time faculty-to-student ratio would lead to higher research output. Still, whether this would be worth the increased expense is an open question.

6. *Economic stimulus.* Another argument for government funding of universities holds that they are useful as a kind of economic stimulus, especially in the immediate neighborhoods or regions where they exist.

For example, economists Anna Valero and John van Reenen summarize their recent paper on this point:

> We develop a new dataset using UNESCO source materials on the location of nearly 15,000 universities in about 1,500 regions across 78 countries, some dating back to the 11th century. We estimate fixed effects models at the sub-national level between 1950 and 2010 and find that increases in the number of universities are positively associated with future growth of GDP per capita (and this relationship is robust to controlling for a host of observables, as well as unobserved regional trends). Our estimates imply that doubling the number of universities per capita is associated with 4% higher future GDP per capita. Furthermore, there appear to be positive spillover effects from universities to geographically close neighboring regions. We show that the relationship between growth and universities is not simply driven by the direct expenditures of the university, its staff and students. Part of the effect of universities on growth is mediated through an increased supply of human capital and greater innovation (although the magnitudes are not large).[17]

One might worry that even if creating a university caused local economic growth, this would merely be a kind of redistribution. Perhaps new universities attract already skilled people from elsewhere. Or, perhaps universities create local growth only because they are funded by taxes or grants from elsewhere. In either case, the growth would be somewhat illusory—it would mean that overall there was no real growth, but instead that the local gains (in increased spending or brainpower) come at the expense of external losses (the places taxed to provide the funding, or the places that lost population and brainpower).

The good news is that Valero and van Reesen try carefully to measure and control for such merely redistributive effects, and still find that universities are associated with real growth. Nevertheless, while it's clear that growth in universities is positively correlated with economic growth, it's not exactly clear whether universities cause growth or growth causes universities—that is, it could be that creating a university causes growth, or it could be that as places grow richer, they are more likely to create new universities.[18]

Even if one can show that funding universities has certain positive fiscal stimulus effects, one would then want to determine A) what the optimal level of funding is, and B) whether *other* forms of government investment in other industries have an even greater stimulus effect. At any rate, most defenders of the university would be quite depressed to discover that the main justification for funding universities is that they turn out to be decent urban renewal projects.

7. *Making democracy work.* In *Not for Profit: Why Democracy Needs the Humanities*, philosopher Martha Nussbaum attempts to argue that humanities education is essential for developing a public well-equipped to engage in self-rule. She worries that the current push for practical education has a practical downside: It prevents people from learning the skills they need to understand each other, deliberate about politics, and rule together.

Early on in her book, Nussbaum gives us a plausible wish list of the skills good democratic citizens need, including:

- the ability to think well about issues affecting the nation, to examine, reflect, argue, and debate, deferring to neither tradition nor authority.
- the ability to recognize fellow citizens as people with equal rights. . . .

- the ability to have concern for the lives of others, to grasp what [effects policies have on others].
- the ability to judge political leaders critically. . . .
- the ability to think about the good of the nation as a whole. . . .
- the ability to see one's own nations . . . as part of a complicated world order in which issues of many kinds require intelligent transnational deliberation for their resolution.[19]

Nussbaum provides a plausible a priori argument for why a well-functioning democracy needs citizens, in general, to have these skills. She does not, however, offer empirical evidence that real-life democratic dysfunction results from citizens lacking these skills.

Furthermore, she provides little evidence that the humanities, in fact, impart such skills. Her book is mostly a summary of others' speculation. She discusses at great length how various famous philosophers, poets, and novelists have speculated in one way or another how a certain kind of humanistic education might ennoble or enlighten people in various ways. She describes a handful of case studies or pedagogical experiments, some old and some new, and some of which indicate education has some positive effect. However, in the end, she leaves us with a number of plausible but largely untested hypotheses about how humanistic education could help make us better citizens.

In principle, her hypotheses can be tested socially and scientifically. We could measure students' skills (to see how much they realize Nussbaum's wish list listed here), then put them through some of her favored humanistic educational methods, then measure them again after the class, and then again 5, 10, and 20 years later, to see if the methods had any lasting positive effect. We'd have to control carefully for selection versus treatments, as we discussed in Chapter 3. But, unfortunately, as of now, we just don't know whether humanities education does or even can deliver the goods Nussbaum hopes it will. Nussbaum may be right that we need the humanities, but she needs the social sciences to discover whether she's right.

It's worth noting that level of education, as an independent variable, seems to have little effect on voters' basic political knowledge. As Ilya Somin discusses in *Democracy and Political Ignorance*, studies generally find that going from a high school diploma to a bachelor's degree predicts, when controlling for confounding variables, that a person will get 1.3 more questions correct on a 30-question battery of basic political knowledge.[20] Of course, this lumps together all college-educated people. The data don't tell us how humanities versus science majors do. They don't measure whether students have acquired any of Nussbaum's favored skills. But at least they clarify that college education has little independent effect on basic knowledge.

At any rate, even if Nussbaum were right, this wouldn't necessarily defend all or even most of the research and teaching in the humanities or the social sciences. It would at best justify the research and teaching that turn out to improve civic virtue and civic performance. It's possible that certain classes or even humanities have no effect, or even a negative effect. Maybe having students read Cicero and Douglas makes them better democratic participants, while having them read critical studies makes them worse participants. Or, maybe it all goes the other way around. We don't really know. (We went through Google Scholar and couldn't find studies validating or even testing such hypotheses.)

SO, WHAT ARE UNIVERSITIES FOR?

We are largely agnostic about what universities are really "for." We don't think there's some essential function or *telos* a university, or higher ed as a whole, must by nature perform or serve. Different schools can legitimately pick different missions. Some schools might be about empowering women, or minorities, or the poor. Some might be about helping farmers farm better. Some might be about producing original and ground-breaking physics research. Some might be about creating an educated class of workers. Some are for keeping the classics alive. Some are for reimagining what the "classics" are. And so on.

Our only deep normative commitment is that if a university embarks on some mission at the public's expense, it had better be a good steward of the public's trust, and it better deliver on its promises. In particular, it had better provide an output of greater value than the value of the inputs it consumes. Consider this our minimum theory of just expenditures: If a university takes government money for a particular purpose, then society should as a result be better off. Perhaps even that's too strong—after all, sometimes we need to take risks, and sometimes the risks don't pay off. When you go looking for a cure for cancer, most of the time, you'll fail. Many pedagogical experiments fail, but were worth trying. So, let's instead offer a *bare* minimum theory of just expenditures: If a university takes government money for a particular purpose, society should generally *expect* to be better off, taking into account appropriate experimental risks.

JUSTICE AND GOVERNMENT SPENDING

Some people might say we can't put a price on education or knowledge. They're wrong. Justice *demands* we put a price on it.

The world forces us to put a price on it regardless of whether we want to or not. Whatever we give up to fund higher education is the price we pay for higher ed. Every time we make a choice, we implicitly put a price on what we choose and what we didn't.

For an activity to make a contribution, every dollar spent must be offset by more than a dollar's worth of output. Everyone understands this when it comes to *for-profit* business. But when thinking about *nonprofit* activities—such as government, schools, or charities—people often forget this basic point. But if we care about justice, it's not the thought that counts. Meaning well is no substitute for doing good.

The same reasoning applies to universities. Here's the basic ethical test of any university: The world should be better off with it than without it. The college should make the world a better place. If a given college consumes more than it produces, it's destroying resources and wasting time. It should either reform, or shut its doors. We might disagree about what goes into the calculus of costs and benefits, but we should all agree that the benefits, whatever they are, should exceed the costs, whatever they are.

Now here's a basic corollary of that point: All things equal, an increase in cost makes it harder to justify a given university's existence.

Basic economics tells us that inputs usually have diminishing marginal returns. In general, each additional unit of an input yields less output than the previous unit of input did. The first worker you hire does more good for the firm than the second, and the 1000th does more good than the 1001st. The first turbo you add to the engine increases power more than the second. The first slice of pizza you eat provides more satisfaction than the second. And so on. In fact, at some point, adding more units is no longer worth it. Eating another slice of pizza just gives you a stomach ache.

Now, universities are not like big factories producing just one good. They are more like shopping malls or industrial parks, with lots of little factories or stores producing lots of different goods and services. Some university centers might be low and others high on their diminishing marginal return curves. Still, the basic point holds: In general, every time the university spends an additional dollar, it's harder to justify spending that dollar than it was to spend the last one.

Higher ed in the US already costs about $500 billion a year when you add up all of its components: university operations, publishing, educational support, and the ever-growing financial sector of student loans. If you ask almost any academic, on the Left or the Right, they'll tell you that amount is not enough. They need *more*.

Let's consider, though, how the sticker price of an education—including tuition, fees, room and board, and other associated costs—has changed over the past several decades. According to statistics maintained by the College Board, a non-profit entity that administers the SAT exam, the average price of an education has skyrocketed in recent decades. When adjusted for inflation to reflect 2016 dollars, the average tuition at a private university in 1976 was $10,680 per year. In 2016, it averaged $33,480. Public universities have followed this same pattern. The average tuition in 1976 (again expressed in 2016 dollars) was $2,600. Today, it sits just shy of $10,000 per year.[21]

Room and board will cost you extra. At both types of institutions, expenses for housing and other accoutrements have similarly exploded. In 1976, fees and room and board at both public and private colleges added about $6,000 to the annual price tag when reflected in 2016 dollars. Today, they average about $12,000.[22] All things considered, a typical student currently spends about $45,000 for a degree from a private institution or $20,000 for a degree from a public institution. Note that these levels also increase substantially at elite institutions. An Ivy League college experience may easily exceed $60,000 per year, although Ivy League schools discount their tuition for less well-off students.

Holding all else constant, these figures demonstrate one unambiguous trend in higher education. On average, it costs about 2.5 to 3 times as much money to receive a degree today than it did to receive the equivalent degree forty years ago. Again, these figures are adjusted for inflation, so they reflect the actual purchasing power of the dollar. Of course, this assumes, perhaps mistakenly, that a degree today and a degree forty years ago are the same thing and have the same value.

Higher education's annual operating costs make up one of the largest components of its expenses, and these, too, have skyrocketed. In 2015—the most recent year with complete statistics—the one-year operating expenses of the US university system topped $536 billion. Again, adjusting for inflation to current dollars, this figure is up from $167 billion in 1976. Those are absolute figures, but the cost per pupil has also risen dramatically, indicating that universities are educating *fewer* people per dollar that they spend. Although statistics did not record differences between public and private institutions until relatively recently, the average spending per equivalent full-time student at all universities in 1976 was about $21,000 in current dollars. Today, when we look at four-year institutions, it averages $54,000 at private universities and $41,000 at public universities.[23] Again, these figures are in current dollars; we have adjusted for inflation.

No matter how you look at it, the trends in university finances show that (1) college is costing its student consumers a lot more and (2) colleges are spending more per student educated. Compared to four decades ago, tuition intake and spending are up across the board. There are many reasons for these trends, including the distortions caused by student loan subsidies, the costs of regulatory compliance, the growth in spending on nonclassroom functions as well as the administrators who oversee them, and cost disease.[24]

Harvard University's endowment is its own money. If it wanted to spend $30 billion researching hip-hop poetry, the school would have our blessing, not that it needs it. But when Harvard gets over $600 million in federal funding, it better be serving the public good, doing more than $600 million worth of good for us.[25]

We won't belabor this point, but *how* the government pays for higher ed—that is, what kinds of taxes pay the costs—also matters. Different kinds of taxes impose differential burdens. For instance, basic sales taxes tend to be highly regressive. To the extent that higher ed is funded through sales taxes, which are a common form of public finance at the state level, it represents significant redistribution or subsidy of the upper middle class and privileged by the poor and underprivileged. On the other hand, income taxes tend to be extremely progressive (the upper 20 percent pay almost *all* income tax), and so income tax–financed higher ed is more like the upper classes paying for a shared good they all tend to consume and benefit from.

Government spending is a matter of justice. Government is supposed to be a fiduciary agent of the people, acting in good faith, competently, and in their various interests. Money has to come *from* somewhere. Government spending is financed through taxes, debt (i.e., future taxes), or inflation, so to justify the government spending whatever amount on whatever priority, we have to ask whether it would have been better to leave that money in private hands. Furthermore, government spending always has a political opportunity cost, as any money allocated toward one item in the budget could have been spent elsewhere. In short, government owes us a duty of care, to spend money carefully, wisely, and without waste, although, of course, the US federal government doesn't come anywhere near discharging this duty.

We're not calling for the federal or state governments to micromanage universities to a greater degree. Our colleagues in Europe spend a great deal of time filing paperwork, filling out forms, applying for grants, and generally having to "prove" they're good stewards of the public trust. It's far from clear to us that there's much benefit from such requirements. European universities tend to be less expensive overall, not because they have faculty fill out more forms, but because they spend less on student activities and maintain generally higher student-to-faculty ratios. The problem is that the kinds of incentive and behavioral problems which plague American universities also similarly plague government bureaucracies—including the bureaus that would oversee universities if we increased their fiduciary watchdog roles. We wouldn't reduce waste by shifting it one level higher. We're worried that universities are bad stewards of public money, but we're equally worried that state legislatures and bureaucracies are also bad stewards of public money.

Perhaps the best argument for continuing to fund higher ed at its current levels is cynical: Federal spending priorities are so awful that, realistically speaking, if the money wasn't spent on possibly useless education, it might be spent on something much worse.

CONCLUSION

Let's review the main complaints of Chapters 2 through 9:

2. Faculty, administrators, and students have selfish interests and face bad incentives that may induce them to act in ways that undermine the common good of their university.

3. Universities regularly engage in negligent advertising. They promise to deliver a whole range of benefits, but lack the evidence to prove that they deliver these benefits. Worse, researchers have uncovered strong evidence that universities simply don't deliver on some of their promises. Most students learn close to nothing, don't develop their skills very much, and don't know how to transfer those skills outside the classroom.

4. Administrators use student evaluations to determine hiring and promotion, but student evaluations do not track teaching effectiveness. They may also reflect other biases that, ethically speaking, should not be used to determine hiring and promotion.

5. Professors haven't coordinated on a common meaning for grades, and GPA calculations are mostly incoherent. The main form of feedback and certification that faculty thus provide to students is a conceptual mess.

6. Academics frequently use moral language to disguise their pursuit of their own self-interest. Certain forms of activism, including activism on behalf of tenure, appear to be little more than rent-seeking.

7. Gen eds generally don't work. Faculty exploit students by forcing them to take useless and ineffective courses that students don't want to. The purpose of many gen eds is to transfer money from students to professors.

8. Professors and administrators maintain low-quality doctoral programs that produce too many PhDs in glutted employment markets as a way to increase their own prestige, obtain subsidized graders and assistants, and justify higher salaries and more resources.

9. Most students cheat a little, and many cheat a lot.

We've barely scratched the surface here. We've almost entirely ignored how faculty from all over the political spectrum use the university for political activism. We've ignored how some faculty use their status to sexually harass their students. We've ignored all the serious ethical problems that arise from universities running semi-professional sports teams. We've ignored whether universities act too paternalistically toward their students or, conversely, do too little to protect them from the dangers of college life. We've ignored whether admissions or hiring practices are fair or biased.

We admit these are important problems, many even *more* important. But we have two sets of reasons for avoiding these questions. First, some of them are inherently political, pitting the Left versus the Right. We wanted to discuss issues that people from all sides of the aisle can admit are real problems. Second, some of the other problems we just identified are, in a weird way, secondary rather than fundamental problems. Ethics issues plague college sports, but college sports are rather obviously a secondary function of the university at best. In contrast, gen eds are seen as a normal part of US and Canadian higher ed, but they seem to be mostly a way of exploiting students to the benefit of faculty in certain disciplines.

In addition, some of the problems we have not covered, though important, are relatively easy to solve. Consider this: Suppose, plausibly, that universities admit too few poor students. The reason: Poor students often had to work at low-paying jobs in high school and thus listed fewer or less impressive extracurricular activities on their résumés. Solution: We direct admissions officers to request income information and give extra weight to poorer students' extracurriculars. But now consider the problem we discussed in Chapter 3: A liberal arts education presumes a false model of how students learn. How do you fix *that*?

Universities are a moral mess. The problem isn't bad people. Universities are made up of decent people, if not angels. The problem is bad incentives. If you want to fix the problem, you need to change the incentives. Just *how* to change the incentives is itself a big problem— even we the authors have no incentive to change the bad incentives! But the bottom line is: You won't fix what ails universities unless you fix the incentives. Good luck with that.

NOTES

Chapter 1

1. North 1990, 3.
2. For example, see UnKochMyCampus.org, which claims that Koch money is ruining higher education.
3. For example, see Giroux 2014; Nussbaum 2016.
4. https://www.eeoc.gov/laws/statutes/titlevii.cfm
5. Epley and Dunning 2000.
6. Simler and Hanson 2018.
7. Dutton 2012.
8. Incidentally, Nancy MacLean accuses Buchanan of being a gremlin, backed by a big conspiracy, in MacLean 2017.
9. See, for example, Caplan 2007; Mueller 2003.
10. Acemoglu and Robison 2012.
11. Brennan and Magness 2018a.
12. Shira Buchsbaum, "Paxson Releases Final Diversity, Inclusion Action Plan," *Brown Daily Herald,* Feb. 2, 2016. http://www.browndailyherald.com/2016/02/02/revised-diversity-inclusion-plan-released/
13. Mulligan 2018, 27.
14. https://ocw.mit.edu/index.htm
15. https://nces.ed.gov/fastfacts/display.asp?id=75
16. See Lombardi 2013, 69–95.
17. Schmidtz 2001.
18. On this point, see Brennan and Jaworski 2016, 55–59.
19. David Lucca, Taylor Nadauld, and Karen Shen, "Credit Supply and the Rise of Tuition: Evidence from the Expansion in Federal Student Aid

Programs," *FRBNY Staff Reports* 733 (2015) https://www.newyorkfed.org/medialibrary/media/research/staff_reports/sr733.pdf

20.   Katy Reilly, "Why Banning Hard Alcohol on College Campuses May Not Be the Answer," *Time,* Aug. 24, 2016. http://time.com/4463227/stanford-hard-liquor-ban/

21.   Andrew Adams, "Do Bans of Texting While Driving Actually Increase Accidents?", Oct. 22, 2012. http://www.ksl.com/?sid=22657873&nid=148&title=do-bans-on-texting-while-driving-actually-increase-accidents&s_cid=featured-1

22.   Indeed, we could no find peer-reviewed articles on this topic beyond arguments to the effect that for-profit education was inherently wrong.

23.   Franklyn-Stokes and Newstead 1995; Nowell and Laufer 1997; Baird 1980.

Chapter 2

1.   Even this can be explained by incentives. Georgetown undergrads generally don't pay for college themselves; their parents pay their tuition. Furthermore, the undergrad business students have a placement rate fairly close to 100 percent. MBA students, on the other hand, have just quit their high-paying jobs to go back to school. They pay $56,000 in yearly tuition out of pocket. *Of course,* they're a bit less interested in chatting about Ursula Le Guin short stories for the sake of pure knowledge.

2.   Coalition on the Academic Workforce, "A Portrait of Part-Time Faculty Members," June 2012. http://www.academicworkforce.org/CAW_portrait_2012.pdf

3.   Coalition on the Academic Workforce, "A Portrait of Part-Time Faculty Members," June 2012. http://www.academicworkforce.org/CAW_portrait_2012.pdf. Table 17 there indicates that only 4.7 percent of the adjunct survey respondents indicated that they taught at more than two universities. The majority—77.9 percent—complete their entire teaching obligation at only one university.

4.   Various surveys routinely find that college professors have low stress and are relatively happy. Susan Adams, "The Least Stressful Jobs, 2013," *Forbes,* Jan 3, 2013. https://www.forbes.com/sites/susanadams/2013/01/03/the-least-stressful-jobs-of-2013/#238490ab6e24; Melissa Stanger, "Here and the Most and Least Happy Careers," *Yahoo! Finance,* Dec. 9, 2012. https://finance.yahoo.com/news/most-least-happiest-careers-235600662.html

5.   https://www.aaup.org/sites/default/files/ARES_2017-18.pdf

6.   Tanza Loudenback, "Middle-Class Americans Made More Money Last Year than Ever Before," *Business Insider,* Sep. 12, 2017. http://www.businessinsider.com/us-census-median-income-2017-9; https://www.census.gov/data/tables/time-series/demo/income-poverty/historical-income-households.html

7.   https://en.wikipedia.org/wiki/Harvard_University_endowment

8.   https://data.chronicle.com/category/sector/2/faculty-salaries/

9. https://data.chronicle.com/221953/Tusculum-College/faculty-salaries/

10. Scott Jaschik, "Faculty Pay: Up and Uneven," *Inside Higher Ed*, Mar. 16, 2016. https://www.insidehighered.com/news/2015/03/16/survey-finds-increases-faculty-pay-and-significant-gaps-discipline

11. "The 10 Highest Paid College Professors in the US," *The Quad*. http://www.thebestschools.org/blog/2013/11/25/10-highest-paid-college-professors-u-s/

12. Brandon Dixon, "Faust Made $1.4 Million in 2015," *Harvard Daily Crimson*, March 13, 2017. http://www.thecrimson.com/article/2017/5/13/tax-forms-2015/

13. See the syllabi discussed here: Emily Hegarty, "Teaching Eco-Composition at the Community College." https://emilyhegarty.mla.hcommons.org/2017/01/02/mla-2017-session-119-teaching-eco-composition-at-the-community-college/.

14. "Which Professional Sports Leagues Make the Most Money?" https://howmuch.net/articles/sports-leagues-by-revenue

15. https://nces.ed.gov/fastfacts/display.asp?id=66

16. Author calculations using data from https://www.bls.gov/ooh/education-training-and-library/kindergarten-and-elementary-school-teachers.htm; https://www.bls.gov/ooh/education-training-and-library/middle-school-teachers.htm.

17. HERI faculty surveys, 1989 versus 2013. https://heri.ucla.edu/heri-faculty-survey/

18. Bowen and Tobin 2015.

19. Ginsberg 2011, 2.

20. https://finaid.georgetown.edu/cost-of-attendance/undergraduate

21. https://nces.ed.gov/collegenavigator/?q=georgetown+university&s=all&id=131496#netprc

22. https://ocw.mit.edu/index.htm

23. Jeffrey Kauffman, "20,000 World-Class Univeristy Lectures Made Illegal, So We Rescured Them," March 15, 2017. https://lbry.io/news/20000-illegal-college-lectures-rescued

24. https://www.edx.org/school/harvardx

25. Caplan 2018.

26. Caplan 2018.

27. Arum and Roksa 2011, 59, 120, 135.

28. Arum and Roksa 2011, 3.

29. Arum and Roksa 2011, 71–85, passim.

30. Arum and Roksa 2011, 5.

31. Buchanan and Devletoglou 1970.

32. Consider: All things equal, a 200-person large lecture has a lower cost per student than a 5-person seminar. A chemistry lab course that allows students to use a $200,000 mass spectrometer is more expensive than a class that requires no equipment. A course with a high-salary business

professor is more expensive (all other things equal) than a course with a low-salary religion prof.

33. That is, imagine that if we offered each a choice between $2,999 in cash or rock climbing, they'd pick rock climbing, but we offered them $3,001 or rock climbing, they'd take the cash.

34. Kress 1989; Ginsberg 2011.

35. Ginsberg 2011, 26–40, admits that compliance with increased federal and state regulation explains some of the increase, but argues it does not explain the majority of it.

36. Ginsberg 2011, 39.

37. Ginsberg 2011, 25.

38. Jay Greene, "Administrative Bloat at American Universities: The Real Reasons for the High Costs in Higher Education." https://goldwaterinstitute.org/wp-content/uploads/cms_page_media/2015/3/24/Administrative%20Bloat.pdf; note that they use US Department of Education data for their calculations.

39. https://www.usnews.com/education/best-colleges/articles/how-us-news-calculated-the-rankings

40. According to *U.S. News and World Report: Find the Best Colleges for You, 2017 Edition*, faculty salaries are worth 7 percent of a school's raw scores (pp. 70–72). We pick Chicago because it has the highest rank for faculty resources. Chicago gets a raw score of 97, and a 7 percentage point reduction reduces its score to 90.

41. We pick Yale because it has the highest rank for financial resources, which are worth 10 percent of its score. It gets a raw score of 97, and a 10 percentage point drop gives it a raw score of 87.

42. Total spending is worth 10 percent of a raw score, while faculty resources are worth 7 percent. The rankings do not provide raw data, but only ranks. Since William and Mary is ranked right in the middle in terms of financial resources, we're conservatively estimating it gets *half* the raw financial resources score of Yale, which is ranked #1. In fact, this *overestimates* its score, because there is a high level of inequality, and the *mean* national university financial resources are higher than the *median*. So, let's assume William and Mary gets a 5 percentage point total boost to its score.

43. Ginsberg 2011, 30–44, 87, passim.

44. Ginsberg 2011, 34.

45. Carrell and West 2010; Stark and Freishtat 2014; De Vlieger, Jacob, and Strange 2017; Braga, Paccagnella, and Pellizzari 2014; Uttl, White, and Wong Gonzalez 2017.

46. Carpenter et al. 2016; Ho, Thomsen, and Sidanius 2009; Boring, Ottoboni, and Stark 2016; Mittal, Gera, and Kumar Batra 2015; MacNell, Driscoll, and Hunt 2015; Driscoll and Cadden 2010; Roberto A. Ferdman, "Why Overweight Women Are More Likely to Earn Less

than Overweight Men," *The Washington Post,* Oct. 28, 2014. https://www.washingtonpost.com/news/wonk/wp/2014/10/28/why-overweight-women-are-more-likely-to-earn-less-than-overweight-men/?utm_term=.7f3f9435138c.

47. Ginsberg 2011, 41–50.
48. See US Department of Education, 2014, *Digest of Education Statistics,* Table 316.80, https://nces.ed.gov/programs/digest/.

Chapter 3

1. Steve Kolowich, "88 College Taglines, Arranged as a Poem," *Chronicle of Higher Education,* Aug. 4, 2015. http://www.chronicle.com/article/88-College-Taglines-Arranged/232003
2. https://www.extension.harvard.edu/about-us
3. https://www.extension.harvard.edu/registration-admissions
4. https://www.extension.harvard.edu/teaching-opportunities-harvard-division-continuing-education
5. https://www.usnews.com/education/best-colleges/articles/how-us-news-calculated-the-rankings
6. https://college.harvard.edu/admissions
7. https://college.harvard.edu/admissions/choosing-harvard
8. http://www.hbs.edu/mba/the-hbs-difference/Pages/default.aspx
9. https://uadmissions.georgetown.edu/applying-georgetown
10. https://college.harvard.edu/admissions/choosing-harvard. Last accessed March 18, 2017. The quotation has since been removed with the selection of a new dean. A similar claim appears at https://msb.georgetown.edu/executive-programs.
11. https://admissions.yale.edu/liberal-arts-education
12. https://admission.princeton.edu/academics/what-does-liberal-arts-mean
13. https://www.amherst.edu
14. https://www.smith.edu/viewbook/#2
15. https://www.mtholyoke.edu/admission
16. http://www.northwood.edu/academics/graduate
17. https://admissions.unh.edu
18. https://www2.gmu.edu/admissions-aid
19. https://www.jmu.edu/about/index.shtml
20. https://www.jmu.edu/engagement/learning/index.shtml
21. http://www.smu.edu
22. https://www.hillsdale.edu
23. https://www.hillsdale.edu
24. See Primary Research Group, 2010, *Survey of College Marketing Programs,* Table 1.12, https://www.primaryresearch.com/.
25. Primary Research Group 2010, 19.
26. Primary Research Group 2010, 19.

27. For example, see Bob Brock, "College Advertising at an All-Time High," *Educational Marketing Group*, Oct. 5, 2017. https://emgonline.com/2017/10/college-advertising-at-all-time-high/.

28. http://www.montclair.edu/chss/why-study-liberal-arts/

29. http://www.wheaton.edu/Student-Life/My-Wheaton/2013/10/6-Benefits-of-Liberal-Arts-Education

30. https://ls.berkeley.edu/liberal_arts_education

31. https://clas.uiowa.edu/students/why-study-liberal-arts-sciences

32. http://www.park.edu/academics/college-of-liberal-arts-and-sciences/why-study-liberal-arts.html

33. https://clas.asu.edu

34. http://www.stlawu.edu/strategic-map/introduction-and-goals

35. Though, oddly, we noticed the following pattern. Liberal arts schools generally look to recruit enthusiastic, well-rounded, disciplined, critically thinking students who care about the world. At the same time, they are all going to transform their students into something different and awesome—namely, enthusiastic, well-rounded, disciplined, critically thinking people who care about the world.

36. On the lack of progress in philosophy, see Brennan 2010.

37. For example, see http://philosophy.wisc.edu/undergraduate/whystudy.

38. http://dailynous.com/value-of-philosophy/charts-and-graphs/

39. https://phil.washington.edu/why-study-philosophy

40. http://philosophy.wisc.edu/undergraduate/whystudy

41. http://www.lsu.edu/hss/philosophy/why-study-philosophy.php

42. https://www.wlu.edu/philosophy-department/about-the-department/why-major-in-philosophy

43. http://www.depauw.edu/academics/departments-programs/philosophy/why-major-in-philosophy/

44. This is a paraphrase. It may also have been that she recommended using a neti pot.

45. http://eddiejackson.net/web_documents/Whystudyphilosophy.pdf

46. We borrow this example from Gladwell 2010.

47. Malcolm Gladwell, "Getting In: The Social Logic of Ivy League Admissions," *The New Yorker*, Oct. 10, 2005. *http*://www.newyorker.com/magazine/2005/10/10/getting-in

48. http://www.collegedata.com/cs/data/college/college_pg02_tmpl.jhtml?schoolId=1016

49. https://www.bmwusa.com/vehicles/3series/sedan.html

50. For example, see Murray 2012; Charles S. Rugaber, "Pay Gap between College Grads and Everyone Else at an All-Time High," *USA Today*, Jan. 12, 2017. https://www.usatoday.com/story/money/2017/01/12/pay-gap-between-college-grads-and-everyone-else-record/96493348/; Philip

Trostel, "It's Not Just the Money: The Benefits of College Education to Individuals and Society," *Lumina Issue Papers.*

51. Philip Trostel, "It's Not Just the Money: The Benefits of College Education to Individuals and Society," Lumina Issue Papers. https://www. luminafoundation.org/files/resources/its-not-just-the-money.pdf

52. Philip Trostel, "It's Not Just the Money: The Benefits of College Education to Individuals and Society," Lumina Issue Papers. https://www. luminafoundation.org/files/resources/its-not-just-the-money.pdf

53. http://www.pages.drexel.edu/~pa34/philexcel.htm

54. "IQ Estimates by Intended College Major," http://www.statisticbrain. com/iq-estimates-by-intended-college-major/

55. Burke et al. 2013.

56. See Ortiz 2007 for a review.

57. Schwitzgebel 2013.

58. Dale and Krueger 2002; Dale and Krueger 2014.

59. Gregg Easterbrook, "Who Needs Harvard?," *Brookings Institute.* https:// www.brookings.edu/articles/who-needs-harvard/

60. Caplan 2018.

61. Arum and Roksa 2011.

62. Arum and Roksa 2011, 21.

63. Arum and Roksa 2011, 121.

64. "Study Finds Large Numbers of College Students Don't Learn Much," *Inside Higher Ed,* Jan 18, 2018. https://www.insidehighered.com/news/ 2011/01/18/study_finds_large_numbers_of_college_students_don_t_ learn_much

65. Arum and Roksa 2011, 219n15.

66. Arum and Roksa 2011, 54.

67. Arum and Roksa 2011, 56. Some researchers dispute these results. Benjamin Page of the Council for Aid to Education released a non-peer-reviewed study that claims, on average, students improve about 0.73 standard deviations on the measured skills. Let's say, charitably, that Page is right. But this doesn't help so much. Even then, the effect size is small, and Page finds that roughly half of students are receiving no gains. See http://cae.org/images/uploads/pdf/Three_Principal_Questions_About_ Critical_Thinking_Tests.pdf.

68. Caplan 2018, 50. See also Detterman and Sternberg 1993; Haskell 2001; Gick and Holyoak 1993.

69. Haskell 2001, xiii.

70. Deterrman 1993, 21.

71. Hyland and Johnson 2006.

72. Caplan 2018, 50–59.

73. Leshowitz 1989, 1160.

74. Caplan 2018, 56.

Chapter 4

1. For an account of why weird behaviors were often functional, see Leeson 2017.
2. Simler and Hanson 2018; Haidt 2012.
3. Emery, Kramer, and Tian 2001, 37.
4. We take this example from Stark and Freishtat 2014. Of course, height and weight are correlated somewhat, so we can predict that, on average, a 200-pound person is taller than a 50-pound person.
5. Hobson and Talbot 2001, Cruse 1987.
6. Clayson 2009, 19.
7. Stark and Freishtat 2014.
8. Now, Stark and Freishtat would presumably admit that we could, in principle, uncover experimental or empirical evidence that students treat such scores as cardinal numbers. If they did, that would help, but no such evidence exists. They would also admit, we presume, that statistically savvy researchers have known about this problem for decades, and there are ways to use ordinal data without committing such errors. However, students, administrators, deans, and most faculty are unaware of this problem and continue to use meaningless averages as if they represent something real.
9. Uttl, White, and Wong Gonzalez 2017, 40.
10. Uttl et al. 2017, 38.
11. Uttl et al. 2017, 23.
12. Clayson 2009, 21–22.
13. Clayson 2009, 26. In addition, see Isely and Singh 2010, 39; Krautman and Sander 1999; Marsh and Cooper 1981; Short et al. 2008; Worthington, 2002; Centra 2003; Vasta and Sarmiento 1979; Ewing 2012. They also find a negative correlation between SET scores and student effort/class rigor, or that professors can "buy" higher SET scores by grading more leniently.
14. Clayson 2009, 19–20.
15. Clayson 2009, 28.
16. Stark and Freishtat 2014, citing Carrell and West 2010, and Braga, Paccagnella, and Pellizzari 2014.
17. Cruse 1987.
18. McKeachie and Kulik 1975; Wittrock and Lumsdaine 1977.
19. Naftulin, Ware, and Donnelly 1973.
20. Granzin and Painter 1973.
21. Murray 1983.
22. Clayson and Sheffet 2006.
23. Clayson and Sheffet 2006, 157.
24. Michael Huemer, http://www.owl232.net/sef.htm#N_16_, citing Ambady, Nalini, and Rosenthan 1993.
25. Riniolo et al. 2006. See also Ambady and Rosenthal 1993.

26.   Centra 1993.
27.   Marsh and Roche 1997, 1190.
28.   Adams 1997, 10.
29.   Mary and Bergmann 2003.
30.   Ryan, Anderson, and Birchler 1980.
31.   Dowell and Neal 1982, 61.
32.   Here, we paraphrase a former dean and friend of ours. But the argument doesn't appear in print, so we won't attribute it to him by name.
33.   Morgan, Sneed, and Swinney 2003, 25.
34.   Gump 2007; Beran, Violato, and Kline 2007; Crumbley and Fliedner 2002; Campbell and Bozeman 2007.
35.   Crumbley and Fliedner 2002, 216.
36.   Crumbley and Fliedner 2002, 217.
37.   For a review of this literature, see Brennan 2016.
38.   Lombardi 2013.
39.   Cushman 2003, 53.
40.   Leeson 2017.

Chapter 5

1.   There are, of course, exceptions, such as the fraudulent MacLean 2017.
2.   As Caplan 2018 shows, students forget most of what they learn in school.
3.   Danzinger, Levav, and Avnaim-Pess 2011.
4.   Schinske and Tanner 2014. See also Branthwaite, Trueman, and Berrisford 1981 for further evidence that grading is unreliable.
5.   Stark and Freishtat 2014.
6.   To be more precise, technically this need not be a problem. Suppose the truth is that each letter grade is better than the next on some meaningful exponential scale. In principle, then, we could use a logarithmic equation to translate this into a linear curve, just as, say, the decibel or Richter scales are logarithmic. However, this will save faculty from complaint only if they carefully fit their letter grades to a meaningful exponential equation in the first place.
7.   Similarly, on that same scoring system, suppose the professor uses the following conversions: A– = 90, B– = 80, and C– = 70. Suppose Sally gets an A–, B–, and C–. She'll average an 80, a B–. But now let's see if this works when we switch to the more realistic "An A is twice as good as a B" scale. On that scale, an A– = 6.68, a B– = 3.34, and a C– = 1.67. Her average grade is a 3.90.
8.   https://www.hampshire.edu/admissions/ faq-for-parents-and-families-of-prospective-students#evals
9.   Brennan and Jaworski 2016.
10.   See Schinske and Tanner 2014.
11.   Guy Montrose Whipple, "Editor's Preface," in Finklestein 1913, 1.

12. For example, Google and Goldman Sachs largely ignore grades: Max Nisen, "Do Grades Matter: Depends on If You're Asking Google or Goldman Sachs," *Quartz,* April 20, 2015. https://qz.com/382570/goldman-sachs-actually-google-gpas-arent-worthless/.

13. For example, McAbee and Oswald 2013 claims that a high correlation exists between conscientiousness and college GPA. So, we might expect that insofar as GPA is a measure of conscientiousness, it will predict other things (marital satisfaction, propensity to save for retirement, employment rates) positively correlated with conscientiousness.

14. Bretz 1989.

15. Schmidt and Hunter 1998.

16. French et al. 2015.

17. Schinske and 2014; Rojstaczer, Stuart, and Healy 2012.

18. Butler and Nisan 1986.

19. Schinske and Tanner 2014.

20. Kohn 2009, 2.

21. Adelman 2009, 39.

22. See Brighouse 2009.

23. Murray 2012.

24. Adelman 2009, 15.

25. Adelman 2009, 25.

26. Adelman 2009, 15–16.

27. See the chart at https://www.brown.edu/about/administration/institutional-research/sites/brown.edu.about.administration.institutional-research/files/uploads/TABLE20_1.pdf, which shows that the percent of As has increased in most of the major subdivisions at Brown. However, even this chart doesn't tell us what number of students majored in each field, so we cannot determine whether the changes are statistically significant.

28. https://www.brown.edu/about/administration/institutional-research/sites/brown.edu.about.administration.institutional-research/files/uploads/admission_0.pdf

Chapter 6

1. www.whosdrivingyou.org.

2. http://www.whosdrivingyou.org/about

3. Jason first discussed this example in Brennan and Hill 2014.

4. Yes, his argument was that voting signified consent, so we needed to force voters to vote in order to ensure they consent to their government.

5. See Apps's May 2, 2011, speech to the Empire Club of Canada, available at http://pdopav2.blogspot.com/2011/06/alfred-apps-speech-empire-club-of.html, last accessed October 5, 2012. As of August 20, 2013, the author appears to have made this blog open by invitation only.

6. Adler 2009, 9.

7. Bovard 1999, 1.
8. https://www.adm.com/our-company/community-giving/strong-roots
9. https://www.adm.com/our-company/community-giving
10. https://www.adm.com/our-company/community-giving/
    strong-communities
11. Dutton 2012; https://www.theguardian.com/commentisfree/2014/jun/03/
    how-i-discovered-i-have-the-brain-of-a-psychopath.
12. Simler and Hanson 2018, 205–244.
13. Simler and Hanson 2018, 216.
14. Yandle 1983; Yandle 2014.
15. Megan McArdle, "Why Walmart Will Never Pay Like Costco,"
    Bloomberg, Aug. 27, 2013. https://www.bloomberg.com/view/articles/
    2013-08-27/why-walmart-will-never-pay-like-costco
16. Ryan Young, "Costco CEO Favors Minimum Wage Hike," Mar. 6, 2013.
    https://cei.org/blog/costco-ceo-favors-minimum-wage-hike
17. Alia Wong and Adrienne Green, "Campus Politics: A Cheat Sheet," *The
    Atlantic*, Apr. 4, 2016. https://www.theatlantic.com/education/archive/
    2016/04/campus-protest-roundup/417570/. A full list of demands is
    available at http://www.thedemands.org.
18. For instance, we hope to remind students that for any non-Irish person to
    celebrate Halloween is racist cultural appropriation; Halloween is for Irish
    people only.
19. Katherine Shaver, "Georgetown University to Rename Two Buildings that
    Reflect School's Tie to Slavery," *Washington Post*, Nov. 15, 2015. https://
    www.washingtonpost.com/local/georgetown-university-to-rename-two-
    buildings-that-reflect-schools-ties-to-slavery/2015/11/15/e36edd32-8bb7-
    11e5-acff-673ae92ddd2b_story.html?utm_term=.6262881b607a
20. For a full list, see http://www.thedemands.org.
21. https://new.oberlin.edu/petition-jan2016.pdf
22. Marvin Krislov, "Response to Student Demands," https://www.oberlin.
    edu/news/response-student-demands
23. "Yale Launches Five Year, $50 Million Initiatie to Increase
    Faculty Diversity." https://news.yale.edu/2015/11/03/
    yale-launches-five-year-50-million-initiative-increase-faculty-diversity
24. https://paw.princeton.edu/article/forging-faculty-diversity
25. "Brown University Latest to Be Hit with Anti-Racism Protests,"
    CBS News, Nov. 16, 2015. https://www.cbsnews.com/news/
    brown-university-latest-to-be-hit-with-anti-racism-protests/
26. Kevin Stacy, "Brown Releases Final Action Plan to Create a Diverse and
    Inclusive Campus," Feb. 1, 2016. https://news.brown.edu/articles/2016/
    02/diap
27. Brogaard, Engelberg, and van Wesep, 2017.
28. Brogaard, Engelberg, and van Wesep, 2017, 3.
29. Brogaard, Engelberg, and van Wesep, 2017, 11–13.

30.   Brogaard, Engelberg, and van Wesep, 2017, 8–9.

31.   Brogaard, Engelberg, and van Wesep, 2017, 13.

32.   Goodwin and Sauer 1995.

33.   Holley 1977.

34.   Lewis 1980.

35.   Williams and Ceci 2007.

36.   Epley and Dunning 2000.

37.   Ceci, Williams, and Mueller-Johnson 2006.

38.   McKenzie, 1996. See also Carmichael 1988.

39.   For example, Bartlett 1991; Shils 1995; De George 2003; Carroll 2000.

40.   Whicker 1997.

41.   Colleen Flaherty and Kaitlin Mulhere, "Day of Protest," *Inside Higher Ed,* Feb. 26, 2015. https://www.insidehighered.com/news/2015/02/26/adjuncts-deem-national-walkout-day-success

42.   Sarah Kendzior, "Academia' Indentured Servants," *Al Jazeera,* Apr. 11, 2013. http://www.aljazeera.com/indepth/opinion/2013/04/20134119156459616.html

43.   Nicole Troxell, "My Life as an Adjunct." https://www.popularresistance.org/academic-sweatshop-my-life-as-an-adjunct/

44.   David Perry, "Migrant Workers. Sharecroppers. Adjuncts?" *Chronicle Vitae,* Apr. 24, 2014. https://chroniclevitae.com/news/461-sharecroppers-migrant-workers-adjuncts

45.   Sarah Kendzior, "The Adjunct Crisis Is Everyone's Problem," *Chronicle Vitae,* Oct. 17, 2014. https://chroniclevitae.com/news/762-the-adjunct-crisis-is-everyone-s-problem

46.   James Hoff, "Are Adjunct Professors the Fast-Food Workers of the Academic World," *The Guardian* Jan. 24, 2014. http://www.theguardian.com/commentisfree/2014/jan/24/exploitation-of-adjunct-professors-devalues-higher-education

47.   Lawrence Harmon, "Exploited Adjuncts Ripe for a Union," *The Boston Globe,* Apr. 12, 2014. https://www.bostonglobe.com/opinion/2014/04/11/exploited-adjuncts-ripe-for-union/aptwoxrSxvoNvomI2YXtJK/story.html

48.   Robert Lopez, "Adjunctivitis: Colleges Would Implode without Exploited Freelance Professors," *The Observer,* Sep. 16, 2015. http://observer.com/2015/09/educated-observer-spring-2015/

49.   Tiffany Kraft, "I Quit," *Inside Higher Ed,* Apr. 21, 2016. https://www.insidehighered.com/views/2016/04/21/adjunct-explains-why-she-has-quit-her-job-essay

50.   Justin Miller, "When Adjuncts Go Union," *The American Prospect,* Jun. 30, 2015. http://prospect.org/article/when-adjuncts-go-union

51.   David Leonard, "Adjuncts Aren't Slaves. Let's Stop Saying They Are." *Chronicle Vitae,* Dec. 4, 2013. https://chroniclevitae.com/news/200-adjuncts-aren-t-slaves-let-s-stop-saying-they-are

52. Rob Jenkins, "Straight Talk about Adjunctification," *The Chronicle of Higher Education,* Dec. 15, 2014. http://www.chronicle.com/article/ Straight-Talk-About/150881

53. US Department of Education 2014; authors' calculations derived from Tables 315.10 and 303.10 in this *Digest of Education Statistics.*

54. For example, see Flaherty, 2015. See also Boston University Faculty Union, 2015.

55. A 2012 Coalition on the Academic Workforce (hereafter CAW) survey found that only 30 percent of adjunct respondents had completed a doctorate. A more extensive analysis conducted in 2003 by the US Department of Education showed that about 18 percent of adjuncts held doctorates. In both studies, the highest level of education was a master's degree. See CAW 2012, Table 9, "Integrated Postsecondary Education Data System" (hereafter referred to as IPEDS; Table 315.70). The Higher Education Research Institute at UCLA found in a 2010 survey of undergraduate faculty that only 24 percent of adjuncts held a PhD, while an additional 4 percent had obtained terminal equivalents, such as an EdD, MD, or DDS. See http://www.heri.ucla.edu/monographs/HERI-FAC2011-Monograph-Expanded.pdf, p. 173. The American Federation of Teachers (AFT) in 2010 similarly found that only 26 percent of adjuncts held a PhD.

56. John Ziker, "The Long, Lonely Job of Homo academicus," *The Blue Review*, Boise State University, March 31, 2014, http://thebluereview.org/ faculty-time-allocation/

57. IPEDS, Table 315.3. *Note:* These findings were also consistent with an earlier 1994 American Association of University Professors (AAUP) study, itself based on earlier Department of Education data going back to 1987. See Rosenthal 1994. Similar statements with regard to faculty time allocation may be found in the 2010–2011 Higher Education Research Institute survey, particulary pp. 26–27 (http://www.heri.ucla. edu/monographs/HERI-FAC2011-Monograph-Expanded.pdf). The consistency of these study results suggests that full-time faculty teaching obligations have remained relatively stable for several decades.

58. According to the HERI 2010–2011 survey, the median course load for full-time university faculty is two classes per semester. This increases to a median of three classes for four-year colleges, a designation that includes a large number of regional and liberal arts institutions (HERI 2010–2011, 20). Although not directly comparable on account of differences in institutional designation categories, similar course load differences may be seen in the US Department of Education survey. More than two-thirds of all faculty at private liberal arts colleges and regional comprehensive undergraduate institutions teach at least three courses per semester and more than a third teach four or more. See IPEDS, Table 315.30.

59. IPEDS, Table 315.30. See also HERI 2010–2011, pp. 26–27, which suggests a similar increase in teaching-related time allocation for faculty at four-year colleges when compared to full universities.

60. The same 2003 survey reported that over 75 percent of adjuncts teach two or fewer courses per semester. Only a small fraction of less than 10 percent teach a "full" four-course load or higher (https://nces.ed.gov/programs/digest/d09/tables/dt09_252.asp). These findings are consistent with a more recent CAW survey (2012), Table 16, and the time allocation frequency distributions of the HERI 2010 part-time undergraduate faculty survey, pp. 180-181.

61. IPEDS 315.40

62. Percentages calculated from IPEDS tables 315.30 and 315.40. The average adjunct works 39.9 hours per week, including all other jobs outside of the university, whereas the average full-time faculty works 53.3 hours per week.

63. Academic salaries vary widely by rank, academic discipline, and institution type. We selected this figure as an approximation of an entry-level salary for a full time teaching position at a baccalaureate institution in 2010. See Curtis and Thornton 2013.

64. CAW 2012, Table 19.

65. The Bureau of Labor Statistics (BLS) uses 2,080 hours, including paid time off, as its hourly baseline for full-time employment. See "Occupational Employment and Wages Technical Note," updated March 30, 2016, http://www.bls.gov/news.release/ocwage.tn.htm.

66. As we point out in Brennan and Magness 2018b, adjuncts are for the most part paid a living wage, calculated per hour, but the reason they fail to earn a "living salary" over the course of the year is that they are only working part-time jobs. Even an adjunct who teaches four courses a semester would work, if he is at all reasonable in how he allocates his time outside of class, only about 1,300 hours a year—a part-time job.

67. Unfortunately, few data sources document the frequency of benefits offered to adjuncts. A 2010 pro-unionization survey by the AFT reported that 28 percent of adjuncts receive some form of employer-provided health benefits, although these figures vary widely by institution type (see p. 13). Available at http://www.aft.org/sites/default/files/aa_partimefaculty0310.pdf.

Chapter 7

1. "175. Adam Smith to William Cullen, September 20, 1774," in Mosner & Ross 1987. .

2. Cheeseman and Boon 2001; Lyons et al. 1998; Rodríguez-Vera et al. 1995; Goldsmith 1976.

3. https://nces.ed.gov/programs/digest/d15/tables/dt15_325.92.asp

4. Scott Jaschik, "Econ Jobs Are Up," *Insude Higher Ed,* Dec. 29, 2016. https://www.insidehighered.com/news/2016/12/29/hiring-economics-phds-appears-strong-2017-starts

5. Scott Jascik, "Econ Jobs, Money, Love," *Inside Higher Ed,* Jan. 6, 2014. https://www.insidehighered.com/news/2014/01/06/study-tracks-economics-phds-and-their-career-paths

6. https://ncsesdata.nsf.gov/doctoratework/2013/html/SDR2013_DST4_1.html

7. https://nces.ed.gov/programs/digest/d15/tables/dt15_325.50.asp

8. Coalition on the Academic Workforce, "A Portrait of Part-Time Faculty Members," http://www.academicworkforce.org/CAW_portrait_2012.pdf

9. "Preliminary Report on the MLA *Job Information List,* 2016-17," *The Trend.* https://mlaresearch.mla.hcommons.org/2017/10/17/preliminary-report-on-the-mla-job-information-list-2016-17/

10. See National Science Foundation (NSF), 2015, *Survey of Earned Doctorates,* https://www.nsf.gov/statistics/srvydoctorates/.

11. https://www.bls.gov/oes/2015/may/oes251123.htm

12. Even with adjuncts included, the BLS still estimated that the median salary for English professors was $61,990 in 2015. The 10th percentile salary sat at $34,180, which is above that corresponding to a typical full-time adjunct course load, suggesting the number of adjuncts included in this total is still a small minority of the discipline even after factoring in its acute adjunctification patterns.

13. https://www.bls.gov/oes/2015/may/oes_stru.htm

14. https://www.humanitiesindicators.org/content/indicatordoc.aspx?i=11037

15. Technically, this could be a quantity demand change rather than a demand change; we don't explore here whether this is a shift in the demand curve or just a change due to relative prices and rewards.

16. US Department of Labor, Bureau of Labor Statistics, 2015, *Occupational Employment Survey*; US Department of Education, Institute of Education Sciences, National Center for Educational Statistics, 2015, *Digest of Education Statistics,* https://nces.ed.gov/programs/digest/

17. Hart Research Associates, "Falling Short? College and Career Success." https://www.aacu.org/sites/default/files/files/LEAP/2015employerstudentsurvey.pdf

18. https://www.humanitiesindicators.org/content/indicatordoc.aspx?i=39 https://www2.ed.gov/rschstat/research/pubs/empircurr/empircurric.pdf

19. Smith 1974; Moghtader, Cotch, and Hague 2001.

20. College Board, "Program Summary Report 2016" https://secure-media.collegeboard.org/digitalServices/pdf/research/2016/Program-Summary-Report-2016.pdf

21. US Department of Education 2015, Table 325.55.

22. Goldberg and Welles 2001, 183.

23. See https://webapp4.asu.edu/catalog/classlist?t=2187&s=ENG&hon=F&p romod=F&e=open&page=4. Note that 550 is an estimate; the department lists a large number of "honors thesis" and "individualized instruction" courses that have a course code assigned to each possible faculty member, but we do not know how many students enroll in such "courses." So, we instead count a traditional professor plus students in a classroom course.

24. Yandle 2014.

25. Arum and Roksa 2011, 35–36

26. Arum and Roksa 2011, 36–37, and 219f15.

27. We note that one study of a single community college system did demonstrate the effectiveness of a specific approach to remedial writing instruction through a newly implemented "Accelerated Learning Program" when participant performance was compared to the traditional remedial writing track. These results speak to the potential effectiveness of tailoring program design and pedagogy. See https://files.eric.ed.gov/fulltext/ED512398.pdf.

28. Levin and Calgano 2008.

29. Perin 2013.

30. http://www.postsecondaryresearch.org/i/a/document/4924_BettingerLong2006.pdf

31. https://eric.ed.gov/?id=ED512398

32. Caplan 2018, 48.

33. Caplan 2018, 48.

34. MLA, "Foreign Languages and Higher Education: New Structures for a Changed World." https://www.mla.org/Resources/Research/Surveys-Reports-and-Other-Documents/Teaching-Enrollments-and-Programs/Foreign-Languages-and-Higher-Education-New-Structures-for-a-Changed-World

Chapter 8

1. NSF 2015.

2. https://www.nsf.gov/statistics/2017/nsf17306/data.cfm

3. https://www.nsf.gov/statistics/2017/nsf17306/datatables/tab-51.htm

4. https://humanitiesindicators.org/content/indicatordoc.aspx?i=220

5. https://www.nsf.gov/statistics/2017/nsf17306/datatables/tab-46.htm; https://www.nsf.gov/statistics/2017/nsf17306/datatables/tab-69.htm

6. https://humanitiesindicators.org/content/indicatordoc.aspx?i=10831

7. Scott Jaschik, "The Shrinking Humanities Job Market," *Inside Higher Ed.* Aug. 28, 2017. https://www.insidehighered.com/news/2017/08/28/more-humanities-phds-are-awarded-job-openings-are-disappearing

8. Budget cut explanations are exceedingly common, particularly in light of a widely observed contraction in state-level support for higher education in the wake of the 2008 financial crisis. A decade later, state-level spending appears to be on the rebound. Illinois State University's

Grapevine Project, which tracks state-level trends, estimates that total state spending on higher education increased by 20 percent between 2013, or roughly the tail end of the financial crisis contraction in spending, and 2018. Per-pupil state funding grew from a national average of $233 per $1,000 in personal income to $271 during the same period (see https:// education.illinoisstate.edu/grapevine/tables/). Revenue from all sources increased dramatically across this period as well, from $273 million (inflation-adjusted) in 2008 to $347 million in 2015, the most recent available year from the US Department of Education. See the *Digest of Education Statistics*, Table 333.10.

9. "State Higher Education Association Finance: FY 2017," State Higher Education Executive Officers Association, p. 16 http://www.sheeo.org/ sites/default/files/SHEF_FY2017.pdf

10. "Federal and State Funding of Higher Education: A Changing Landscape," Pew Charitable Trusts Issue Brief, June 11, 2015. https://www. pewtrusts.org/en/research-and-analysis/issue-briefs/2015/06/federal-and-state-funding-of-higher-education; "Total Pell Grant Expenditures and Number of Recipients over Time." The College Board, 2017. https:// trends.collegeboard.org/student-aid/figures-tables/pell-grants-total-expenditures-maximum-and-average-grant-and-number-recipients-over-time

Gordon, G., & Hedlund, A. (2016). "Accounting for the Rise in College Tuition" (Working Paper No. w21967). National Bureau of Economic Research. https://www.nber.org/papers/w21967.pdf

11. Magness 2016.

12. For example, the bottom 10th percentile wage for English faculty in 2016 was $35,790. As a point of comparison, for history, it sat at $38,000. Although these figures sit well below the median wages for entry-level, full-time academic jobs (roughly $50,000), they are also well above what a full-time adjunct teaching a 4-4 course load would make at the national average of $3,000 per course.

13. HERI surveys 1989 versus 2013. The HERI survey only examines full-time faculty.

14. University of Akron Academic Program Review: Individual Ph.D. degree programs and tracks identified for phase-out, August 15, 2018. https:// www.uakron.edu/provost/priorities-and-initiatives/apr/docs/apr-degree-status.pdf

15. http://www.bls.gov/emp/ep_chart_001.htm

16. For example, Katina Rogers, in her "Humanities Unbound" report for the University of Virginia's Scholarly Communication Institute (http://katinarogers.com/wp-content/uploads/2013/08/Rogers_SCI_ Survey_Report_09AUG13.pdf) finds that most PhDs find alternative full-time jobs.

17. Nerad, Aanerud, and Cerny 1999.

18. https://www.nsf.gov/statistics/2017/nsf17306/datatables/tab-35.htm
19. https://www.nsf.gov/statistics/2017/nsf17306/datatables/tab-38.htm
20. Colander and Zhuo 2015.
21. Colander and Zhuo 2015, 145.
22. Colander and Zhuo 2015.
23. Herlihy-Mera 2015.
24. Kuhn 1962.
25. Chronicle of Higher Education, "Faculty Salaries Vary by Type, Discipline." https://www.chronicle.com/article/Faculty-Salaries-Vary-by/127073
26. https://data.chronicle.com/category/ccbasic/15/faculty-salaries/
27. https://data.chronicle.com/category/ccbasic/22/faculty-salaries/
28. https://data.chronicle.com/category/ccbasic/22/faculty-salaries/
29. Gumport 1993.
30. Di Leo 2013.
31. See, in particular, Coates and Humphreys 2002; Coates, Humphreys, and Vachris 2004.

Chapter 9

1. McCabe, Butterfield, and Treviño 2017, 58; Lang 2013, 15–16.
2. Park 2011, 533.
3. Warren Blumenfeld, "A Culture of Cheating at the University," *Huffington Post*, Oct. 31, 2016. https://www.huffingtonpost.com/warren-j-blumenfeld/a-culture-of-cheating-at-_b_8443528.html
4. Buckner and Hodges 2016, 603.
5. Bowers 1964.
6. Crowne and Marlowe 1960.
7. McCabe, Butterfield, and Treviño 2017, 58.
8. McCabe, Butterfield, and Treviño 2017, 41–42.
9. Lang 2013, 15–16.
10. McCabe, Butterfield, and Treviño 2017, 83–84.
11. McCabe, Butterfield, and Treviño 2017, 161.
12. Ariely 2013.
13. Liljenquist, Zhong, and Galinsky 2010.
14. Ariely 2013.
15. Ariely 2013.
16. Paraphrasing Lang 2013, 35.
17. Lang 2013, 45.
18. McCabe, Butterfield, and Treviño 2017, 31.
19. McCabe, Butterfield, and Treviño 2017, 31.
20. Shubik 1971.
21. In Shubik's version, one can just choose not to bid and thus suffer no loss. I have modified the rules so that all losing players suffer a loss, regardless

of whether they bid, and so that bidding always directly harms other players. This makes the game more analogous to rent-seeking.

22. Axelrod 1984.
23. Fish and Hura 2013.
24. Greene and Saxe 1992.
25. McCabe, Butterfield, and Treviño 2017, 83–84.
26. Naude and Hörne 2006.
27. Lang 2013.
28. McCabe, Butterfield, and Treviño 2017.

Chapter 10

1. James Turk, "The Canadian Corporate-Academic Complex," *AAUP* Nov-Dec. 2010. https://www.aaup.org/article/canadian-corporate-academic-complex#.WSMoAmjytEY
2. Tuchman 2009.
3. Buchanan and Devletoglou 1970.
4. Delta Cost Project, "Trends in College Spending, 2003-2013." http://www.deltacostproject.org/sites/default/files/products/15-4626%20Final01%20Delta%20Cost%20Project%20College%20Spending%2011131.406.P0.02.001%20....pdf
5. There is actually a small academic literature on the existence of campus bikeshare programs of this type, showing not only the associated budgetary waste but their tendency to succumb to problems afflicting common ownership, leading to their eventual abandonment. Other universities nonetheless persist in repeating—and allocating money—to this idea. See Alban, D. L., & Stephenson, E. F. (1999). The "Berry Bikes": A Lesson in Private Property. *The Freeman*, 49:8-9; Thomas, Diana Weinert and Yonk, Ryan and Young, Stephen, "In and Out of the Commons: Extractive Public Entrepreneurship and the Aggie Blue Bikes Program" (November 29, 2010). Available at SSRN: https://ssrn.com/abstract=1716974
6. https://www.aier.org/article/pejorative-origins-term-%E2%80%9Cneoliberalism%E2%80%9D
7. See, for example,http://www.hup.harvard.edu/catalog.php?isbn=9780674979529.
8. Google NGram shows the term was extremely uncommon before roughly 1980, with occasional uses often applying to completely unrelated figures and concepts.
9. Oliver 1960.
10. Yearly published mentions of the term "neoliberalism," as measured by Google's Ngram tool, went from practically nonexistent in 1980 to one of the trendiest academic buzzwords by 2008. For a major contributing factor in its popularization, see Foucault, Michel. 2004. *The Birth of*

Biopolitics: Lectures at the College de France, 1978–1979. Translated by
Graham Burchell, Picador USA.

11. Boas and Gans-Morse 2009.
12. Google Scholar citations revealed over 23,900 hits for "neoliberalism"
    in 2015. This compares to a total of 293 between 1930 and 1980. See, for
    example, http://142.207.145.31/index.php/acme/article/view/1342.
13. Bowen and Sosa 2014.
14. Bousquet 2003, 208.
15. Giroux 2014, 156.
16. Giroux 2014, 2.
17. Giroux 2014, 6.
18. Giroux 2014, 137.
19. Olssen and Peters 2007.
20. Sam Abrams, "Professors Moved Left Since 1990s, but Rest of the
    Country Did Not." http://heterodoxacademy.org/2016/01/09/
    professors-moved-left-but-country-did-not/
21. See the 1984 Carnegie Commission survey on higher ed, https://www.
    icpsr.umich.edu/icpsrweb/ICPSR/studies/7501.
22. Samuel J. Abrams, "Think Professors are Liberal? Try School
    Administrators." *The New York Times*, October 16, 2018.
23. Matt Mitchell, Michael Leachman, and Kathleen Masterson,
    "A Lost Decade in Higher Education Funding," Aug. 23,
    2017. https://www.cbpp.org/research/state-budget-and-tax/
    a-lost-decade-in-higher-education-funding
24. Carey 2015, 255–256.
25. Amanda Ripley, "College Is Dead. Long Live College!" *Time*, Oct. 18, 2012.
    http://nation.time.com/2012/10/18/college-is-dead-long-live-college/6/
26. Joseph Aoun, "A Shakeup of Higher Education," *Boston Globe*, Nov. 17,
    2012. https://www.bostonglobe.com/opinion/2012/11/17/shakeup-higher-
    education/Wi5FQz2JYstDnYDlUaUfdI/story.html
27. Greg Graham, "How the Embrace of MOOCs Could Hurt Middle
    America," *Chronicle of Higher Education*, Oct 1, 2012. https://www.
    chronicle.com/article/after-the-buzz-how-the/134654
28. Kevin Carey, "Here's What Will Truly Change Higher Education: Online
    Degrees That Are Seen as Official," *The New York Times*, Mar. 5, 2015.
    https://www.nytimes.com/2015/03/08/upshot/true-reform-in-higher-
    education-when-online-degrees-are-seen-as-official.html

Chapter 11

1. https://nces.ed.gov/fastfacts/display.asp?id=75. The total amount
   spent on all forms of postsecondary training is closer to $1.1 trillion.
   See https://cew.georgetown.edu/wp-content/uploads/2015/02/
   Trillion-Dollar-Training-System-.pdf.
2. https://nces.ed.gov/fastfacts/display.asp?id=75

3. Pew Charitable Trusts, "Federal and State Funding of Higher Education: A Changing Landscape," Jun. 11, 2015. http://www. pewtrusts.org/en/research-and-analysis/issue-briefs/2015/06/ federal-and-state-funding-of-higher-education

4. See Pew Charitable Trusts, "Federal and State Funding of Higher Education: A Changing Landscape," Jun. 11, 2015. http://www.pewtrusts. org/~/media/assets/2015/06/federal_state_funding_higher_education_ final.pdf, Figure 6.

5. Sachs 2005. For a summary of various critiques of Sachs, see van der Vossen and Brennan 2018.

6. Cadie Thompson, "There's a $1 Trillion Crisis Threatening the American Way of Life as We Know It," *Business Insider,* Mar. 6, 2017. http://www. businessinsider.com/american-infrastructure-falling-apart-2017-2

7. David Lucca, Taylor Nadauld, and Karen Shen, "Credit Supply and the Rise of Tuition: Evidence from the Expansion in Federal Student Aid Programs," *FRBNY Staff Reports* 733 (2015) https://www.newyorkfed.org/ medialibrary/media/research/staff_reports/sr733.pdf; Greg Gordon and Aaron Hedlund, "Accounting for the Rise in College Tuition," http:// www.nber.org/papers/w21967.pdf.

8. Caplan 2018, 238–261.

9. https://files.eric.ed.gov/fulltext/ED558166.pdf, p. 3.

10. For example, Caplan 2018.

11. Caplan 2018.

12. http://archive.news.indiana.edu/releases/iu/2016/02/carnegie-classification-institutions-of-higher-education.shtml

13. https://www.heri.ucla.edu/monographs/HERI-FAC2014-monograph-expanded.pdf, p. 30.

14. https://www.heri.ucla.edu/monographs/HERI-FAC2014-monograph-expanded.pdf, p. 30, authors' calculations.

15. https://www.heri.ucla.edu/monographs/HERI-FAC2014-monograph-expanded.pdf, p. 29, authors' calculations.

16. https://www.heri.ucla.edu/monographs/HERI-FAC2014-monograph-expanded.pdf, p. 29, authors' calculations. To get this low estimate, we assume that all the surveyed faculty in the lower categories hit the maximum for their category, and all the surveyed faculty in the two higher categories hit the minimum. This gives us a ratio of the top two groups having published 684.3 papers for every 412.8 the bottom five groups published.

17. Valero and van Reenen 2016.

18. Caplan 2018, 113–118.

19. Quoting from Nussbaum 2016, 25–26.

20. Somin 2013, 84.

21. https://trends.collegeboard.org/college-pricing/figures-tables/tuition-and-fees-and-room-and-board-over-time-1976-77_2016-17-selected-years

22. https://trends.collegeboard.org/college-pricing/figures-tables/tuition-and-fees-and-room-and-board-over-time-1976-77_2016-17-selected-years

23. 2004 *Digest of Education Statistics*, Table 343, https://nces.ed.gov/fastfacts/display.asp?id=75.

24. According to William Baumol and William Bowen, as technology changes, certain forms of work become more productive, while others do not. For instance, thanks to technological advancements, factory workers are much more productive now than previous factory workers or early craftspeople, while a symphony is not more productive today than it was in Beethoven's time. However, an orchestra company does not just need to compete with other orchestra companies for labor, but must also compete with other employers in industries that have enjoyed productivity growth. The problem, Baumol and Bowen conclude, is that firms in low productivity fields may thus have to pay workers above their marginal productivity. Baumol believed academia was a paradigmatic example of an industry suffering from a cost disease. So, while spending is up, part of the problem is that costs are up—you have to pay professors and staff significantly more this year than yesteryear, even though professors and staff today are not significantly more productive now than in the past.

25. Meg. P. Bernhard, "Harvard's Federal Research Funding Declines Slightly in FY 2014," *The Harvard Crimson*, Jan 22, 2015. http://www.thecrimson.com/article/2015/1/22/federal-funding-decreases-2014/

BIBLIOGRAPHY

⋙◆⋘

Data Sets

American Academy of Arts and Sciences. *Humanities Indicators*. https://www.humanitiesindicators.org/default.aspx

American Association of University Professors (AAUP). *Economic Status Reports*. 2012-present. https://www.aaup.org/our-work/research/annual-report-economic-status-profession

American Federation of Teachers (AFT). 2010, March. *Survey of Part-Time/Academic Faculty*. http://www.aft.org/sites/default/files/aa_partimefaculty0310.pdf

American Institutes for Research. *Delta Cost Project*. https://deltacostproject.org

Carnegie Foundation. 1969–Present. *National Surveys of Higher Education*. https://eric.ed.gov/?id=ED042425

Chronicle of Higher Education. *Chronicle Data*. https://data.chronicle.com/category/sector/2/faculty-salaries/

Coalition on the Academic Workforce (CAW). "A Portrait of Part Time Faculty Members" (2012) http://www.academicworkforce.org/CAW_portrait_2012.pdf

Higher Education Research Institute (HERI). 1989–Present. *Faculty Surveys*. https://heri.ucla.edu/heri-faculty-survey

Illinois State University. *Grapevine Project*. https://education.illinoisstate.edu/grapevine/tables/

National Science Foundation, National Center for Science and Engineering Statistics. 2015. *Survey of Earned Doctorates*. https://www.nsf.gov/statistics/srvy/doctorates

Primary Research Group. 2010. *Survey of College Marketing Programs.* https://www.primaryresearch.com/

US Department of Education, Institute of Education Sciences, National Center for Educational Statistics. 2004, 2014, and 2015. *Digest of Education Statistics.* https://nces.ed.gov/programs/digest/

US Department of Education, Institute of Education Sciences, National Center for Educational Statistics. *Integrated Postsecondary Education Data System (IPEDS).* https://nces.ed.gov/ipeds/

US Department of Labor, Bureau of Labor Statistics (BLS). 2015. *Occupational Employment Survey.* https://www.bls.gov/

Bibliography

Acemoglu, Daron and James Robinson. 2012. *Why Nations Fail.* New York: Crown Business.

Adams, J. V. 1997. "Student Evaluations: The Rating Game." *Inquiry* 1(2): 10–16.

Adelman, Clifford. 2009. "Undergraduate Grades: A More Complex Story than 'Inflation.'" In Lester Hunt, ed., *Grade Inflation: Academic Standards in Higher Education,* pp. 13–44. Albany: SUNY Press.

Adler, Jonathan. 2000. "Clean Politics, Dirty Profits: Rent-Seeking Behind the Green Curtain." In Terry Anderson, ed., *Political Environmentalism: Going Behind the Green Curtain,* pp. 1–30, Stanford, CA: Hoover Institution Press.

Ambady, Nalini and Robert Rosenthal. 1993. "Half a Minute: Predicting Teacher Evaluations from Thin Slices of Nonverbal Behavior and Physical Attractiveness." *Journal of Personality and Social Psychology* 64: 431–441.

Ariely, Dan. 2013. *The (Honest) Truth about Dishonesty.* New York: HarperCollins.

Arum, Richard and Josipa Roksa. 2011. *Academically Adrift: Limited Learning on College Campuses.* Chicago: University of Chicago Press.

Axelrod, Robert. 1984. *The Evolution of Cooperation.* New York: Basic Books.

Baird, John S. 1980. "Current Trends in College Cheating." *Psychology in the Schools* 17: 515–522.

Bartlett, Linda. 1991. "Tenure and Academic Freedom." *Journal of Collective Negotiations* 20: 119–130

Basow, S. A. and N. T. Silberg. 1987. "Student Evaluations of College Professors: Are Female and Male Professors Rated Differently?" *Journal of Educational Psychology* 79(3): 308–314.

Beran, Tanya, Claudio Violato, and Don Kline. 2007. "What's the 'Use' of Student Ratings of Instruction for Administrators? One University's Experience." *Canadian Journal of Higher Education* 37(1): 27–43.

Boas, Taylor C. and Jordan Gans-Morse. 2009. "Neoliberalism: From New Liberal Philosophy to Anti-Liberal Slogan." *Studies in Comparative International Development* 44: 137–166.

Boring, Anne, Kellie Ottoboni, and Philip B. Stark. 2016. "Student Evaluations of Teaching (Mostly) Do Not Measure Teaching Effectiveness." *ScienceOpen Research*. doi:10.14293/S2199-1006.1.SOR-EDU.AETBZC.vi

Boston University Faculty Union. 2015. *Our Bargaining Goals*. http://www.seiu509.org/files/2015/08/BU-Open-Letter-081715.pdf

Bousquet, Marc. 2003. "The Rhetoric of 'Job Market' and the Reality of the Academic Labor System." *College English* 66: 207–228.

Bovard, James. 1995. "Archer Daniels Midland: A Case Study in Corporate Welfare." *Policy Analysis* 241.

Bowen, William G. and Julia Ann Sosa. 2014. *Prospects for Faculty in the Arts and Sciences: A Study of Factors Affecting Demand and Supply, 1987–2012*. Princeton, NJ: Princeton University Press.

Bowen, William G. and Eugene M. Tobin. 2015. *Locus of Authority: The Evolution of Faculty Roles in the Governance of Higher Education*. Princeton, NJ: Princeton University Press.

Bowers, William J. 1964. *Student Dishonesty and Its Control in College*. New York: Bureau of Applied Social Research, Columbia University.

Braga, Michela, Marco Paccagnella, and Michele Pellizzari. 2014. "Evaluating Students' Evaluations of Professors." *Economics of Education Review* 41: 71–88.

Branthwaite, Alan, Mark Trueman, and Terry Berrisford. 1981. "Unreliability of Marking: Further Evidence and a Possible Explanation." *Educational Review* 33: 41–46.

Brennan, Jason. 2010. "Scepticism about Philosophy." *Ratio* 23: 1–16.

Brennan, Jason. 2016. *Against Democracy*. Princeton, NJ: Princeton University Press.

Brennan, Jason and Lisa Hill. 2014. *Compulsory Voting: For and Against*. Cambridge, UK: Cambridge University Press.

Brennan, Jason and Peter Jaworski. 2016. *Markets without Limits*. New York: Routledge.

Brennan, Jason and Phillip Magness. 2018a. "Estimating the Cost of Adjunct Justice: A Case Study in University Business Ethics." *Journal of Business Ethics* 148: 155–168.

Brennan, Jason and Phillip Magness. 2018b. "Are Adjuncts Exploited? Some Grounds for Skepticism." *Journal of Business Ethics* 152: 53–71.

Bretz Jr., Robert D. 1989. "College Grade Point Average as a Predictor of Adult Success: A Meta-Analytic Review and Some Additional Evidence." *Public Personnel Management* 18: 11–22.

Brighouse, Harry. 2009. "Grade Inflation and Grade Variation: What's All the Fuss About?" In Lester Hunt, ed., *Grade Inflation: Academic Standards in Higher Education*, pp. 73–92. Albany: SUNY Press.

Brogaard, Jonathan, Joseph Engelberg, and Edward van Wesep. 2017. "Do Economists Swing for the Fences after Tenure?" https://papers.ssrn.com/sol3

Buchanan, James and Nicos Devletoglou. 1970. *Academia in Anarchy: An Economic Diagnosis*. New York: Basic Books.

Buckner, E. and R. Hodges. 2016. "Cheating or Cheated? Surviving Secondary Exit Exams in a Neoliberal Era." *Compare: A Journal of Comparative and International Education* 46: 603–623.

Burke, Brian L., Sharon R. Sears, Sue Kraus, and Sarah Roberts-Cady. 2013. "A Comparison of Critical Thinking Changes in Psychology and Philosophy Classes." *Teaching of Psychology* 41: 28–36.

Butler R. and M. Nisan. 1986. "Effects of No Feedback, Task-Related Comments, and Grades on Intrinsic Motivation and Performance." *Journal of Educational Psychologyu* 78: 210–216.

Campbell, Judith Prugh and William C. Bozeman. 2007. "The Value of Student Ratings: Perceptions of Students, Teachers, and Administrators." *Community College Journal of Research and Practice* 32: 13–24.

Caplan, Bryan. 2007. *The Myth of the Rational Voter: Why Democracies Choose Bad Policies.* Princeton, NJ: Princeton University Press.

Caplan, Bryan. 2018. *The Case Against Education.* Princeton, NJ: Princeton University Press.

Carey, Kevin. 2015. *The End of College: Creating the Future of Learning and the University of Elsewhere.* New York: Riverhead Books.

Carmichael, H. Lorne. 1988. "Incentives in Academia: Why Is There Tenure?" *Journal of Political Economy* 96: 453–472.

Carpenter, Shana K., L. Mickes, S. Rahman, and C. Fernandez. 2016. "The Effect of Instructor Fluency on Students' Perceptions of Instructors, Confidence in Learning, and Actual Learning." *Journal of Experimental Psychology: Applied* 22: 161–172.

Carrell, Scott and James West. 2010. "Does Professor Quality Matter? Evidence from Random Assignment of Students to Professors." *Journal of Political Economy* 118: 409–432.

Carroll, Linda. 2000. "Tenure and Academic Excellence." *Academe* 86: 22–25.

Ceci, Stephen J., Wendy M. Williams, and Katrin Mueller-Johnson. 2006. "Is Tenure Justified? An Experimental Study of Faculty Beliefs about Tenure, Promotion, and Academic Freedom." *Behavioral and Brain Sciences* 29: 553–569.

Centra, J. A. 1993. *Reflective Faculty Evaluation.* San Francisco: Jossey-Bass.

Centra, J. A. 2003. "Will Teachers Receive Higher Student Evaluations by Giving Higher Grades and Less Coursework?" *Research in Higher Education* 44: 495–518.

Cheeseman, G. A. and N. Boon. 2001. "Reputation and the Legibility of Doctors' Handwriting in Situ." *Scottish Medical Journal* 46: 79–80.

Clayson, Dennis E. 2009. "Student Evaluations of Teaching: Are They Related to What Students Learn? A Meta-Analysis and Review of the Literature." *Journal of Marketing Education* 31: 16–30.

Clayson, Dennis E. and M. J. Sheffet. 2006. "Personality and the Student Evaluation of Teaching." *Journal of Marketing Education* 28: 149–160.

Coates, Dennis and Brad R. Humphreys. 2002. "The Supply of University Enrollments: Administrators as Utility Maximizing Bureaucrats." *Public Choice* 110: 365–392.

Coates, Dennis, Brad R. Humphreys, and Michelle A. Vachris. 2004. "More Evidence That University Administrators Are Utility Maximizing Bureaucrats." *Economics of Governance* 5: 77–101.

Colander, David and Daisy Zhuo. 2015. "Where Do PhDs in English Get Jobs? An Economist's View of the English PhD Market." *Pedagogy: Critical Approaches to Teaching Literature, Language, Composition, and Culture* 15: 139–156.

Crowne, D. P. and D. Marlowe. 1960. "A New Scale of Social Desirability Independent of Psychopathology." *Journal of Consulting Psychology* 24: 349–354.

Crumbley, D. Larry and Eugene Fliedner. 2002. "Accounting Administrators' Perceptions of Student Evaluation of Teaching (SET) Information." *Quality Assurance in Education* 10: 213–222.

Cruse, Daniel B. 1987. "Student Evaluations and the University Professor: Caveat Professor." *Higher Education* 16: 723–737.

Curtis, John and Saranna Thornton. 2013. "The Annual Report on the Economic Status of the Profession, 2012–2013" *Academe* March–April 2013: 4–19.

Cushman, Thomas. 2003. "Who Best to Tame Grade Inflation?" *Academic Questions* 16: 48–56.

Dale, Stacy Berg and Alan B. Krueger. 2002. "Estimating the Payoff of Attending a More Selective College: An Application of Selection on Observables and Unobservables." *Quarterly Journal of Economics* 107: 1491–1527.

Dale, Stacey Berg and Alan B. Krueger. 2014. "Estimating the Return to College Selectivity of the Career Using Administrative Earning Data." *Journal of Human Resources* 49: 323–358.

Danzinger, Shai, Jonathan Levav, and Loira Avnaim-Pesso. 2011. "Extraneous Factors in Judicial Decisions." *Proceedings of the National Academy of the United States* 108: 6889–6892.

De George, Richard T. 2003. "Ethics, Academic Freedom, and Academic Tenure." *Journal of Academic Ethics* 1: 11–25.

De Vlieger, Pieter, Brian A. Jacob, and Kevin Strange. 2017. "Measuring Up: Assessing Instructor Effectiveness in Higher Education." *Education Next* 17. http://educationnext.org/measuring-up-assessing-instructor-effectiveness-higher-education/

Deterrman, Douglas. 1993. "The Case for the Prosecution: Transfer as an Epiphenomenon." In Douglas Detterman and Robert Sternberg, eds., *Transfer on Trial: Intelligence, Cognition, and Instruction*, pp. 1–24. New York: Praeger.

Detterman, Douglas and Robert Sternberg, eds. 1993. *Transfer on Trial: Intelligence, Cognition, and Instruction*. New York: Praeger.

Di Leo, Jeffrey R. 2013. *Corporate Humanities in Higher Education: Moving beyond the Neoliberal Academy*. New York: Springer, 2013.

Dowell, D. A. and J. A. Neal. 1982. "A Selective Review of the Validity of Student Ratings of Teaching." *Journal of Higher Education* 53: 51–62.

Driscoll, Jennifer and David Cadden. 1010. "Student Evaluation Instruments: The Interactive Impact of Course Requirement, Student Level, Department and Anticipated Grade." *American Journal of Business Education* 3: 21–30.

Dutton, Kevin. 2012. *The Wisdom of Psychopaths*. New York: Scientific American/Farrar Straus and Giroux.

Emery, Charles, Tracy Kramer, and Robert Tian. 2001. "Customers vs. Products: Adopting an Effective Approach to Business Students." *Quality Assurance in Education* 9: 110–115.

Epley, Nicolas and David Dunning. 2000. "Feeling 'Holier than Thou': Are Self-Serving Assessments Produced by Errors in Self- or Social Prediction?" *Journal of Personality and Social Psychology* 79: 861–875.

Ewing, A. M. 2012. "Estimating the Impact of Relative Expected Grades on Student Evaluations." *Economics of Education Review* 3:141–154.

Finklestein, I. E. 1913. *The Marking System in Theory and Practice*. Baltimore: Warwick and York.

Fish, Reva M. and Gerri M. Hura. 2013. "Student's Perceptions of Plagiarism." *Journal of the Scholarship of Teaching and Learning* 13(5): 33–45.

Flaherty, Colleen. 2015, February 9. "15K per Course?" *Inside Higher Ed*. https://www.insidehighered.com/news/2015/02/09/union-sets-aspirational-goal-adjunct-pay

Franklyn-Stokes, Arlene and Stephen E. Newstead. 1995. "Undergraduate Cheating: Who Does What and Why?" *Studies in Higher Education* 20: 159–172.

French, Michael T., Jenny F. Homer, Iona Popovici, and Philip K. Robins. 2015. "What You Do in High School Matters: High School GPA, Educational Attainment, and Labor Market Earnings as an Adult." *Eastern Economic Journal* 41: 370–386.

Gick, Mary and Keith Holyoak. 1983. "Schema Induction and Analogical Transfer." *Cognitive Psychology* 15: 1–38.

Ginsberg, Benjamin, 2011. *The Fall of the Faculty*. Princeton, NJ: Princeton University Press.

Giroux, Henry. 2014. *Neoliberalism's War on Education*. New York: Haymarket Press.

Gladwell, Malcolm. 2010, October 10. "Getting In." *The New Yorker*.http://www.newyorker.com/magazine/2005/10/10/getting-in.

Goldberg, David and Elizabeth Welles. 2001. "Successful College and University Foreign Language Programs, 1995–1999: Part I." *Profession* 2001: 171–210.

Goldsmith, H. 1976. "The Facts on the Legibility of Doctors' Handwriting." *Medical Journal of Australia* 2: 462–463.

Goodwin, Thomas H. and Raymond D. Sauer. 1995. "Life Cycle Productivity of Academic Research: Evidence from the Cumulative Histories of Academic Economists." *Southern Economic Journal* 61: 728–743.

Granzin, Kent L. and John J. Painter. 1973. "A New Explanation for Students' Course Evaluations." *American Educational Research* 10: 115–124.

Gray, Mary and Barbara R. Bergmann. 2003. "Student Teaching Evaluations: Inaccurate, Demeaning, Misused." *Academe* 89: 44–46.

Greene, A. S. and L. Saxe. 1992. "Everybody (Else) Does It: Academic Cheating." https://eric.ed.gov/?id=ED347931

Gump, Steven E. 2007. "Student Evaluations of Teaching Effectiveness and the Leniency Hypothesis: A Literature Review." *Educational Research Quarterly* 30: 55–69.

Gumport, Patricia J. 1993. "The Contested Terrain of Academic Program Reduction." *Journal of Higher Education* 64: 283–311.

Haidt, Jonathan. 2012. *The Righteous Mind*. New York: Pantheon.

Haskell, Robert. 2001. *Transfer of Learning: Cognition, Instruction, and Reasoning*. San Diego: Academic Press.

Herlihy-Mera, Jeffrey. 2015 "Academic Imperialism; Or, Replacing Nonrepresentative Elites: Democratizing English Departments at Top-Ranked US Institutions." *Minnesota Review* 85: 80–106.

Ho, A. K., L. Thomsen, and J. Sidanius. 2009. "Perceived Academic Competence and Overall Job Evaluations: Students' Evaluations of African American and European American Professors." *Journal of Applied Social Psychology* 39: 389–406.

Hobson, S. M. and D. M. Talbot. 2001. "Understanding Student Evaluations: What All Faculty Should Know." *College Teaching* 49: 26–31.

Holley, John W. 1977. "Tenure and Research Productivity." *Research in Higher Education* 6: 181–192.

Hunt, Lester, ed. 2009. *Grade Inflation: Academic Standards in Higher Education*. Albany: SUNY Press.

Hyland, Terry and Steve Johnson. 2006. "Of Cabbages and Key Skills: Exploding the Mythology of Core Transferable Skills in Post-School Education." *Journal of Further and Higher Education* 22: 163–172.

Isely, Paul and Harinder Singh. 2010. "Do Higher Grades Lead to Favorable Student Evaluations?" *Journal of Economic Education* 36: 29–42.

Kohn, Alfie. 2009. "The Dangerous Myth of Grade Inflation." In Lester Hunt, ed., *Grade Inflation: Academic Standards in Higher Education*, pp. 1–12. Albany: SUNY Press.

Krautman, Anthony and William Sander. 1999. "Grades and Student Evaluations of Teachers." *Economics of Education Review* 18: 59–63.

Kress, Shirley. 1989. "Niskanen Effects in the California Community Colleges." *Public Choice* 6: 127–140.

Kuhn, Thomas. 1962. *The Structure of Scientific Revolutions*. Chicago: University of Chicago Press.

Lang, James M. 2013. *Cheating Lessons: Learning from Academic Dishonesty.* Cambridge, MA: Harvard University Press.

Leeson, Peter. 2017. *WTF?: An Economic Tour of the Weird.* Stanford, CA: Stanford University Press.

Leshowitz, Barry. 1989. "It Is Time We Did Something about Scientific Illiteracy?" *American Psychologist* 44: 1159–1160.

Lewis, Lionel S. 1980. "Academic Tenure: Its Recipients and Its Effects." *Annals of the American Academy of Political and Social Science* 448: 86–101.

Levin, Henry M., and Juan Carlos Calcagno. 2008. "Remediation in the Community College: An Evaluator's Perspective," *Community College Review* https://doi.org/10.1177/0091552107310118.

Liljenquist, Katie, Chen-Bo Zhong, and Adam D. Galinsky. 2010. "The Smell of Virtue: Clean Scents Promote Reciprocity and Charity." *Psychological Science* 21: 381–383.

Lombardi, John. 2013. *How Universities Work.* Baltimore: Johns Hopkins University Press.

Lyons, Ronan, Christopher Payne, Michael McCabe, and Colin Fielder. 1998. "Legibility of Doctors' Handwriting: Quantitative Comparative Study." *British Medical Journal* 317: 863.

MacLean, Nancy. 2017. *Democracy in Chains: The Deep History of the Radical Right's Stealth Plan for America.* New York: Viking Press.

MacNell, Lillian, Adam Driscoll, and Andrea N. Hunt. 2015. "What's in a Name: Exposing Gender Bias in Student Ratings of Teaching." *Innovative Higher Education* 40: 291–303.

Magness, Phillip W. 2016. "For Profit Universities and the Roots of Adjunctification in US Higher Education." *Liberal Education* 102: 50–59.

Marsh, H. W. and T. L. Cooper. 1981. "Prior Subject Interest, Students' Evaluations, and Instructional Effectiveness." *Multivariate Behavioral Research* 16: 83–104.

Marsh, H. W. and L. A. Roche. 1997. "Making Students' Evaluations of Teaching Effectiveness Effective." *American Psychologist* 52: 1187–1197.

McAbee, Samuel T. and Frederick L. Oswald 2013. "The Criterion-Related Validity of Personality Measures for Predicting GPA: A Meta-Analytic Validity Competition." *Psychological* Assessment 25: 532–534.

McCabe, Donald, Kenneth D. Butterfield, and Linda K. Treviño. 2017. *Cheating in College: Why Students Do It and What Educators Can Do about It.* Baltimore: Johns Hopkins University Press.

McKeachie, Wilbert and James A. Kulik. 1975. "Effective College Teaching." *Review of Research in Education* 3: 165–209.

McKenzie, Richard B. 1996. "In Defense of Tenure." *Zeitschrift für die gesamte Staatswissenschaft* 152: 325–341.

Mittal, Sanjiv, Rajat Gera, and Dharminder Kumar Batra. 2015. "Evaluating the Validity of Student Evaluation of Teaching Effectiveness (SET) in India." *Education+ Training* 57: 623–638.

Moghtader, Michael, Alanna Cotch, and Kristen Hague. 2001. "The First-Year Composition Requirement Revisited: A Survey." *College Composition and Communication* 52: 455–467.

Morgan, Donald Ace, John Sneed, and Laurie Swinney. 2003. "Are Student Evaluations a Valid Measure of Teaching Effectiveness: Perceptions of Accounting Faculty Members and Administrators." *Management Research News* 26: 17–32.

Mosner, E.C. and I. S. Ross. 1987. *The Correspondence of Adam Smith*. Glasgow Edition, the Works of Adam Smith. Oxford, UK: Oxford University Press.

Mueller, Dennis. 2003. *Public Choice III*. Cambridge, UK: Cambridge University Press.

Mulligan, Thomas. 2018. *Justice and the Meritocratic State*. New York: Routledge.

Murray, Charles. 2012. *Coming Apart: The State of White America, 1960–2010*. New York: Crown Forum.

Murray, H. G. 1983. "Low-Inference Classroom Teaching Behaviors and Student Ratings of College Teaching Effectiveness." *Journal of Educational Psychology* 75: 138–149.

Naftulin, Donald H., John E. Ware Jr., and Frank A. Donnelly. 1973. "The Doctor Fox Lecture: A Paradigm of Educational Seduction." *Journal of Medical Education* 48: 630–663.

Naude, E. and T. Hörne. 2006. "Cheating or 'Collaborative Work': Does It Pay?" *Issues in Informing Science & Information Technology* 3: 459–466.

Nerad, Maseri, Rebecca Aanerud, and Joseph Cerny. 1999. "So You Want to Become a Professor? Lessons from the PhDs—Ten Years Later Study." In Donald Wulff, Ann Austin, and Associates, *Paths to the Professoriate: Stategies for Enriching the Preparation of Future Faculty*, pp. 137–58. New York: Jossey-Bass.

North, Douglas. 1990. *Institutional Change, and Economic Performance*. New York: Cambridge University Press.

Nowell, Clifford and Doug Laufer. 1997. "Undergraduate Student Cheating in the Fields of Business and Economics." *Journal of Economic Education* 28: 3–12.

Nussbaum, Martha. 2016. *Not for Profit: Why Democracy Needs the Humanities*. Princeton, NJ: Princeton University Press.

Oliver Jr., Henry M. 1960. "German Neoliberalism." *Quarterly Journal of Economics* 74: 117–149.

Olssen, Mark and Michael A. Peters. 2007. "Neoliberalism, Higher Education and the Knowledge Economy: From the Free Market to Knowledge Capitalism." *Journal of Education Policy* 20: 313–345.

Ortiz, Claudia María Álvarez. 2007. "Does Philosophy Improve Critical Thinking Skills?" Master's thesis, University of Melbourne. https://www.reasoninglab.com/wp-content/uploads/2017/05/Alvarez-Final_Version.pdf

Park, Chris. 2011. "In Other (People's) Words: Plagiarism by University Students—Literature and Lessons." In Robert Barrow and Patrick Keeney, *Academic Ethics*, pp. 525–544. New York: Routledge.

Perin, Dolores. 2013. "Literacy Skills Among Academically Unprepared Students," Community College Review. https://doi.org/10.1177/0091552113484057

Riniolo, Todd C., Katherine C. Johnson, Tracy R. Sherman, and Julie A. Misso. 2006. "Hot or Not: Do Professors Perceived as Physically Attractive Receive Higher Student Evaluations?" *Journal of General Psychology* 133: 19–35.

Rodríguez-Vera, F. Javier, Y. Marin, A. Sánchez, C. Borrachero, and E. Pujol. 1995. "Illegible Handwriting in Medical Records." *Journal of the Royal Society of Medicine* 95: 545–546.

Rojstaczer, Stuart and Christopher Healy. 2012. "Where A is Ordinary: The Evolution of American College and University Grading, 1940–2009." *Teachers College Record* 114: 1–23.

Rosenthal, Joel T. 1994 "The Work of Faculty: Expectations, Priorities, and Rewards." *Academe—The Bulletin of the AAUP* 80: 35–48.

Ryan, James J., James A. Anderson, and Allen B. Birchler. 1980. "Student Evaluations: The Faculty Responds." *Research in Higher Education* 12: 317–333.

Sachs, Jeffrey. 2005. *The End of Poverty*. New York: Penguin.

Schinske, Jeffrey and Kimberly Tanner. 2014. "Teaching More by Grading Less (or Differently)." *CBE-Life Sciences Education* 13: 159–166.

Schmidt, Frank L. and John E. Hunter. 1998. "The Validity and Utility of Selection Methods in Personnel Psychology: Practical and Theoretical Implications of 85 Years of Research Findings." *Psychological Bulletin* 124: 262–274.

Schmidtz, David. 2001. "A Place for Cost-Benefit Analysis." *Philosophical Issues* 11: 148–171.

Schwitzgebel, Eric. 2013. "Do Ethics Classes Influence Student Behavior?" Unpublished manuscript, University of California at Riverside. http://www.faculty.ucr.edu/~eschwitz/SchwitzPapers/EthicsClasses-131210a.pdf

Shubik, Martin. 1971. "The Dollar Auction Game: A Paradox in Noncooperative Behavior and Escalation." *Journal of Conflict Resolution* 15: 109–111.

Shils, Edward. 1995. "Academic Freedom and Tenure." *Minerva* 33: 5–17.

Short, H., R. Boyle, R. Braithwaite, M. Brookes, J. Mustard, and D. Saundage. 2008. "A Comparison of Student Evaluation of Teaching with Student Performance." In Helen L. MacGillivray and Michael A. Martin, eds. *OZCOTS 2008: Proceedings of the 6th Australian Conference on Teaching Statistics*, pp. 162–170. Canberra: Statistical Society of Australia.

Sidanius, J. and M. Crane. 1989. "Job Evaluation and Gender: The Case of University Faculty." *Journal of Applied Social Psychology* 19: 174–197.

Simler, Kevin and Robin Hanson. 2018. *The Elephant in the Brain*. New York: Oxford University Press.

Smith, Ron. 1974. "The Composition Requirement Today: A Report on a Nationwide Survey of Four-Year Colleges and Universities." *College Composition and Communication* 25: 138–148.

Somin, Ilya. 2013. *Democracy and Political Ignorance.* Stanford, CA: Stanford University Press.

Stark, Philip B. and Richard Freishtat. 2014. "An Evaluation of Course Evaluations." *ScienceOpen Research* 9: 2014. doi:10.14293/S2199-1006.1.SOR-EDU.AOFRQA.v1

Tuchman, Gaye. 2009. *Wannabe U: Inside the Corporate University.* Chicago: University of Chicago Press.

Uttl, Bob, Carmela A. White, and Daniela Wong Gonzalez. 2017. "Meta-Analysis of Faculty's Teaching Effectiveness: Student Evaluation of Teaching Ratings and Student Learning Are Not Related." *Studies in Educational Evaluation* 54: 22–42.

Valero, Anna and John van Reenen. 2016. "The Economic Impact of Universities: Evidence from Across the Globe." Paper no. 22501. National Bureau of Economic Research, Cambridge, MA.

van der Vossen, Bas and Jason Brennan. 2018. *In Defense of Openness: Why Global Freedom Is the Humane Solution to World Poverty.* New York: Oxford University Press.

Vasta, Ross and Robert F. Sarmiento. 1979. "Liberal Grading Improves Evaluations but Not Performance." *Journal of Educational Psychology* 71: 207–211.

Whicker, Marcia Lynn. 1997. "An Economic Perspective on Tenure." *PS: Political Science and Politics* 30: 21–25.

Williams, Wendy and Stephen Ceci. 2007. "Does Tenure Really Work?" *Chronicle of Higher Education* 53. https://www.chronicle.com/article/Does-Tenure-Really-Work-/25565

Wittrock, M. C. and A. A. Lumsdaine. 1977. "Instructional Psychology." *Annual Review of Psychology* 28: 417–459.

Worthington, A. C. 2002. "The Impact of Student Perceptions and Characteristics on Teaching Evaluations: A Case Study in Finance Education." *Assessment and Evaluation in Higher Education* 27: 49–64.

Yandle, Bruce. 1983. "Baptists and Bootleggers." *Regulation* 7: 12–16

Yandle, Bruce. 2014. *Baptists and Bootleggers.* Washington, DC: Cato Institute.

Ziker, John. 2014, March 31. "The Long, Lonely Job of *Homo academicus.*" *The Blue Review.* http://thebluereview.org/faculty-time-allocation/

INDEX